CONVERSATIONS

WITH Nelson Algren

H. E. F. DONOHUE
AND
NELSON ALGREN

THE UNIVERSITY OF CHICAGO PRESS

CHICAGO AND LONDON

D1572172

Nelson Algren and H. E. F. Donohue
dedicate this book to
C. M. A. D.

The University of Chicago Press, Chicago 60637
The University of Chicago Press, Ltd., London
Copyright © 1963, 1964 by H. E. F. Donohue and Nelson Algren
All rights reserved. Originally published 1964
University of Chicago Press edition 2001
Printed in the United States of America

05 04 03 02 01   6 5 4 3 2 1

Sections of the first three chapters of this book appeared in the Fall,
1963, issue of *The Carleton Miscellany*, Chapter 12, "The Writer at
Fifty-five," first appeared in the October, 1964, issue of *The Atlantic
Monthly*.

Library of Congress Cataloging-in-Publication Data

Donohue, H. E. F.
    Conversations with Nelson Algren / H. E. F. Donohue and Nelson Algren.
        p.   cm.
    ISBN: 0-226-01383-9 (pbk. : alk. paper)
    1. Algren, Nelson, 1909– —Interviews. 2. Novelists, American — 20th
century — Interviews. I. Algren, Nelson, 1909– II. Title.

PS3501.L4625 Z665 2001
813.'52 — dc21
[B]
                                                            00-050779

CONVERSATIONS WITH
NELSON ALGREN

Contents

CONTENTS

Foreword

About Nelson Algren

The strong set expression on his face—an alert, angular concordance of total acceptance and bemused surprise—has caused some spectators to tell Nelson Algren he looks like a dishonest Art Carney. This always pleases him. He is even more pleased when someone tells him he looks like a healthy Baudelaire.

It is his shock of hair that does it. He has the highest widow's peak in the world, and he keeps brushing it with one hand the wrong way—from nape of neck to forehead—so that the whole thatch rises torturously, crowning him with the cheerful aspect of a noble Mohawk gone berserk. When, at some woman's insistence, he combs it back, he can exude what Mark Twain has called "the calm confidence of a Christian with four aces." Even without his glasses, which he usually does not wear, his eyes miss nothing. He seems constantly ready to observe everything, particularly something that is about to go crazy or wrong.

Often he will sport a cigar. He drinks when he pleases and enjoys food. Just under six feet tall, Algren has the slightly rounded but tough stomach of the mature man who takes good care of the rest of his body. He swims. He walks. With men he strides slightly ahead; with women he stays quite close, paying strict attention.

When Algren speaks about anything "good" he may sound somber, but when he speaks of horrendous or bizarre things one can understand what Charles Lamb meant when he said, "Anything awful makes me laugh."

As he speaks he often telegraphs what he is going to say, what the key phrase is going to be. He repeats himself, splicing the repetitions with "you know" and "I mean" and "well." But when the crucial phrase or word finally arrives, it usually comes clean and fresh. His interest in what he is saying, together with his listener's attention, fills in the gaps and tides them both over. If he does not sense interest in what he is saying, he simply will not speak.

Most of what he wants to talk about is funny, but he cannot tell set jokes. His pace is often jumbled and he usually drowns the punch line with his own premature, tentative laughter. When you do not howl with glee over the finished joke, he questions your sense of humor. When speaking of a friend, he is always loyal and discreet; but if he thinks the person has been "conned" or compromised, his sarcasm can be merciless. Often he appears to be slightly imperious, except when children are present.

Aside from his work, and all the actions of other humans, Algren's interests range from beating the horses to comprehending and exploiting E.S.P. He is convinced one can do both. He watches a great deal of TV. He attends the theatre and the movies regularly. He likes most sports and Dixieland music. He is still confounded by a sign he once saw in Greenwich Village: "Nonconformist meeting at 8:30—Be On Time."

He shunts aside all rules, regulations, and dicta, except for three laws that he says a nice little old Negro lady once taught him:

Never play cards with any man named "Doc."

Never eat at any place called "Mom's."

And never, ever, no matter what else you do in your whole life, *never* sleep with anyone whose troubles are worse than your own.

H. E. F. DONOHUE

New York, 1964

PART I

FROM THE GRANDFATHERS

1   *The Child*

QUESTION: Tell us about you and your life.

ALGREN: I was told during the war by a fortuneteller in Germany, a woman who pretended to be able to tell, to read your palm, that I had a long life line which would come to an abrupt end.

Q: Do you believe that?

ALGREN: Well I had no reason to doubt it. And I asked the fortuneteller, "How?" She said, "A blonde woman, well proportioned, is going to hit you with a blunt instrument and she will get off completely free saying she thought it was a rose." That's how I'm going to meet my end. But I will be seventy-seven at the time.

Q: Where were you born?

ALGREN: Detroit, Michigan, March 28, 1909. Detroit was a fort. I was born in a place called Mack Avenue across the street from something called Northeastern High School. My mother had a candy store.

Q: Have you been back there lately?

ALGREN: I was there in 1960 when Wayne University was buying up culture in a very big way. They had about ten days of nothing but culture, and they were taking all of that automobile money and distributing it in packages of five hundred dollars and so I took a plane. I got there in an hour, just in time to go up on the platform. I spoke for one hour, received my package, and went home. In between I went down to Mack Avenue, 867 Mack Avenue, and the old homestead is now gone. Yeah, it's gone. No address.

Q: What kind of a house was it? How long did you live there?

ALGREN: Until I was three. My father worked there for about ten years, I think. He was a machinist. He worked at the screw works. I have no idea what the screw works is, but I always remember talking about the screw works, the screw works. He worked there for years and then he also worked for Packard. Those were the first two words I remember—the screw works, and, right about then, Packard!

Q: According to *my* father, who also was a machinist—he finished his apprenticeship about five years before you were born—a machinist was pretty much of a radical in those days because no one believed lathes would last. It was like being a rocket scientist during the last war.

ALGREN: Well, I don't know where my father picked it up. He had no formal education.

Q: Do you remember the candy store?

ALGREN: I remember incidents in Detroit. I remember getting lost. I ran away from home when I was two or two and a half, looking for an uncle. My mother had a younger brother named Theodore who was the family hero. Both my mother and father came from Chicago. My mother's family was a big family of about five girls and three boys, something like that. And Theodore somehow got work on one of the lake boats. He worked on boats all his life. It was sort of a family legend. I remember she had Uncle Theodore mixed with God or somebody, she talked about him so much. So I went looking for him. I certainly wasn't three but I was old enough to walk. I think maybe I was two and a half. And I picked up some other kid next door. It was my idea. This other kid didn't know where he was going, a kid about my age. We went the whole day—I remember that very vividly. I remember sidewalks out of town. I pretended to him that I knew where I was going. Uncle Theodore was a ship captain, that was it. I had the idea this guy was a ship captain and I'm looking for Uncle Theodore, the ship captain. I must have been very determined because I was gone the whole day and I still remember the sidewalks that were newly laid out of town. Some guy came along and gave us some candy—I remember him a little vaguely. Then we came to a railroad track and a train came by and the engineer leaned out—a lot of smoke—and we waved and I told this other kid, "That was Uncle Theodore." I was satisfied. But I couldn't find my way home. So a tailor picked us up, a little Jewish tailor, I remember him and I remember his shop—there were a lot of kids around and I think they lived in the back. I remember he gave us rye bread and he called the police and the police took us down to the station. I can still remember the guns behind the desk. They sat us on the desk and gave us ice cream and finally someone came down for me. It took the whole day.

Q: How did you like the police?

ALGREN: Oh I guess I got along pretty well. I think I liked being the center of attention there.

Q: You are of Scandinavian and Jewish background? Everybody thinks you are Polish.

ALGREN: No Polish whatsoever. The Swede was my father's father, a man I never saw. From Sweden. His name was Nels Ahlgren, A-h-l-g-r-e-n. He came to America when he was about eighteen just before our Civil War. He had changed his religion. He had got hold of the Old Testament and he changed his name to Isaac Ben Abraham—he did this on his own, nobody asked him to—and he got out of Sweden. What he was thinking of I don't know, but he was very literal-minded. He decided to take the Old Testament at its literal truth. If the Old Testament said, "Thou shall make no graven image" and "Man is made in the image of God," then somebody has goofed by putting George Washington on the dollar bill because that man is God and there's the graven image of God on the money.

Q: Why did he come to America?

ALGREN: I imagine if you became a Jew in Stockholm at that time, the best thing to do was to go to America. He married a little servant girl over here. She was German. I think she was Jewish, but I don't know. But she was certainly no kind of a believer in anything, and he turned out to be a deserter. He deserted them. First he went to Minnesota by himself and traded in furs and he was burned out—I looked this up once —he was burned out in the last Indian raid east of the Mississippi. My father said something about it once so I looked it up and it corresponded. Some little joint. He was a fur trader and you know that's where the Swedes went, for some reason. Then he came down to Chicago and married this little German servant girl and he squatted in Indiana. He had a farm. He became a squatter with more crank ideas, always with a con angle to them. He was always trying to outthink everybody. He had no claim to the land. And when he had a little country store there just before he went to farming, he brought a load of Swedish pennies that were worth about two-thirds of the American cent and resembled the American money, so when people came into this little country store and they wanted three pennies change, he gave them Swedish pennies, which they would take out of curiosity. It saved him one cent right there. When he ran out of Swedish pennies, he began making them, he began manufacturing them, stamping them out himself. He was inventive. He worked for a while on perpetual motion. I'm trying very hard to avoid saying he was a nut.

Q: Did you know him?

ALGREN: No, no, but I remember his picture at my grandmother's. He was a very stern Zionist and he deserted his family. He had several children in Indiana and he left them. He decided he was going to the Holy Land. He was a Zionist. He was a Jew's Jew, a rabbi's rabbi. None of them could get orthodox enough. He went to San Francisco and it was very slow. I mean there was no money so in order to get to the Holy Land he had to live in San Francisco two or three years before he got passage, and in San Francisco he identified himself to the Jewish community there as a rabbi. They weren't orthodox enough for him. They're Russian and Polish and European Jews and they're supposed to know the Bible and a Swede comes in and tells them they aren't Jewish enough—he found all sorts of heresies. They didn't want to bother with him, but he could catch the official rabbis because he knew the Bible word for word. I mean he knew the *whole* thing, word for word. And he kept making a pest of himself there. He kept calling on the Chief Rabbi, telling him what he was doing wrong, until finally someone would simply meet him at the door and say, "Well, the rabbi isn't home," so he left a note the last time he was there, saying that there's nobody home upstairs at the rabbi's house, meaning there's nobody up there. He was an intellectual before his time, which was his trouble, inasmuch as he didn't want to work. He was doing *every*thing he could not to work and he always had this con thing going because he was a Zionist. Finally he did go to the Holy Land. He took the family—my father was born in San Francisco on the way so they had to take him, and the first thing my father remembered was camels. I don't know where he thought he was at.

Q: Camels?

ALGREN: Yeah, when he woke up. I mean my father was about two years old and he woke up to find himself in Jerusalem with a lot of camels. I'm sure he never knew how he got there, but the first thing he remembered were a lot of camels with Arabs riding them. It was a very funny beginning for my father, a very odd memory for a man who would spend his whole life working for the Yellow Cab company in Chicago and the screw works—Arabs on a lot of camels. He remembered that. He also remembered that his father, the old man, the grandfather, wanted to be an authority. He was a Zionist and he was a Socialist and he liked the idea very much of sitting with the other Prophets and being waited on. The woman, the servant girl, did all the cooking. He didn't have to work at all. He could just prophesy. He loved that. He would philosophize and leave the making of a living up to her. So she had to cook and sew and take care of all these other bums, you know. He was an authority, patriarchal, and he had his own way out there for a while until she got tired of it. She was being conned and she didn't like the country and she had other kids back here, so she said she was going, she was going home. But he says, "You can't go; you don't have a dime." But she said, "Good-by," and went to the American Consulate and told them she didn't want to stay with the man, and they gave her money to go. My father remembers that, too. She said good-by to the old man without much regret, I guess. My father was about three then.

Q: When was your father born?

ALGREN: 1868, or something like that. That's my idea of it. Let's see: He died in 1940 and he was seventy-two when he died, so this happened then about 1871. My father said he remembered walking down this road with his mother when he was three, leaving Jerusalem, and the old man, my grandfather, was standing in the door and when they were almost out of sight the old man said, "Hey! I'm coming with you!" He saw his meal ticket going and he caught her. He went along with her and on the boat he ran into trouble again. He looked at the money the American Consulate had given her to get home, and that was the point at which he got this graven image idea and threw the money overboard.

Q: How much?

ALGREN: It was their passage money. But it's always interested me that he didn't take the money and *say,* "I threw it overboard last night." It was done publicly and people saw him do it. Oh he explained to them, you know: Man is made in the image of God; thou shalt make no graven image, so it's a crime to have money and he threw George Washington overboard. He pauperized them doing that. A guy took up a collection on the boat, but they carefully gave it to her. When they got back to Indiana, he deserted them and he came back when they were living in Chicago and my father was about twenty years old.

By that time he was sort of small, I'm told. He was blue-eyed with a long white beard. He hadn't been home for many years. They had not seen him for sixteen–seventeen years. He'd been all over. And he'd abandoned Judaism. He'd abandoned Judaism for Socialism, Socialism for Methodism, Methodism for—I believe his first conversion to Judaism and then to Socialism was sincere. Then my guess is that it became more and more that he simply wanted to keep going and going and going, so he finally wound up a kind of missionary because he was pretty good on the con. He went all over the world just adopting any faith that would send him somewhere. He became a missionary for anybody who would pay his way. And then he came back then. He was an old man. He stayed with them one winter. He had nothing. He was a pauper and they let him stay and he stayed all winter. Then in the spring he said he should go and they said, "No, you can stay," and he said no. He always put it in a pious way. Actually I think he wanted to go. But the way he put it was, "I don't have any right to live on you because I deserted you." So far as religion went, he said, "There is no truth, there is no religion, no truth. It is all nothing." He didn't believe in anything then.

Q: How old was he?

ALGREN: Oh, I don't know. He must have been sixty anyhow, I suppose. A small little white-haired man. And the son, my father, put him on a Madison streetcar in Chicago. I asked my father when did he last see the old man. He said, "He was on a Madison streetcar. I saw him going down the aisle. I give him half a dollar." That was the last they saw of the old man. Word came about ten or fifteen years later. I was in high school when they got word. That guy must have lived to have been eighty, as far as I can see—certainly he was in his middle seventies—and my grandmother died, you know, at ninety-six. But, anyhow, they did get a notice. I remember they got a notice from a county in Florida, Orange County or something, a notice from the authorities there saying that this old man Isaac Ben Abraham, yeah, had died and was a pauper and would be buried as a pauper unless they came and claimed the body or sent the money to bury him. And they didn't. He died as a pauper and that was all there was to it. So when I came along in Detroit, they named me after him. They named me Nelson Algren Abraham on the birth certificate.

Q: Named after the wanderer?

ALGREN: Yeah, yeah. When I started to write I just made it Nelson Algren and when I got into the Army I changed the name legally. I didn't figure that could get on a theatre marquee. Anyhow I've always felt much closer to this guy, to this grandfather. My father was a very passive man. I never had any conversation with my father. When I started reading Ramsay MacDonald, *The Socialist Movement,* it was a complete revelation to me that I was repeating the grandfather's life in a way. I mean when I started talking about Socialism my father would say, "Oh, the old man, he used to talk about the Social—how do you say it in German?—the *Socialisme?"* You know, he put a kind of French pronunciation on it and I looked at my father, you know, because he didn't speak French or German or anything. And then I realized that my father had simply repeated the word he had heard *his* father say. He had heard this word. He had no idea what it meant, but he used it in the Old World way. And he never referred to his father—it was always "the old man."

Q: What about your mother's side of the family?

ALGREN: Well, it's a much more prosy family, much less unique. On my mother's side they were just the usual (Chicago)

West Side German Jews who knocked themselves out to repudiate their Judaism immediately, you know, as they had been in Germany, where the German Jews were always Germans first and very anxious to become blond and blue-eyed, which they succeeded in doing. I don't know how. Here it was the same thing. My mother never had any knowledge of Yiddish or Hebrew because it was *verboten*. See, these people were Prussians. I mean this old German guy, my mother's father—his name was Kalisher—when he was in the house you speak German. You speak the language of the Fatherland in the house. Out of the house you'd speak English. This Yiddish thing is a mongrel language. It was a very common thing among German Jews to assimilate very fast. That was why they immediately managed to get up toward the North Side. Then they had kind of a hard time because they were followed by the Orthodox, the Jews who were Jews first, the ghetto people—this always embarrassed the German Jews who were already assimilated in Chicago. By the 1900's they were Americanized. Sometimes they went a little too far.

Q: How do you mean?

ALGREN: They went for the American Legion thing. The girls were auxiliaries and I saw one of my aunts buried, the goddamndest thing you ever saw. That's the only time I ever saw a Jewish service in which Christ was called on to resurrect the dead. This was Aunt Frances, in my mother's family. They moved out to Harvey and she was married to a Jewish guy and she represented the whole family, all the women—

Q: Did your father come from a family of men and your mother from a family of women?

ALGREN: No. They both came from families of women. My father had a couple of brothers and about five sisters. My mother had about three brothers and five sisters, something like that. But Aunt Frances was buried in a Jewish chapel on North Broadway and the rabbi delivered the service in Hebrew because she was of Jewish extraction. She was also a member of the Ladies' Auxiliary of the American Legion of Harvey, Illinois, so three women of that auxiliary showed up at the chapel with a New Testament and an American flag and after the rabbi had buried the woman in the Jewish tradition without hope of resurrection—at least I've never heard of it before; I think this was the issue between the Jews and Jesus, wasn't it? —well, these three women come up. I'm sure it was all done innocently and the light was very dim. One of them starts reading. One was holding the flag—she was looking *very* determined—and whether the one reading could not read very well or whether it was the bad light I don't know, but she stumbled around trying to read this thing and finally the other one snatched the book from her and read, "Oh death, where is thy sting?" I think that was the passage. But anyhow, all I caught was, ". . . and He is the resurrection and the life and . . ." I said, "Now, *wait* a second!" And I started looking around. Nobody knew what was going on. They're all looking around as if saying "Well" and "Nice." She'll have to lay there, you know, until Christ comes. On the day of the Resurrection you shall arise, you know, and go with the rest of the Gentiles, see. They'd reclaimed her. I said, "Holy Christ, what kind of a—"

Q: How old were you?

ALGREN: This was about ten or fifteen years ago. But it represents a sort of thing in my mother's family. Another aunt still alive is married to a South African. I mean a real South African. He's not an unpleasant guy, but he is an all-out Fatherlander.

He went to Germany and back. Said it was the greatest thing that ever happened. She's blonde Jewish and their country club is for Gentiles only. They wouldn't belong to any other. It's not too unique because it comes from the same streak, the same strata of middle-class German Jewish bunch who made it here first by 1900 and then moved to the North Side only to be embarrassed when around 1905 or so the Polish Jews started coming in, broke, living in the West Side ghetto. The trouble was that the North Side German Jews were willing to help the newcomers, they wanted to give them money, but they didn't want them to come up there in their *yarmulkes* and their black things and the beards. So they would send them packages. They sent them CARE packages over to the West Side. They were bribed. *"Stay away."* They were ashamed of them so they would send them money and they would send them food packages but they kept them away.

Q: When you moved to Chicago at the age of three, where did you live?

ALGREN: At Seventy-first and South Park.

Q: You lived neither in the West Side ghetto nor on the North Side?

ALGREN: No. I went to a Congregationalist Sunday school.

Q: Why?

ALGREN: I don't know. It was the nearest one. The result of all this mixing was that my mother and my father were neither Gentiles nor Jews. They certainly weren't Jews. My mother didn't mind my coming back from Sunday school and telling her stories about Christ that I had learned. The old man would say, "Oh that son-of-a-bitch—He gave us nothing but trouble

—He caused all our wars—lay off that." He just didn't want to bother, you know. And then my mother would say, "Well, he ought to go and learn something." And I wanted to go there. It was a Protestant school in an Irish and Protestant neighborhood. My mother sent me there because she didn't like the Irish.

Q: Why didn't she like the Irish?

ALGREN: Oh whenever anything started she'd say, "It's those Irish bums again." And oh the fights between my mother and my father, the bitterest fights they ever had, were on Tunney and Dempsey. My father was a Dempsey man because he said Dempsey was a real fighter and Tunney was just a sissy. And my mother said, "No, he's a gentleman, and all Dempsey is, he's an Irish bum." And then she worked for Charles Evans Hughes because Wilson, he's just an Irish bum. Dempsey and Wilson, she thought, were both big Irish drunks. The whole neighborhood was Irish there.

Q: Jim Farrell's old neighborhood?

ALGREN: I think he lived in the Fifties, a little farther north. My mother sent me to the Congregationalist Sunday school at Sixty-ninth and South Park. It's still there. I remember being a little confused because the minister's name was Hoover and I remember hearing about how Hoover was the Food Commissioner at the time in 1919, the one saving the lives of Belgian babies. I continued going to that school because the kids I knew went there. They had this annual picnic and I went there because of that picnic. I wanted to go to that picnic with the other kids and I went there and found five dollars, a five-dollar bill, which made me a convert I guess. I couldn't wait until the next year.

Q: Were you a poor kid?

ALGREN: Oh no, no. Only in the American sense. I mean I don't remember a time when we went hungry. We never had a car, but they succeeded in owning that home on the South Side, a two-story thing. They believed in buying a home. When he moved to the North Side, he bought a two-story place but he never got it paid off. We lived there for years as owners because we rented the upstairs or the downstairs. We lost the building ultimately. He didn't ever quite pay it off. I guess in Detroit at the turn of the century they were poor, in the sense that money was close. But I never remember being denied anything, and then when my sisters grew up and started to work, we were just a middle-class family.

Q: How many sisters did you have?

ALGREN: Two. One was a schoolteacher, one an office worker. They both died, one in 1939 and the other in 1960. That was the older sister, the office worker. She was sixty. The other one who died in 1940 was thirty-nine, thirty-eight.

Q: Any brothers?

ALGREN: No, no.

Q: Were you the youngest?

ALGREN: Yes. I was seven years younger than the one sister and nine years younger than the other.

Q: Did you get along?

ALGREN: I never got along with the older sister. We had something going against each other. I didn't like her. I didn't like her when I grew up. With the younger sister I was very close. She was the only one in the family I could talk to. I was close to her because she was a teacher and she liked books. I always went to her. If my mother wanted me to go to the store, she knew better than to ask me because I wouldn't, I didn't take orders. But she'd say to Bernice, "Well, you know, ask him to go." Anything Bernice said was right. She knew everything. If she said, "Do this," I did that. She couldn't do anything wrong.

Q: How did you get along with your father?

ALGREN: Oh, I was contemptuous of him.

Q: Why?

ALGREN: Well, in the first place, he was incredibly simple. He couldn't understand a movie without seeing it three times *and* having it explained. And he always told the same jokes, year after year. I really liked him, but I'd get awfully impatient with him. He was too simple.

Q: How about your mother?

ALGREN: My feeling about her was a little more complex. I always thought she should be more dignified. She was always on her knees, scrubbing, something like that. She was clumsy, a clumsy woman. I wanted a graceful mother. I wanted somebody to be elegant, I guess, I don't know. She was always climbing, sponging the walls. I'd bring someone home, some kid home from school, you know, some kid whose mother was always real well-dressed, or had a servant, or something like that. I'd bring him home and my mother would be in the middle of the floor with a scrub bucket. Oh Christ, you know. Oh Jesus, you know. I'd be really bothered. And it bothered me when she mispronounced words. I wanted her to say words right. She'd refer to somebody: "Oh, he was elexecuted." I'd say, "Elec*tro*cuted, Mother." Elexecuted. Elexecuted. And I never knew anyone else who could get *m*'s and *n*'s mixed.

When she wrote she wrote "moon" for "noon" and she couldn't say "aluminum." I don't know why. I would get impatient about that. Then I'd get impatient with the old man. He had a tire and battery shop on Kedzie Avenue, and I used to help him. There was Johnson's, a big gambling joint about half a block away, upstairs, and we did a lot of tire changing for the gambling people, the guys who worked in the block joint, and the cops used to play up there. So I told the old man. He knew I went up there and I said there was a horseshoe bar in the place. I was about seventeen and I liked to gamble even then. The place was once called "Hunting House Dancing Academy." The cops used to come in the restaurant and then go upstairs. And I told the old man that. He said, "Well, that's crazy." He said, "A cop can't do that; they'd put him in jail. That'd be dishonest." I said, "Cops, Pa, cops take money, cops steal." "Oh," he said, "I don't want to listen to crazy talk like that. A cop, a policeman is made to defend the law! That is why he is a policeman. If he doesn't do that, then he gets put into jail." I said, "Don't act like that, Pa." I mean I said, "Aw, come on . . ." You know he was too gullible to believe.

Q: Are they alive?

ALGREN: The old man died the year after Bernice died, in 1940. Then nobody died until 1960, when the older sister died. Then my mother died in July of 1961. She was eighty-six, I guess.

Q: Where was she?

ALGREN: In a nursing home. There's a whole continent of nursing homes for all the old vegetables, for people you don't want around the house any more. Oh, it's a fantasyland. If you get a license for that and a doctor's connection to send them and you get twenty-five of those people there at eighty-five or a hundred bucks a week, and hire half a dozen nurses to lift them, you will have yourself a great money-maker. It's a real unnatural sight.

Q: Who paid for it?

ALGREN: I paid for it. I got some money from the Welfare people. You're supposed to split it. I didn't get a full claim, but I would go along with them. I got her in there. I had to get her in there right away because she started just falling down. She was all right but there was no one to take care of her. If I don't get her into this nursing home, then she's got to go to County Hospital and she's too alert not to be humiliated by that because she has spent her whole life trying not to take charity and she had succeeded in that, so I put her in this nursing home. But I put her in there without a dime. The first day I didn't even have the dough to pay the ambulance. "Do everything, get her in there," I told the ambulance, "and you can send me the bill." After she was in there I talked to them.

Q: How many years was she in there?

ALGREN: Oh it wasn't a matter of years. I put her in one when I went to Europe and she walked right out of it. She saw the signs: right to the graveyard. She got out of there. She's been living over on Lawrence Avenue all alone for years and she just put on her clothes and got out of there. But she had to go back. She gave in and went back. The people running the place went along with me. When I got five hundred bucks I'd give them two or three hundred. I didn't pay attention to the bills. I was being nice, you know, just giving them enough so they'll keep her there. I said to them, "I'll fight with you later." We're killing each other with kindness. They got plenty out of it. And they got money from the Welfare people, too. Then I had to get hold of the undertaker. So far as I know, that nursing home still feels I owe them money. I don't pay no heed to that. And the undertaker—I just don't know. He still wants about thirteen hundred dollars and I think I am going to give him eight hundred when he's willing to take it. "We don't do things in that way," he said, and, "We had a great expense with your mother, you know. The dress, the dress cost about three hundred dollars, you know." I said, "I understand, but you must realize that my loss is greater than yours." And there was a silence on the other side. He's the funniest guy. They turn that love into money. You can't argue with them. You can't say, "How much are roses going to cost?" You can't say, "Can I get any of the material cheaper?" You have got to go for the thirteen hundred dollars, and that is what I went for. Then after the funeral I dismissed it all from my mind.

2 *The Young Man*

QUESTION: How did you get to college? Where did you go?

ALGREN: I went to the University of Illinois. I worked down there.
I worked all the way through.

Q: Why did you go to college?

ALGREN: It was my sister's idea.

Q: Bernice?

ALGREN: Yeah. I wasn't any good in high school. I fooled around
a lot. I clowned a lot. I was very cocky and really didn't take
the thing too seriously. My father said, "Now it's time for you
to be a draftsman, to be something." The idea of a four-year
college education staggered him because he had about three
months of school. "Now what are you going to do?" he said.
And I said, "I'll get by." I asked him, "You want me to stick
around here?" He couldn't see that, he couldn't see that at
all. But I really had a bad scholastic record. I flunked everything in high school. It took me five years before I could get
out.

Q: What high school?

ALGREN: It's called Roosevelt now. It was Hibbard then. And this sister of mine is the one who said, "He is going to college," and she put the old man down. The old man never went against anything she said. He had the same feeling the rest of us did: that Bernice knew what was right. If the other sister had said it, they would have had a fight, but if Bernice says I go to college then I go. My mother always went along with Bernice. So I went. I went down to the University of Illinois with fifty bucks tuition, and you worked. Everybody worked down there. We'd go to the YMCA and we'd get a job with a fraternity, waiting on tables. I worked for four years. Down there I picked up. I mean I got good grades all the way—just about straight "B" or something—which was shocking because when I had gone to high school I couldn't catch on. I mean it was sort of a joke.

Q: Why was that? What were you interested in in high school?

ALGREN: Well, I think what I was interested in in high school was what every adolescent is interested in, in proving himself to be a man.

Q: How?

ALGREN: Why, I tried to do it by being a renegade rather than a good student. I don't know, but roughly dividing that school the way all schools can be divided into the good boys and the bad, I preferred the bad boys, I guess. I didn't want to succeed with a book under my arm the way some of the kids were determined to be good students and to get college scholarships. They went home early and didn't smoke. They weren't interested in baseball or the girls either. I didn't want any association with them. I wanted to associate with the guy who was about three years older than anybody else, who was a pretty

good third baseman and he could field a grounder with a cigarette in his teeth without taking it out. He didn't give a damn
for anybody. I mean, nobody could tell him what to do. I
wanted to be like that kind of guy.

Q: Why?

ALGREN: I don't know why. I don't know why. I thought that was
more of a way of being a man, and that's a pretty common
sort of struggle.

Q: Well, I was always interested in being a man. I worked very
hard through grammar school and high school and in the first
year of college, but then when I really got into college, I didn't
work hard at my studies. I pulled the other switch.

ALGREN: Oh, I see what you did. Well, I pulled just the opposite
thing then, because when I got to college I had a room of my
own and I went to work in a fraternity waiting on tables and
went home and read. I switched to a program of austerity. I
picked it up somewhere, I believe, from Marcus Aurelius, or
somewhere, where I began to think that you didn't even have
the right to eat more than you needed. The only justification
for eating what you did eat was to sustain your energy to
live with nobility. I went around being noble.

Q: You were interested in nobility?

ALGREN: Yeah. In dignity.

Q: In dignity.

ALGREN: It was a very absurd kind of dignity in the sense that you
not only ate, even though you were very hungry, you only ate
a proportion of what was in front of you. For instance, even
though I had a sweet tooth, I would say, "No, I don't want any
dessert." I didn't need the dessert physically. If somebody

spoke to me, I would decide in my own mind whether
the question was worth answering. If it was a silly question, I would just ignore it. This would give you some per-
plexed looks. People thought you didn't hear them and then
they'd press the question. It was a very aloof sort of plane to
live on. It also involved an almost compulsive way of doing
things. You didn't waste time. You didn't just walk around.
The first thing you did in the morning, you took a cold bath.

Q: What time?

ALGREN: Early. Six o'clock. And then you went to work by the
shortest route and you took the same route every day and you
ate very plainly. You said, "Good morning," when you came
in. That was all you said. You didn't join in a conversation
because it was better that you thought of some of Shakespeare's lines while you were waiting on tables instead of going
into this nutty conversation. In other words, I was trying to
live isolated inside myself, too. Now this went on for some
time.

Q: This was in 1928?

ALGREN: Yeah.

Q: During the heights of the big twenties period before the Depression?

ALGREN: Yeah. Well, I very seldom came home then, so I didn't
even know when I got out of school in thirty-one that there
was a depression.

Q: You found that out then?

ALGREN: Yeah, I found that out. It was sort of a bring-down.

Q: Before we get to that, tell me more. You must have gotten
interested in books.

ALGREN: Well, I had always liked books. I had always read, but I got interested in specific writers. I began—I read and reread Matthew Arnold's "Dover Beach" and I read Byron and Chaucer. I spent one summer in a Shakespeare course there with a teacher named Bruce Weirich, who I think was the only teacher that I remember down there that I really got something out of, who really liked Shakespeare himself. I doubt that he's still there. That was so long ago. I got something out of his course and I remember I was also moved by a course given by a sociologist named Taft. It made me decide to be a sociologist.

Q: In your freshman year?

ALGREN: Second year.

Q: But you began to start?

ALGREN: Well, it was a kind of an amateur stoicism. It was a very Calvinistic kind, very deeply puritanical. The kind of feeling that, as I say, I thought I got from reading the Latin stoics.

Q: Why did you feel that this was an appropriate feeling for you at that time?

ALGREN: I don't know. It appealed to me. I felt this was the way to live. I had had a grandfather who had lived this way.

Q: Right. When did you decide that you weren't going to become a sociologist?

ALGREN: Well, that was decided for me, because it became a very impractical time to become a sociologist inasmuch as there weren't any openings for sociologists. In order to become a sociologist, I guess I would have had to take a master's degree. It was always difficult to stay in school.

Q: Any time?

ALGREN: Well, yes, because it just was a survival thing and I had to borrow money for tuition and so forth, so there was no question of going further. . . .

Q: Where did you borrow the money?

ALGREN: From the University, from the School of Journalism at the University, in the last year.

Q: Did you pay it back?

ALGREN: Yeah, I paid it back some years later, maybe ten years later.

Q: You said you were isolated—from the other students or from the world?

ALGREN: I never knew anybody down there.

Q: Why not?

ALGREN: Well, I didn't have anything in common with them. The isolation wasn't my own idea. The fact is that living as an independent you don't go to fraternity parties. I mean, you weren't included in the social life naturally if you're an independent and so there was only the books. I didn't make any friends down there except one or two people very casually.

Q: Did you mind this? Were you lonely?

ALGREN: Oh, yes, it was very lonesome. No, I can't say I minded it. It wasn't painfully lonely. It seemed to be the way I liked it. If I hadn't liked it, I could have bust out of it. It was a kind of interesting struggle. It wasn't a passive thing, it was a struggle, because I was always perpetually falling off this grand plane that I had arranged.

Q: Well, tell me about that.

ALGREN: This program, this program included an austerity diet for one thing. You ate simply. You could eat all you wanted.

I would take oatmeal and put salt on it. No milk, no cream, no sugar. This was enough. That was it. This was enough to sustain you till noon when I would eat something. You stayed this way just long enough so that hunger didn't interfere with the life of the mind, as it were. This must have been what I was trying to do. And the other things that interfered with the mind, of course, were women and drink. There wasn't any drinking question because there wasn't anything available to drink and I didn't have any particular appetite for it. I don't know, sometimes some guys would steal some wood alcohol or something like that, but I never had any interest in it, and of course it was a very closely, it was a very deeply, puritanical campus. The Dean of Men had a very strong and deeply puritanical hold on the morals of the campus and was very proud to say shortly after his wife's death that he was pleased that he had returned his wife to God as he had found her and he was not only—

Q: (*Laughter*)

ALGREN: And he was not only an advocate of virginity, but he had an information bureau going made up of people whom he'd caught. He didn't have any control, of course, over the fraternities and sororities. He couldn't watch that closely, but what he could watch was the outskirts of Urbana and Champaign, where there were prostitutes. These he could find, and he could find out where there was gambling too in independent houses. That is, he had informers, people he'd caught. Well, either you get expelled or you inform, so in an atmosphere like that, sin is much more attractive than ordinarily it would be. It had to be a sneak deal.

Q: But you had a personal, puritanical regime of your own?

ALGREN: I had ruled this out, you see, but, like I say, I had arranged a pattern of behavior that I didn't always live up to.

Q: You weren't supposed to do what you were doing anyway. Did this make it more attractive to you to try to do some of it?

ALGREN: It might have. I certainly would have gone looking, anyhow. Living on this plane, when you do fall off, you do a sort of Jekyll and Hyde thing because you think of nothing but Marcus Aurelius and it's time to go to bed and you wake up and you start walking down Walnut Street, you know, but with a very oppressive sense of sin. This might be the house— all the houses look like warehouses. And I never had any success there, although I went down there. I remember waiting outside of a place because of its dim lighting and deciding that was the place and then going up and knocking at the door and a woman came to the door and asked what I wanted and I said, "Well, I've got a couple of dollars to spend," and she hollered at somebody back there, for some man to come, and I left. After a couple of these efforts, I couldn't find the place. The only women really I found available was an occasional landlady, usually a widow, but I don't think I had a very healthy attitude toward sex then.

Q: How old were you when you stopped being a virgin?

ALGREN: Well, I was no longer a virgin at that time. I stopped being a virgin when I was seventeen in high school. I hadn't had any trouble getting over virginity. I wasn't trying to recover virginity.

Q: You say you had an unhealthy attitude toward sex? What was that?

ALGREN: I don't think that the reaction to sex should be that you had debased yourself. I mean, it was really a refusal to recognize that you're put together as an animal. It was an attempt to repudiate your own very real needs as though those needs weren't legitimate and natural. Fortunately I got a little help.

Q: When?

ALGREN: Oh, down there about the third year.

Q: With another student?

ALGREN: No, with the landlady, and she was sort of a cheerful type so I think I began sliding off a little bit there. I know I began eating better. I think I stopped being quite as repressive to myself. I mean, I think I began to recognize that pleasure wasn't necessarily evil.

Q: How old was the landlady?

ALGREN: Oh, she was a woman, I guess, certainly in her thirties.

Q: How long was the liaison? How long did it last?

ALGREN: There were three semesters I stayed there at her place.

Q: And you went on reading at the same time?

ALGREN: Yeah.

Q: And what did you read?

ALGREN: In the third year I think I read sociology. I read Fielding. I read some of the English novelists. I read somebody named Max Nordau. He was a revolutionary. I had never read anybody who was so critical of organized society. I remember reading him and it was the first I had ever read anybody, for instance, who was against military conscription, and so forth.

Q: And you continued to get good marks?

ALGREN: I made about a "B." Just a little above the average, I would say.

Q: When did you begin to make up your mind what you wanted to do after you got out of college?

ALGREN: I had it decided in the third year that I was going for the sociology thing but it wasn't practical.

Q: What did you decide?

ALGREN: I decided on journalism because there was more of a chance of getting a newspaper job. I went to the School of Journalism, graduated from the School of Journalism.

Q: Then you got out right in the Depression?

ALGREN: Yeah, 1931, yeah.

Q: Did you get a degree?

ALGREN: Yeah, I got a degree, a strange one: B.S.J. Broken down, it means Bachelor of Science in Journalism. It was a very little School of Journalism there.

Q: How old were you?

ALGREN: I was about twenty-two.

Q: What did you do?

ALGREN: Why I had a little card that qualified me. It said, "This card entitles the bearer to consideration as editor, columnist, foreign correspondent, headline writer, copywriter, et cetera" —just a little gimmick the school got out to protect itself I guess. I traveled around the country presenting that card, you know. "I'll go to work for you," I'd say. And they'd say, "No." There wasn't any, there wasn't any work, you know. I tried Chicago. I tried the City News Bureau, and there just wasn't any. Somebody gave me work for a week in Minneapolis—the *Minneapolis Journal*—but I wasn't getting paid. I didn't know I wasn't getting paid.

Q: What were your jobs in college?

ALGREN: I waited on tables at a little graduate fraternity the second year. The first year was just the things a freshman kid did —you mow lawns, you do those things. Then the second year I got the job with a little scientific fraternity, which was a much better job because the fraternity was so small that the waiters had to wash the dishes too, and for that I think we got thirty dollars a month. I mean there were not many jobs where you not only got your food but also you got paid. It wasn't much but I held onto it until I graduated.

Q: What about Minneapolis? Why weren't you paid for that week you worked?

ALGREN: I didn't know. The guy said when I walked in, "Well, sit down and try your hand." I didn't understand that, so when payday came around, there I was, writing headlines, and I was running up a bill at the YMCA, so I said, "When do I get paid?" He said, "We can't pay you. You're just getting experience. There's a man out of town and you are just filling in for him." So I said, "Well, then I have to leave." He said, "Well, thanks for coming around." Well, then I went.

Q: How did you eat?

ALGREN: I was getting credit at the YMCA and my sister sent me money.

Q: Bernice?

ALGREN: No, this was the older one, Irene. She sent me money and I got back home, but I gave up the newspaper idea. I had hit all these newspapers.

Q: How long did you look for a newspaper job?

ALGREN: Oh, all of that year. I still had my graduation suit on when I started hitchhiking and I started going down to the

Southern Illinois papers, then I got down through the South and finally wound up in New Orleans selling.

Q: Selling what?

ALGREN: Oh, selling everything. Selling coffee, selling hair waves —marcel waves, you know—selling beauty parlor appointments that the beauty parlor didn't know about and sending women down to the beauty parlor. Stuff like that. I worked for the Standard Coffee Company and then I had to get out of town and they—

Q: Why did you have to get out of New Orleans?

ALGREN: Well, they closed in on us on this beauty racket, this beauty parlor thing. We had about a thousand certificates for the beauty parlor saying all they had to do was to go down and get this finger wave and shampoo which usually costs about five dollars but this way it's free because they are giving it away free because it is a new thing and they're just making friends and we're just giving away one to a block. But it said in small type, you know, that this whole thing actually costs three-fifty when she gets down there. So she says, "Well I don't understand why it should be for nothing." And we say, "Well, we don't know any more than that about it, but you know you can call up." We always checked the house. There was only about one phone to a block. You can tell if it's wired. And then we'd say, "Just call up, but we'll give it to your next-door neighbor." That always got them—the other woman. None of them had had a finger wave since they'd been married and the idea that the woman next door might, just might, get her hair done when she could have the same thing by paying us twenty-five cents—charity charge, courtesy charge, or something. We had our pockets full of quarters, jingling. And then one of these fools went back and a couple of husbands were waiting for him. They beat the shit out of him. So we got out of there. We went down to the Rio Grande Valley with about eleven bucks between us, which was like a thousand.

Q: Who was with you?

ALGREN: Oh there were two other guys. I was living with two Southerners there, and all in quarters. That was a lot of money. Jesus. Twenty-five cents. My God, for a nickel you could buy a great big poor-boy sandwich. A bunch of bananas was a nickel. And so we got down to the Rio Grande Valley and picked oranges and grapefruit there for a while—made about seventy-five cents a day at the most and tried to get to work in a packing shed—that was the best job you could get, it seemed the ultimate thing, the most fortunate thing that could happen to anybody. I didn't get that. But I did find an abandoned gasoline station. Then one of the guys I was with promoted it. It was abandoned. The Sinclair people owned it. It was way out between Harlingen and Rio Hondo in the Rio Grande Valley and nobody was using it, so this guy I was with went to the Sinclair agent in Harlingen and said, "If you give us a place to live, we'll fix this thing up, we'll dig pits for gas, we'll put in gas, we'll fix the whole place for you—all we want is a place to live." The guy was pleased. It makes him look good—he can write up to Dallas to the main office that he got this station going. It was all falling apart. There were no windows in it. It was a jungle. I mean there *was* a road going by, but there were also deer and wild hogs. There were giant mosquitoes in droves. We fixed it up. We dug the pits and he got an old Studebaker. Of course there was no gas to *be* sold, you understand. It was just an ad for the company and we got to stay in it. We had to walk a ways down the road to get water, but we existed. The guy I was with, he had the idea to use the joint. His idea was that I would be there in charge of the station and he'd run around the Rio Grande Valley picking up produce. He wanted to use the station as a base since no one from the gasoline company had ever contacted us. We didn't tell the agent that, but the agent was—

Q: Picking up what?

ALGREN: Produce. See, of course you couldn't tell the agent that that was what we really wanted the station for, but there was no danger of getting caught. We were twenty-five miles out of town. Maybe the agent is going to come around once a week. But meanwhile during the week this guy figured he'd pick up produce from the farmers around there and resell it. So what he picked up chiefly was black-eyed peas. Then he couldn't sell them. Nobody wanted black-eyed peas, for the same reason I guess that nobody wanted grass. Black-eyed peas were as common as grass. He wasn't a Texan, this guy I was with. He was a Floridian. He didn't know anything about it. It was entirely different. He figures that because he's a Southerner he knows. He knew nothing. He was as strange to the Rio Grande Valley as I was. So he'd run around in this old Studebaker, which was also borrowed, and come back with the black-eyed peas that he couldn't sell, and he could never admit he was wrong. So he said, "Well we can sell them because some place called the 'Jitney Jungle,' a Piggly-Wiggly, a self-help store down there, they said if we put the black-eyed peas up in jars, if we picked them and put them up in jars, then maybe some of the oilmen's wives will buy them to save all the picking." So for days I was picking those things, putting them up in jars while this guy was out promoting all, was promoting everybody.

Q: Did you sell any black-eyed peas in the jars?

ALGREN: No. Nobody ever bought them. I didn't see him again for days. I'm packing black-eyed peas until I'm blind and this guy don't show up. Then I hear a car drive up in the middle of the night. I don't know who it is. I go out there and there's somebody there. It was this guy. I didn't know what the hell he was doing at first. He had come up in another car which he had promoted from somebody else, then he had figured he had all this gas out at the station—we had two tanks with about ninety gallons in each out there—and now he wants to get out of this station deal. He's got another promotion going and he's got a better prospect, so he's going to leave me there, you know, picking and packing black-eyed peas. There he was in the middle of the night siphoning the gas out into his car, saying, "There's about one hundred and eighty gallons of gas I own down there." Well, I'm responsible for the gas. I had signed for the gas. So this nut is driving up in the middle of the night to siphon the stuff away.

Q : Was the gas there to be sold?

ALGREN: Yeah, but there was no chance to sell it. I guess we sold one gallon or something.

Q: In how long?

ALGREN: I don't know. The thing went on for weeks. Sometimes a Mexican would drive up and indicate that he wanted some tequila. He figures we must be making booze out there. He'd look around and say, "No women? No women? What the hell you guys doing here? No tequila? You got tequila? No gas?" Then he'd laugh. They went away laughing because something was wrong.

Q: What about the gas?

ALGREN: Well, there was this Floridian, whom I called Luther Luther because his name wasn't Luther. I got along until he began siphoning the gas and I was legally responsible for it, so I loaded the tanks with sand as against his next siphoning. This got him stuck out in the sticks with sand in his gas pipe in his hired Studebaker and I skipped to El Paso. In El Paso, I recall I wrote a long letter home to a friend in Chicago telling him of my disappointment in the South. In El Paso I went broke in a crap game and I was walking away about a half a block down when a policeman curbed me and asked me where I was going. It turned out that a plate-glass window had been broken up the street. In the station the window's owner came in and he took a look at me and said, "That's not the man." So I got up and started to go but the cop who picked me up asked me, for the second time, where did I think I was going, which made me unsure whether I was going anywhere. He said, "But if we let you go, you will break somebody's window." So that was how I got into the El Paso County Jail. I was in with eight drunks and I noticed the padlock was unlocked so I opened the door and walked out past the turnkey, a colored guy who was sleeping on a stool. When I was going down the steps, I remembered I had been told that there were five hundred cops in El Paso so that if one came up the steps I figured I would just be a visitor going down. But it turned out that the cop coming up the steps was the same one who had pinched me. The third time he asked me where I thought I was going. So I turned around and he said, "Where are you going now?" (*Laughter*) And I still wasn't sure, so he brought me back in and this turnkey, this colored guy, he stood up and he started hollering, "He knows something! He knows something!" Of course, all I know is enough to walk out of an open door. So I got put back in with the eight drunks and this time they really locked the door. And, uh, then the cop began getting friendly. He said, "What you need is a lawyer. I can get you off the hook for two hundred dollars." And I told him I'd wait for the judge. And the judge finally fined me five dollars.

Q: On what charge?

ALGREN: Vagrancy. Then I moved into a small mountain town about eighty miles east of El Paso. I lived on the outskirts of town in a stove-heated room on a deteriorated ranch. I used to walk through that town to a local teachers college into an empty classroom that had thirty desks equipped with type-writers. This was Alpine, Texas. Alpine Teachers College, I think it was. It must have been that I still didn't know I was out of school because I hadn't paid any tuition to Alpine Teachers College. I would just simply walk in and use one of the typewriters. Nobody else was using it. There weren't many students in that year.

Q: Were there any students in it when you were there?

ALGREN: Sometimes students would walk in. There was a hand-ful of students. The college was new and was ready for use, but there weren't many people using it, as there weren't many cars on the highway. Then I felt I had to leave town. I was going to go back to Chicago, but I started becoming attached to the typewriters. Almost a compulsive attachment, a sort of possessiveness, about typewriters, especially about the one I'd been using, an old upright Royal. So I picked it up. Since I was leaving town, I simply picked it up and walked through, straight through the middle of town with this and took it back to my home on the range there and I went to the hard-ware dealer and got a box, packed it, not really realizing in a town as small as that everybody knows you're moving, so all day long they would go and see. People watch as you walk down the street with a typewriter, then come back and go into the hardware store and come out with a big box. People began wondering exactly what are your plans now, especially since I was the only one in the town who was from out of town. But I remember I felt very confident. I told the type-writer to which I had formed an attachment, I said, "I'll see you in Chicago," and then I mailed it in the post office and I hung around town because I wanted to be sure that the type-writer got on its way.

Q: You mailed it to yourself in Chicago?

ALGREN: Yeah, and then I got on a boxcar myself. I thought the whole thing was sort of a shrewd move, you know, and I was in San Antonio, or near San Antonio. The train slowed up and I got out. It was sort of sunny and I'd been in the boxcar and I put my back up against the wall there and started rolling a cigarette with one hand. Everybody had to do that in the South. You had to roll a cigarette one-handed with Bull Durham and the string—the yellow string had to hang down from your pocket. This was ritual. I noticed the sheriff coming along. He looked like he was looking for some-body. I said, "Good morning," and he asked me who I was, and I told him. Well, then I was on my way back to Alpine.

Q: Was he nice about it, or rough?

ALGREN: Oh, no, no. He had a deputy there. There was no need to be rough.

Q: What did he say to you?

ALGREN: Oh, well, he said, you know, "They want to see you back there." I said, "What do they want to see me about?" He said, "You'll find out when you get back there." I had no idea what he could want.

Q: What happened when you got back?

ALGREN: Well, then it was very plain. The guy simply hadn't mailed the typewriter at all. The sheriff went over and found the typewriter. It didn't require a mighty brain to figure that one out. But then the difficulty was that it was a circuit-riding judiciary. That is, in that part of Texas they didn't have a regular judge. He came around twice a year. So, because this was in the fall of the year, I had to wait for trial in the spring. Then I made some interesting friends in there. One, I remember, was a rodeo rider.

Q: In where?

ALGREN: In the jail.

Q: How long were you in jail?

ALGREN: Oh, five, four months, I guess, four months and some days. They came in March. I think I was arrested in November, uh, and then in the middle of March, the circuit judge came around. One of the inmates was a rodeo rider named Jess and he was interesting because he made a shrewd move, too. What he had done was to kill a Mexican on the American side, and then to avoid arrest had gone over to the Mexican side. And there he had killed a Mexican on the Mexican side and so, as a choice between being tried for killing a Mexican on the Mexican side and being tried for killing a Mexican on the American side, he figured it out to be better off back on the American side, so he gave himself up. Especially since he had relatives in the town. I thought this was a very shrewd move at the time. I was very impressed but—and I was given a jury trial, found guilty—what?

Q: Let's talk a little more about the five months in jail.

ALGREN: Oh, well, it was a very sparse diet because I think the warden was allowed sixty cents a day for each prisoner, but his own take came largely off of how much he could save on that, so there were two very thin meals a day, very thin indeed.

Q: What did you eat?

ALGREN: Oh, it was, uh, it was like beans and oatmeal and it was very spare.

Q: How many people were in the cell?

ALGREN: Ah, well, I guess there were two, but the cell doors were open. It was one large cell block with four cells, as I remember—each could accommodate, I guess, four men, but the doors to each cell were open and we could go in and out. We couldn't go into the run-around. The run-around was the space between the cell and the jailhouse wall that had to be cleaned every day. One of the more privileged prisoners would be allowed out in the morning to clean that run-around. That meant he could look out the window after he swept up and he had more freedom. He was a little bit closer to the outside. I think there were only three others that were there at the time. There were many who came in and went out after one day or so. It was a stop for federal prisoners.

Q: You couldn't get out on bail?

ALGREN: Well, I had nobody to bail me out.

Q: What was the bail? Remember?

ALGREN: No. I didn't have a lawyer, no bail was set . . .

Q: And there was no public defender?

ALGREN: Yeah, they gave me a defender.

Q: But you couldn't get bail? Did they offer you bail?

ALGREN: Well, I didn't have a defender until I was tried. Nothing was said at the time.

Q: They just said you would sit here and wait for the judge?

ALGREN: Yeah. The time was very difficult to pass. There was nothing to read.

Q: You were twenty-two? Twenty-three?

ALGREN: Yeah, there was nothing to read. We argued a lot.

Q: What about?

ALGREN: Oh, just about everything, everything there was to argue about.

Q: Were you the only college graduate in there?

ALGREN: Yeah, yeah. My cellmate for a while was a one-armed man, that is, one hand. He had the arm but the hand was off. It was just a sort of a nub. He had a face that was very close to that of one of the first early silent-movie cowboys named Art Acord—I don't know if you remember that sort of Indian profile of Art Acord—and he claimed to be a brother of Art Acord. Art Acord was a big man. He had Art Acord's face, but he was a very little man and he was the boss of the place. That is, he considered himself such.

Q: Why was he in?

ALGREN: Oh, I guess just vagrancy. You know, just a small-time thief.

Q: How did he lose the hand?

ALGREN: He never said. He had developed it. I remember his habit of bending tobacco tins with it. I mean, it was calloused.

There was no sensitivity in it so he could kind of use it as a hammer. I mean he was very egotistic.

Q: How did you pass the time?

ALGREN: Well, I guess we argued, we talked. I remember I drew pictures. And then every once in a while this crazy rodeo rider would think up a game. I can't think of what they called the game. You take your belt—now this was jailhouse humor, see. One guy stands blindfolded. I don't know how we picked him, but one guy had to stand with his eyes closed and these other three or four guys used their belts. He bends over and they hit him in the can with the belt and you guess which one hits you.

Q: What happened if you guessed right?

ALGREN: Well, then, the other guy takes your place. You could do this all afternoon, see.

Q: Did you play that game?

ALGREN: Yeah, but you see, this, this rodeo rider, he was very touchy. He always wanted to do the hitting but he wouldn't take the other position. He would simply deny it. This was another way of good thinking because he never got whipped, see. I didn't particularly enjoy this game, but this was one way we passed the time. And I think there might have been a checker board in there. There was certainly nothing to read. I think I tried to write, but I remember I caught some kind of hives. I began waking up scratching and I looked at them and they were very swollen. I mean they were very itchy, very big lumps. And then a funny thing happened. If you scratched them—"traveling hives" it was. I never heard of such a thing and I never heard of it since. But the fact of the matter was that if you had them on your arm, you did like this and then you put your hand there, you'd have them there. You transferred them almost at a touch.

Q: Kind of like poison ivy.

ALGREN: Yeah, so finally it was from head to foot I had these things and I simply didn't believe it. I'd look down and sure enough, here was some more. I was just one traveling hive, see.

Q: Did they have a doctor look after you?

ALGREN: No, no. One guy came up. I think I asked for something at that time and he brought me up a can of insecticide, something like that. But I thought I was better off with the hives. I know there were always guys hollering out the window at somebody. It was a big event when somebody sent up a can of tobacco or something like that. It was a big event if the sheriff brought in somebody, a federal prisoner, overnight. Once they brought in a guy who had been shot—they shot him somewhere—he'd been shot in the back. We killed that day watching him die because he wouldn't let them operate. He was in too much shock and he didn't understand. They wouldn't take the chance on operating on him and then having him die, so they wouldn't touch him without his permission and he was in too great shock to give permission. So he died there and I suppose the rest of the time just went on listening to this nutty roommate tell, you know, all his conquests.

Q: How did the rodeo man make out on his charge of murder?

ALGREN: Oh, he was freed, he was freed. There wasn't any real prosecution. He had to wait but he wasn't worried about anything and he was privileged. I don't know whether he and the sheriff were cousins, but they might as well have been. He was a home boy. He came from that town. Come to think of it, I think we spent most of the time just razzing each other, especially if there was some kind of slow-witted CCC deserter in there, somebody you could just razz.

Q: Could you write letters to anybody? Did anybody know you were there?

ALGREN: Yeah, I wrote letters, yeah. I got letters out. I don't think there was any censorship on that. Yeah, I wrote several letters from there.

Q: What impression did all of this have on you? How did you like it?

ALGREN: At first I was scared, naturally. Later I got over the scare. The first scare is you don't know what they're going to do with you and then later I began just deciding to sweat it out, that's all. And I didn't write many letters and the letters I did write didn't indicate that I was in jail.

Q: Have you written any stories about this experience?

ALGREN: Yeah, yeah. I did touch on it in a story that's in *The Neon Wilderness*. I remember I called it—it's a story about a Mexican—the story was named after a Mexican who was in there.

Q: What did he do?

ALGREN: Oh, well, he came in there right at the end. He just waved to his wife down below and—oh, I remember the name of the story; I was trying to remember—the name of the story was "El Presidente de Méjico." I used to kid around and tell him he would be President of Mexico someday. He thought that was very funny.

Q: What happened when your trial came up?

ALGREN: Well, that took all day. They do a big thing of it down there. It's not a casual thing at all. They give you a full jury trial and they had a public defender, an old man, who began by pleading not guilty. And there was a recess and then he switched his plea to guilty.

Q: Did he consult you?

ALGREN: Well, I guess he told me what he was going to do. It wasn't a matter of consultation. He was the defender. There was no choice. I wasn't going to tell him what to do in that position. I certainly wasn't going to argue with him. He put up some sort of a formal and conventional defense, I believe. He did this mechanically. I don't know, for whatever his fee was. He did it in a very perfunctory way and then I got on the witness stand. I was on the stand to hear the verdict and the verdict was guilty and the sentence was two years at Huntsville. It was a pea farm, a chain-gang deal. But then after sentence was passed, one of the jurors recommended mercy and then the judge—I had to stand in front of the judge —he said we are recommending mercy. He impressed on me that I was going to serve the time but it wasn't necessary for me to serve it in Texas. He said I could go home and serve it. They don't want to keep you in Texas. There were too many, you know. They want to get you out of the state. They don't want to let you really go free, so the understanding was that if I got out of the state within twenty-four hours and went back home, or at least got out of the way—of course I was fingerprinted; they do fingerprint you, and they do send the prints, one to Washington and one to your home city— that if at the end of two years I would come back to this court and swear that I had not been in any more trouble, then it would be considered that I had served the two years.

I never went back so legally I am still liable. I got out of there within twenty-four hours.

Q: When you go back to Texas, can they do anything to you?

ALGREN: Well, uh, I don't know who would bother, who would bother unless I became a candidate for the governorship of Texas, unless there was some point in that.

Q: Are you going to do that?

ALGREN: No, I'm going to run for Governor of Illinois.

Q: And then you went back to Chicago? How?

ALGREN: Different ways. Sometimes by boxcar.

Q: How many boxcar trips did you take?

ALGREN: Oh, innumerable. I couldn't remember because I took them for three or four years.

Q: How was a boxcar ride in those days?

ALGREN: Oh, it wasn't actually the boxcar riding. It was catching one, it was catching one and also getting out. Just getting to a boxcar was a problem because they didn't want you on the highways. When the thing was coming by, the doors were closed and then sometimes it would be going too fast. They didn't want a bunch of bums just crawling all over the place. It had to be done—they didn't mind you riding so much as long as you stayed out of sight. But the point was to catch the thing and then stay out of sight, and then to be able to duck in and out when you needed water. Actually, riding the boxcar wasn't so tough.

Q: What about food? Did you carry food with you?

ALGREN: Well, sometimes you carried a couple of Hershey bars. Often there'd be some little place where the train would slow down and there would be somebody selling hot dogs or something like that, just a little hot-dog stand or something like that.

Q: Were you pulled out of many boxcars by the railroad police?

ALGREN: No, not so many. In Greenville, North Carolina, once they drove up and took everybody out.

Q: How did they handle you?

ALGREN: Well, they wouldn't let us get back on there. They sent us down to the Salvation Army. They kept the colored guys, the colored guys, I think they separated them and sent them on to the labor camps. The white guys they let go to the Salvation Army and warned them that if they caught them trying to get out of town on the train again, then they would pick them up.

Q: Well, how were you expected to get out of town?

ALGREN: That was your problem. That was your problem. . . .

Q: If you didn't get out of town, you would be picked up for vagrancy?

ALGREN: And if you got out on the highway, you would be picked up for vagrancy, so you just had to sneak it. What you had to do then was just get out on the highway and keep walking without flagging anybody until you were safely out and then try to catch a train. I remember we got off there in the middle of the night and they pulled us out and one of them kept using a flashlight and he flashed it at this one party and ne looked the second time, and it was a woman. Since he had been using very rough language, he was very apologetic.

He said, "Why didn't you say you were a woman?" She was dressed in overalls. He said, "We never use language like that in front of women down here." He apologized to her. He was very gallant.

Q: Did you know it was a woman?

ALGREN: I hadn't noticed, no.

Q: What about your carnival days? I've heard you were in a carnival.

ALGREN: This was some time after I skipped, skipped the—abandoned the gas station and it was before I went on this type-writer bit. I lived in a house with a dozen other people, none of whom were working. It was in the Rio Grande Valley and the sign on top of the house said "Hotel." It was a curious hotel because it was made up of people who were taken in, who had no money, and whom the proprietor hoped would get some. He himself had a job in the grapefruit shed. His wife cooked in the kitchen and everybody lived in the hopes that somebody would get some money. A county fair showed up there, and one of the members of the carnival stayed over-night and asked me if I wanted to go to work so I went out there with him in the morning and he put me to work as a shill. I never saw the man himself again, but he put me to work. The job was simple enough. It was to stand in front of a wheel purporting to be a kind of horizontal roulette wheel with numbers on it. In back of it a small man, a New Yorker, operated the wheel. Behind him there was a Navaho blanket which had been nailed up. It was offered as a prize, but it had nails driven through it so it didn't look like they expected a winner. His partner, a big Texan, a professional Texan, that is, he had the rancher's hat, a man about six three, well-dressed, boots. Four or five shills would stand

around this wheel, just lean on it. Our backs were turned to
the runway where the fair had the usual things along the runway—the strong boy and the freaks and the girlie show and
the cat with two hearts and so forth. We couldn't see who was
coming along the runway. It wasn't our business. That was
the business of the partner outside. Now, when he saw a likely
customer coming, he would signal to the man we were facing,
to the New Yorker, who would begin spinning the wheel.
We'd all have a half a dollar or so apiece to put down and
we'd make a great deal of noise. That is the point: to create
a row as the sucker was passing and then almost everybody
would win. You put down a half a dollar and the guy would
say, "Another winner, another winner," and then you would
get five half dollars or five silver dollars back for the one,
and whenever that happened one of the more trusted shills
would hit you in the side to get the money back and then
you'd play it again. The idea was to attract this guy to see
what was going on and when he was just looking over your
shoulder to very gradually make room for him, and then the
New Yorker would say, "Well, just this one time, a chance to
make a dollar," or something. He made up the rules as he
went along. It made no sense. I mean, it made no kind of
gaming sense. He was working the thing with his foot and it
was a very crude apparatus and he would say, "Just this one
time, a chance to hit the double Black Jack," or something
like that, and, "Only a nickel, only a nickel." So you'd
give him a nickel and say, "I'll take two chances." He'd say,
"Oh, no, no, you can't do that—just one to a customer, no,
no, no, you've had your chance." So then you say to this
sucker who didn't intend to play, you'd say, "Hey, just take
a chance for me, will you? I mean, he won't let me, you
know." You'd give him the nickel and then he'd play it for
you and he'd win and he'd get the money. Then he would

turn it over to you and you'd say, "No, I'll split it with you,"
and he'd say, "No, no, it isn't mine because, you know, I
just played it for you." I says, "No, man, you took a chance
for me." So he's involved. He's already got half the winnings.
He puts it back on and he gets involved in the game that way.
Then he wins. He wins as much as twenty dollars. He goes
to reach for it. He says, the guy running the wheel says,
"Wait a second now, I wouldn't pick the money up because,"
he says, "now, now is your chance to win a hundred." The
sucker says, "Well, I don't know." He says, "All you have to
do is just let the twenty ride and if it comes red, you've got
a hundred coming. There's nothing to it. You don't want
to miss a hundred bucks. Go ahead, you know, you know,
you might make the red." So he goes and the other guy says,
"Wait a second. You know, it'll cost you another two dollars
for the chance to make the hundred." Well, naturally, so he
gets the two. Finally, the guy's so confused. He's got a fantastic amount of money coming. He's got so much coming,
he can't let it go. He has to keep paying a little bit and a
little bit more and this thing would go up to the point where
he would be borrowing three or four hundred dollars from
this guy. I've seen them write checks out there. They accepted
checks. It was a very interesting con but what bothered me
about it was that I wasn't getting anything except hot dogs.
Once in a while they'd let us go to the stands and eat for
nothing. I was handling enough money to get out of Texas but
I couldn't keep my hands on it. Every time I'd win ten dollars or so, the guy next to me would hit me, you know, and
I'd have to put it back in his hands. So this went on for about
four or five days and I thought what if I should go, what if I
should suddenly go legit on them like I had really won it
and walked away? Well, he'd have to expose himself to say,
"Come back here, you've got our money." So I picked my

moment when I saw, when it was at night, and I saw a sheriff coming along. The sheriff made the tour regularly. When I saw him coming, I won a handful of money, I don't know, twelve dollars or something like that in halves, and I picked up the money and then the guy hit me for it. I put it down in my pocket this way and backed off. There was a frozen moment and then I was gone, with the dough. And they didn't chase me because the sheriff was there. They couldn't have. I hadn't thought about this guy who worked for the carnival, who had gotten me the job. I wondered if he would know that I had finked on the game. He might tell them where I lived. So I just moved out of there.

Q: So where did you go? You went to Alpine and the typewriter?

ALGREN: Yeah. That was about the sequence.

Q: Then where did you go?

ALGREN: Oh I went back to Chicago. I hitchhiked out of there. I had gone to New Orleans in the summer. I remember that summer. I'll never forget that summer, it was so hot. I'd never been south before and I remember that heat. Toward Christmas I started home and I remember going through Tulsa around the first of the year and it was cold. It was snowing. I remember eating at a kind of home—I don't think it was a Salvation Army home, it was one of the other joints, the same kind of thing, but a smaller outfit—Army Veterans' God's Blessing Station, or something like that. I remember. I remember it must have been around Christmas and that it was awful cold.

Q: What did you do when you got back to Chicago?

ALGREN: I'd written to somebody. I wrote poems. I was real burned up about the guy siphoning the gas, and there was another guy around there with a steel plate in his skull, a World War I veteran. We had stayed at a number of places before we hit the station and I was always getting conned by these guys. They conned me out of a watch. I don't know. I was always putting up security for these guys. And then this guy, the guy with the steel skull, was willing to work now and then. But the other one, the Floridian, he would never work, he was just a promoter and his name was Luther. Everybody there was named Luther. Everybody I knew—they were all named Luther. What I think happened was that they all had different names once but then they all became anonymous and Luther is the most anonymous name, you know. Everybody was named Luther. We stayed at the landlord's house and the man's name, the old man's name, was Luther.

Q: When did you begin to write?

ALGREN: Just about that time.

Q: Down there?

ALGREN: Yeah. I wrote a letter home. See this guy with the steel skull was a little on the violent side and he said we could get into something. He had a gun and he wanted to stick up this "Jitney Jungle" store. "And how are you going to go out?" He says, "We're going to take Luther's car." Luther is the *other* Luther, the Luther with the Studebaker. We're going to get out of town in a 1928 Studebaker. I thought to myself: Boy, you better pick up that steel strip in his head and see what's underneath it. The guy was nuts. So I wrote a letter, kind of a bitter letter on the condition of the Confederacy. I didn't like the deal I was getting. I wrote a letter home.

Q: To whom?

ALGREN: I'm not sure. I must have written that letter to Murray Gitlin. Somewhere along the line I saw an ad, there was an ad, an ad in the paper. Of course I'd always wanted to write. I'd been writing at the University of Illinois, but—

Q: When did you decide you wanted to write?

ALGREN: Oh I don't know. I was always trying to write. Even in grammar school I think I was trying to write, in high school I was trying to write, and at the University of Illinois I was trying to write. It was just something that I never thought of not doing.

Q: Well, why did you always try to write instead of trying to become, say, a crooked cop?

ALGREN: Because I guess I sensed I was better at writing. I didn't need to be a crooked cop and I needed to write. I mean it was just something you did, you know, just like a race horse runs. But I never thought really it came to anything. I thought you could write if you had a trade or if you were a teacher or newspaperman. Then you could write.

Q: But you still haven't answered my question at this point—why you or anybody else should write. Let's just take you first. Why did you always want to write? You weren't raised in any literary group. You didn't come from writers. You had to find out about writing on your own, but you say that since high school you wanted to write. Why?

ALGREN: I wanted to write in the sense that everybody needs some form of expression. Let me say that I think just wanting to write doesn't necessarily mean that you really want to write. When I run into many people, as I have for a long time, who say, when they introduce themselves, "I want to write," this doesn't mean they really want to write. Very few people really want to write. What they want is what I wanted in high school: I wanted somebody or some means to distinguish me from everybody else. Why I would pick on writing was just a mechanical facility. Developing it is accidental. The fact that I wanted to write, when I say it was mechanical, it was just the easiest way of finding out, to borrow James Baldwin's recent phrase, what my name is, who am I? If I had been a hundred ninety-six pounds and six four, I would have found my name by becoming an all-state football player or something. I mean you write or you play football or you paint, or you become a pimp, or you steal, or you become a politician, in an accidental way. I mean, you go where you have a certain proclivity. I mean, a certain tendency. All this means is that you want to be yourself. You want to, you need—you're nobody unless somebody says you're somebody and you need some recognition. If you're in sixth grade and you win a spelldown, then you begin to know who you are. You're the kid who can spell the best. People do this just to try to distinguish themselves from the day they were born, of course. But this doesn't mean you really want to write. This just means you want sufficient attention just to justify yourself and so that people won't get you mixed with anybody else. And not only that, but they'll think you're better than anybody else. And they'll like you more, and so forth. This is just the same reason that a girl always wants to be the prettiest one in the class. She wants to be somebody. But this doesn't mean you really want to write. I wanted to write in this sense all through the University, I guess. When we did themes I wanted to write good themes. I wanted to be a writer in the literary sense. That is, I wanted to find a place in the literary world and, in this sense, I wanted to write. But the experience on the road gave me something to write about. It was just an accidental, just a fortuitous thing. I didn't go on the road in order to have something to write about. You do see what it's like, what a man in shock who is dying looks like. He knows he's going to die and he's shocked by the idea that he's dying. Or you're waiting for a boxcar and it seems to be going a little too fast and some kid makes a try for it and you see him miss and then you get the smell of blood and you go over and you see it sliced off his arm. And all the whores in New Orleans. And all the tens of thousands of Americans literally milling around at that time trying to survive. All these thousands of little scenes—sitting around a little kitchen in New Orleans with three other guys trying to sell something. One was an old man, I was the youngest, and then two middle-aged men. Sitting around a little, a little kind of night bulb, with four bowls of some kind of soup somebody had cooked up with one piece of meat in it, and the man who cooked the soup was distributing it. Everybody knew he was going to try to keep that. We all knew there was one piece of meat in there. We were wondering who was going to get it. We assumed that he was going to keep that piece for himself. When he poured mine, I noticed he just tilted that ham just enough so that the meat didn't slip out and he did it for the other guys, but he slipped with the old man. The old man was a guest. I don't know what the old man was doing there except a free meal or something. And he slipped. Overconfidence I guess, and the meat went into the old man's plate. We just looked at it there. We couldn't take it back but it just seemed a shame that it was only one piece of meat. All these scenes, one after another, piled up into something that made me not just want to write but to really say it, to find out that this thing was all upside down. Everything I'd been told was wrong. That I see with my own eyes. I'd been told, I'd been assured that it was a strive and succeed world. What you did: you got yourself an education and a degree and then you went to work for a family newspaper and then you married a nice girl and raised children and this was what America was. But this is not what America was. America was not socialized and I resented very deeply that I'd been lied to. I'd not only been lied to morally, I'd been lied to even insofar as the information that I had about journalism. I'd been told how to write headlines for newspapers. I'd been told in the School of Journalism the way you wrote headlines when you tried to write a headline, but the way you'd been taught, this got you fired immediately from a newspaper. You had to reverse everything from what you'd been taught, mechanically as well as morally.

Q: But a lot of people who experienced what you experienced did not become writers, so there must be some other things working here, too. What about the possibility that as a writer you work on your own? How important is that to you?

ALGREN: Well, I hadn't thought of it but, now you mention it, I'm sure that this was part of it because it was a way out of dealing with other people.

Q: As you tried to express yourself?

ALGREN: Yes. I think, now that you mention it, remembering the four years, the four years at the University of Illinois I was separated from people, was independent of them, I think that without thinking about it, I wanted a condition where I would not have to take orders from anybody, where I would be able to tell them what to do, I think. And I believe that in writing I felt that they had to listen to me.

Q: Because you had listened to other writers as you read them?

ALGREN: Well, not because of that but because if I was a good writer and had an experience that was true and knew how to say it, they would have to listen.

Q: But also isn't it true that when you first got interested in books at the University of Illinois, you were influenced by people whom you didn't even know and who were dead and who lived in other countries? You did see the power of the written—

ALGREN: Oh yeah. Oh yeah.

Q: —word because it had worked on you.

ALGREN: Oh, yeah. Well, when I saw the kind of lives that writers had led, I mean, the kind of satisfaction that could accrue for a writer, I wanted that satisfaction more than the satisfaction that might accrue to being the owner of a chain of successful newspapers.

Q: But you were finding yourself a protester, a dissenter, right? All along the line, from the days of high school—

ALGREN: Yes.

Q: —when you decided that what you saw was not the same as what you were told—

ALGREN: Yes.

Q: —and you resented this. Is it possible that you decided that to become a writer was the best way of expressing your protest?

ALGREN: No, not quite that simple. It worked out that way, but there might have been more than one facet to the protest because almost everybody who was out of a job then was protesting—

Q: Right.

ALGREN: —so I would have protested whether I could read or write or not. But I think, as I remember it, even in high school long before the Depression when there was no problem of hunger, I was protesting this before I graduated from high school. The kids that I went to high school with were getting jobs, were going to work, for instance, for Sears, Roebuck in a sensible capacity with the idea of becoming a reliable salesman in order to rise higher.

Q: But they weren't protesting?

ALGREN: No, they accepted this. They accepted a long-term job, a job that would give them security, at Sears, Roebuck or the post office, or a job which, if they were faithful to it, would provide them with security for their lifetime and, in fact, I still have friends who are still at Sears, Roebuck, and I wouldn't say well-to-do, but have no fear of insecurity. They've grown with Sears, Roebuck and they've lived well, I mean, they've lived comfortably. But there's still that gap between us because, even at that time, I resented doing a thing like this, because I was sure that you can't reduce living to working for survival. This made me very angry and very, very irritable without knowing why, and it's just that life had to give you something more than security. And these other kids, as I remember, didn't understand that. They didn't share my feeling that life should be something rich or something more than just a guarantee of respectable survival. I couldn't accept that.

Q: Do you think that all writers are protesters against the difference between what they're told and what they find out to be true?

ALGREN: No, I think most writers are protesters against what is true and—

Q: Against what is true?

ALGREN: I'm not talking about great writers. Uh, yeah, I'm talking about the contemporary scene. It seems to me that most writers are insisting that the contemporary scene is real. Well, I think it is unreal.

Q: But there must have been some other reason for these people becoming writers, then.

ALGREN: No, not necessarily, because a lot of them began, began with dissent in the thirties. I'm talking about men of my own age, who began by leading bread lines and writing very effective plays. The example that comes to mind is Irwin Shaw's *Bury the Dead*. This was a man who protested war and what war did. Of course, when war actually came, he refused to have the play put on. I'm sure that at the time he wrote this play *Bury the Dead* that he was against war in all its forms but this wasn't hard to do because it was a time of peace. When the war actually came along, he withdrew the play.

Q: But he was also quite anxious about the rise of Fascism and what was happening to Jews when the war came along.

ALGREN: But this wasn't protest; he's Jewish.

Q: But a lot of people who aren't Jews were quite upset by that and a lot of people who were Jews or otherwise were very worried about the rise of Hitler. We'll talk later about contemporary writers. I just wanted to find out from you what drove you into being a writer and I think you've helped on that. And from here we can go back to when you said you saw an advertisement, right? Now, have you said what you wanted to say, about why you write, why you always wanted to be a writer?

ALGREN: That's as much as I care to say at the moment.

Q: All right. What about the advertisement?

ALGREN: Anyhow, there was a little piece, a little advertisement, and I forget where I saw it. It must have been in some neighborhood newspaper. Maybe it was in the *Saturday Review of Literature.* Maybe some small magazine. Anyhow it said that the Writers' Circle, 3600 Douglas Boulevard, is interested in manuscripts. So when I got back to Chicago I went over to 3600 Douglas Boulevard, which was the Jewish People's Institute, and I went to this little group and the guy named Murray Gitlin—he was the club director there—had a lot of young people in trying to write. He wanted to write himself and he was very friendly. He was a very friendly guy. I didn't have a typewriter at the time and my brother-in-law wouldn't let me use his, but Murray gave me his in his office. We were up in Albany Park then, up on Lawrence Avenue, so in order to use the typewriter, I'd ride the Kedzie Avenue car to Douglas Boulevard and transfer over. It was about an hour's trolley ride. I don't know what he used while I was using it, but he gave me the corner. And either I wrote the letter to him or at any rate this letter I wrote about my hassle in this gasoline station got into his hands and he said, "This is a story; make it a story." So I did and called it "So Help Me" and I sent it to *Story* magazine, which I hadn't heard about, but Murray Gitlin knew about *Story,* and they took it and published it in 1933. Because they took it, I got a form letter from Vanguard Press. I was twenty-four and I got this letter from Vanguard Press: "Are you working on a novel? We are interested in a novel on the basis of this piece in *Story* magazine." I had nothing else to do so instead of answering the letter, I rode to New York. I was so used to hitchhiking by that time, I was so used to walking out the door and getting on Route 66—it was just as easy as getting into a car, and although I never knew exactly what route I was going to take, I never had any trouble. By that time I was a professional transient so I knew all the places to go by then. So I rode to New York. Some kids—two guys with a lot of bedding in the car—picked me up and they were going to New York by way of Niagara Falls. I said, "All right, I've never seen Niagara Falls." So I came down. We saw the Falls and it seems to me I helped them somewhere along the line. I think I helped to buy food or something. I think I helped buy gas once or twice. Anyhow we came down the Palisades. That was the first time I saw New York. And I went right up to Vanguard Press and met James Henle. And he said, "What'll you need? What would you do? How would you write a novel?" I said, "I'd go back to the Southwest." He said, "What would you need to do that?" I said, "I need thirty dollars a month." I mean I knew it would cost that much. You get room and board for twenty dollars a month and that leaves ten dollars for tobacco and so forth. And so we made a deal. He gave me ten dollars to get out of town and a promise of thirty dollars a month for three months, a total of one hundred dollars. I wrote *Somebody in Boots* on that. I didn't finish it in three months, but I delivered it. It was delivered in 1935. That was the only work I did between graduation and 1936 when the WPA opened up. I got married in 1936 and the book wasn't a success at all, so I didn't try writing another novel until 1940. I got divorced then.

Q: In 1940?

ALGREN: In 1939.

Q: You were married three years?

ALGREN: Something like that. Then I went off by myself to Chicago's Northwest Side and wrote *Never Come Morning,* which got better notices.

Q: You say that you did not write a book for three or four years while you were married. Why didn't you write during the time you were married?

ALGREN: Now, this question doesn't have, if applied to just one marriage, doesn't have any particular meaning because just one wretched marriage—there's so many, but the question does have meaning if it raises the question of why it is so seldom that a writer has a good marriage, or an actor, or an actress? I don't know the figures, but I think the incidence of failed marriages or marriages that simply exist, because there are children, marriages that don't emotionally succeed are much commoner, much commoner, among artists or people in the arts.

Q: Why is that?

ALGREN: I think something goes on. Now I'm not talking about the hack writer, a surface writer. I don't mean that kind of writer because I think these are journalists who report and I don't think there's any emotional conflict. Or with such an artist, say, as Norman Rockwell, and with some painters, yeah. But I think that the artistic impulse is related to the sexual impulse very deeply. The most extreme example I can think of is with Toulouse-Lautrec. I think Edmund Wilson does this thing in the book *The Wound and the Bow,* kind of explaining Dickens and Hemingway, and I think it accounts for what Dickens called the "wretchedest marriage that anybody ever made," the "unhappiest couple that ever was," he called it. And maybe Hemingway had something out of his marriages, but it is true that he had at least four wives and what I think happens there is that the writer needs, as much as anybody, he needs this steady situation with one woman and he knows, as everybody knows, that it's not good to scatter yourself. I mean, if you stay with one woman then it gets better. But, if you do that, the conflict arises in this because he not only wants that, but he also wants to use this particular ability he has. Everybody he knows, anybody can get married and have children. He wants to be the one who does it differently. Anybody just by falling in love and having somebody fall in love with him can achieve that, but not many people can get love the way Dickens had, where people, an ordinary housewife, would follow him down the street and thank him for the people that he had given her. So this is a very rare opportunity and if you see this, and even if you only see it or even if you begin to get through letters from people you've never seen a kind of a love and a kind of a recognition that you're helping them, this is something more from the plain artistic viewpoint. This is something that can seem to the writer to make it worth while giving up the stable situation.

Q: Can he maintain both?

ALGREN: No, he can't.

Q: Why not?

ALGREN: Well, he can. But as your question indicated and as my answer indicated, it certainly didn't work with me, because once you commit yourself to a marriage and life is unrealized, you become a purely negative person. I mean, you are giving yourself to a negative situation.

Q: What is that?

ALGREN: Well, a negative situation is one in which you can't write. All your attention and your energy is drawn off by things that don't matter, without even the satisfaction of children. So all it comes to really, it simmers down to this: You're living with somebody who's living with you simply because she doesn't want to go to work, which would be all right, but what you're giving up is really yourself. And since you don't see it clearly and you regard yourself as being obliged, if she makes you *feel* obligated, all you do is just get very irritable. This makes you hard to live with. And, so then you have to, you tear the thing apart somehow and this is all I see in that. I don't know whether that answers anything.

Q: Yes, I think it does. When did *Neon Wilderness* come out?

ALGREN: Oh, right after the war.

Q: Then you were publishing short stories before the war?

ALGREN: Yeah, I published several before the war and then in 1942 I went into the Army and I got out in 1945.

Q: How long were you with the WPA?

ALGREN: I think from 1936 to 1940.

Q: What did you do in the WPA?

ALGREN: I was an editor. I guess I was an editor.

Q: For whom?

ALGREN: For the Writers' Project, Illinois Writers' Project.

Q: Was that any good?

ALGREN: The WPA? Yeah, it was very good. I believe that the first thing it was, it served to humanize people who had been partially dehumanized. There had been, I believe, in those years between 1929, 1930, '31, when people had been self-respecting, lost their self-respect by being out of work and then living by themselves began to feel the world was against them. To such people the WPA provided a place where they began to communicate with people again. They got a little self-respect back and, uh, I know it put me in touch with people again, and it also put me in touch with people who were politically alert and I know there are oftentimes now when I think, well, where did everybody go? There is—

Q: But at the time—

ALGREN: There were all shades of opinion. There was a lot of human communication.

Q: Was there any good writing done, any—

ALGREN: The best writing perhaps was on the Illinois project. Dick Wright turned out a book. I mean, he was using the project time.

Q: What book did he turn out?

ALGREN: He turned out a book of short stories. I believe the title of it was—the first, top story was, I believe, "Bad Boy Leaves Home." It was published by Martha Foley. I guess it had gotten sufficient recognition.

Q: Did you have anything to do with that?

ALGREN: No, no, nothing to do with that. I knew Wright when he wrote *Native Son* but it gave him a means to write further and I used it. Everybody used it to the extent that it was a place where you could report at ten in the morning and then leave at two and then you had the rest of the day to yourself. And it meant too that when my salary went up to a hundred and twenty-five dollars a month I had a leeway of half of that.

Q: So, that it *was* good.

ALGREN: Well, it kept me alive. It certainly improved my economy. When I started out with the WPA, I think I got eighty-seven dollars a month, then ninety-six, and then I was making one hundred and twenty-five dollars a month, which was the most money I had ever made. One hundred and twenty-five dollars a month was more than— It was in easy circumstances because I was paying twenty-five dollars a month rent, so I had a hundred bucks and I was going to the race track. It was a kind of affluence. . . .

3 *The Army and the Writing*

QUESTION: What did you do in the Army for three years?

ALGREN: Oh, I was a private. I started out with the field artillery and wound up with the medics. I was a litter-bearer in the medics. When I was with the field artillery I jumped around a 105 howitzer at Fort Bragg and then again at Camp Maxey, Texas. I got awfully bored with it. I mean the *monotony* was the most miserable thing about the Army, the monotony of practicing the hand salute. I had no desire at first to go overseas but after a year I know I'm not going home and I want to go *some*where, anywhere to get away from all the hand salutes. So I asked to go overseas. I mean the Army makes heroes out of you. The Army thinking is that no matter how reluctant a man is when he gets into the Army to risk his neck overseas, that after about a year stateside he will either blow his top or ask to go overseas. At first I was certainly contented to stay stateside. At first I felt the longer I can stay stateside the better, but my feelings completely changed after a year. By the time my outfit was ready to go overseas, I was scared that I was going to get left behind, so I went up to a lieutenant in the morning and I said, "Am I going?" And he said, "Yes, you're going, don't worry." And so I took his word. But that same afternoon a couple of my buddies who were going told me, "You're not going." They had made it their business to look in the barracks room where they were stenciling the bags, see, and there were about a dozen bags there put to one side. These were the bags that were *not* being stenciled because these bags weren't going anywhere. They belonged to one guy who is a nut, to one guy who is A.W.O.L., one guy is supposed to be court-martialed, and one guy is too sick to go. Obviously they weren't taking these guys and my bag was over there. I really got apprehensive. I really honestly got scared that I wasn't going to go. So I actually went into the orderly room and I saluted and I said, "Sir—" and they had this kid there who was crying. He was just scared. He was begging not to go. He just went in there and cried and I stood at the side there while this guy was begging off—his wife's family, or something—and they ain't paying him no heed. But there was a young sergeant there, a young Greek guy, and very reasonable, a very quiet guy. Now I *knew* that if I came up formally and all, and saluted and everything, that *no*body is going to make any common-sense connection between a guy who wants to go and a guy who don't want to go. This doesn't make any sense in the Army. So I quietly said to this other guy, "Can I talk to you personally, Sergeant?" You know you could do that with him; he was not a stiff guy. I talked to him personally. I said, "You know my bag ain't being stenciled." And he said, "Well I don't know anything about that." I said, "Well, I don't want to get left behind, you know. I want to go. I just don't want to stay and this other guy, that kid in there, he don't want to go." So he said, "You sure you want to go?" "Oh yes," I said. "Sure I want to go. What do you want me to say?" "Well," he said, "you've been goofing off." I said, "Of course I'm going to be goofing off here—I mean this is goof-off country."

Q: Did you get to go?

ALGREN: I went and I'm very glad now that I did go.

Q: Did you see any action?

ALGREN: Yeah, later.

Q: Where?

ALGREN: In Germany and France. First we went to Wales for two or three months, someplace called Camp Penally.

Q: How long were you in Wales?

ALGREN: Oh, we were in Wales from near Christmas until the following spring—I'd say three months. This was the Christmas of forty-four. The last Christmas of the war.

Q: Who did you think was winning the war?

ALGREN: I thought that the United States and its allies were winning the war and that I was losing it. I was wrong. We were all losing it. We were going to go overseas just for the last big victory and I remember when we were told that it wasn't going to be that easy because we weren't winning the war any more, and that we were losing it. That was the time of the Battle of the Bulge and the von Rundstedt business. So, uh, we went there at the tail end of the Battle of the Bulge.

Q: Were there any good things in the Army for you?

ALGREN: Yes. Overseas there was. I can't remember anything good while we were stateside, but overseas where there was much less discipline, where we didn't have to be saluting all the time, there was a kind of freedom to move. Seeing London and the German cities. I liked London and, of course, Paris.

Q: Why were you in the Army to begin with?

ALGREN: Well, there was no alternative. I wouldn't even qualify as a conscientious objector, because you have to have some record of conscientious objection. You can't just go up and say, well, I don't believe in war.

Q: But you thought Hitler should have been beaten?

ALGREN: Oh, yes, yes, I had been interested in the anti-Fascist movement in the thirties. I had done leg work for the Abraham Lincoln Brigade around Chicago. I had my name in all the anti-Fascist literature, the League for American-Soviet Friendship and all of that.

Q: And you wanted to see Hitler beaten?

ALGREN: Oh, yeah, but I wasn't sure that the purpose of the war was altogether to beat Hitler. Yeah, I knew Hitler had to be beaten. I knew Germany had to be defeated, but I wasn't ever sure that there wasn't an overlapping in what we stood for in fighting Hitler and, of course, this kind of doubt was felt much more keenly by the Negro, by Negro troops. It was also interesting, too, that if I had been actually in the Abraham Lincoln Brigade, instead of just doing leg work, I wouldn't have been taken by the Army because these were anti-Fascists, the guys who went in the thirties really did not want Fascism. They went overseas and because of that they went to Spain, and these men were not wanted in the Armed Forces. These men didn't get in in the Second World War. They were, they were dangerous. They were Communists. And—

Q: Were they actually all Communists?

ALGREN: Well, at least they were all anti-Fascists. What I mean is that our feeling—

Q: Are all anti-Fascists Communists?

ALGREN: No.

Q: You mean they were *called* Communists.

ALGREN: Yeah, they were called Communists. That was the general label, but my feeling was although the Nazis had to be beaten, because of what they stood for, this didn't necessarily mean that we believed in exactly the opposite, that, if we won the war, then everything was going to be as it should be.

Q: Then the war experience for you must have been very sad because you're a militant, profound anti-Fascist, aren't you?

ALGREN: No, I don't think so. I don't think I've ever been either militant or profound as an anti-Fascist. When the issue has come up, when certain things have come up and I've been called on to express, literally when I've been cornered, then I take a left-wing stand. So far as I was concerned, I didn't really do much about the McCarthy era. I spoke once or twice. But I didn't try to take matters into my own hands until the Rosenberg trial came up. Then I was asked to serve as an Honorary Chairman of the Chicago Committee to Save the Rosenbergs, which I did, but I didn't save them. All I did was to lose my passport. I felt all right in that. I felt it was a kind of a phony, they didn't want me around the office. I never went to the office. They had their own functionaries, the people who were doing what they wanted, but their names were not known around Chicago. And my name was. I felt all right going along with the Rosenbergs. I felt that their execution or the attempted execution was a kind of a punitive thing. It was a way of blaming the stalemate in Korea or the defeat in Korea and that when this sort of thing happens, it has to be accounted for in terms of espionage. I thought that just the fact that the lack of conviction on the Government's part that they were spies was a damning thing. And just the fact that this line was kept open right up to the last minute of execution in case the woman should want to inform, showed a lack of certainty, a lack of conviction on the part of the Government. And even from a conservative viewpoint, the idea of putting people to death for a political offense, I think, was foolish, making martyrs out of schlemiels. Nevertheless, I didn't want to go along with the people who saw in it an opportunity, especially American Jews, who saw in it an opportunity to assert their own loyalty. I think particularly of the professor from the University of Montana, who was very emphatic. He said he thought they deserved the death penalty, because it made him personally, as an American Jew, look like a good American. This sort of thing I felt infuriating and I didn't want to go to the other side either, which regarded it as the beginnings of the American pogrom, which some of the members of the committee wanted to do. I mean, this is an inciting thing. "They're getting executed because they're Jews." I didn't want to go that line either and, in fact, the only time I talked for the committee, I disassociated myself from that viewpoint that this is the beginning of an American pogrom. I didn't want to go with that easy line. I thought they were being executed because they were Communists or as scapegoats, because somebody was needed there. I didn't think they were being executed because they were Jews. The incident made me wary of businessmen who regard themselves as liberals by putting out money but remain anonymous themselves. Liberals by surrogate—how can you be a liberal and risk nothing but money?

Q: But in the Army—I'm trying to get to your feelings of, you know, when you were in the Army, that you, that if Hitler hadn't been defeated, you would have been unhappy.

ALGREN: I may never have thought that Germany would win that war. I never got scared about it. I always assumed that I was on the winning side. This was pretty naïve, I guess. It could very well, as I know, have gone the other way. I felt earlier in the war in Spain it was a war with which I really felt more profoundly. This I felt was a pretty clear business of warfare between people who believed in human rights above property rights and it was a war in which a demand for recognition of human dignity was being pitted against an entrenched sense of property.

Q: Why didn't you enlist?

ALGREN: Well, I'll tell you, this sort of war, against the kind of people you have to fight, that has to be won by hand. That is, it had to be won in the way, in the way that the men who went there tried to win it, by the bayonet and the grenade, and I didn't go. I wanted that war to be won, too. I didn't go for this reason: Because given a bayonet against a Moor with a bayonet, the Moor was going to win. In other words, I didn't go to the war in Spain although I was asked. It was assumed that I would go. My defense when asked why aren't you there was that I don't want to get killed. That was why I didn't go. By the time World War II came around, I didn't feel that the Army should take me seriously as a soldier.

Q: As a killer.

ALGREN: Yeah. I was willing to do perfunctory, mechanical jobs. I was willing to clean up around the barracks. When I got overseas, I didn't feel any reluctance about carrying a litter. There were things that had to be done. Hospitals had to be kept clean and so forth, but I can't ever say that I ever took on myself, either in the war in Spain or in this war, the actual job which had to be done, of killing certain people. There isn't any other way of doing it. They have to be shot in the head or they have to be blown up or they have to be bombed.

Q: Why aren't you a killer?

ALGREN: I wasn't brought up right. I don't know. I believe that there are people who ought to be shot in the head and I think there are people that—

Q: Can you do that? If, under a legal system where certain people that you thought should be shot in the head, you were asked to do it, would you accept the job?

ALGREN: Well, the temptation is to say yes.

Q: What's the truth?

ALGREN: Well, I don't know. I've never been in that situation. There aren't many people who can. Anybody can who is brought into it young enough, like the young Frenchmen in the F.F.I. who went into it at fourteen or fifteen and learned to kill. If you do get the hang of it, that young, you can do it almost any time.

Q: Are most Americans killers?

ALGREN: All people are killers, potentially. Tigers aren't in it with people. But if you mean, as a trade, yes, there is a trade in killing here, of course, and I've talked, and even had friends, among men whose trade this is. But—

Q: If there were a legal setup where you could not be physically harmed yourself or legally punished for assassinating people you thought should be done away with, could you accept the job?

ALGREN: If I was given no alternative, I would do it.

Q: No, you would be given the alternative, your choice. I'm giving you the choice.

ALGREN: Of *not* doing it?

Q: Of not doing it.

ALGREN: Oh, then I wouldn't do it.

Q: Even though you think—

ALGREN: I don't think killing, under any circumstances, can be right. I don't think there can be any, any justification for killing somebody else.

Q: Yet you think, as you just said, that there are some people who should be killed.

ALGREN: I think I'll take that back. I'll renege on that. Not people that should be killed, but people that have to be killed. They have to. Nobody should be killed, but these are people who, unless they are killed, their existence makes life almost impossible for a lot more people.

Q: Can't they be put away instead?

ALGREN: It's a little risky. The first attempt in Spain at overthrowing the democratic government did fail and the Spanish President had Franco, he had five of them from North Africa, from Spanish North Africa, who lost the first attempt, and he put them away. He just exiled them. The war could have been avoided right then if they had been put up against the wall, right away.

Q: Well, no, but he just exiled them. I don't mean to argue with you about this, but he didn't put them away. He didn't control them.

ALGREN: Yeah.

Q: You're not a killer. You ended up in the medics.

ALGREN: Oh, yeah.

Q: To take care of people.

ALGREN: No. To keep somebody from killing me.

Q: Have you ever killed a man?

ALGREN: Actually, or just in the heart?

Q: Actually.

ALGREN: No.

Q: Ever damaged a man physically in a fight?

ALGREN: Oh, I broke a guy's nose once. I never had any pang of conscience about it.

Q: When was the last time you had a fist fight? Drunk, sober, angry, calm, anything, under any condition? How did you break the man's nose?

ALGREN: Well, I hit him, I hit him with my right hand. It was an argument over a, uh, gambling obligation.

Q: How long ago was it?

ALGREN: Oh, it was, let me see, about ten, eleven years, I guess. It doesn't seem to me it was that long ago.

Q: Was that the last time you hit a man?

ALGREN: Yeah. I had a little wrestling engagement last summer [1962] on the ship I was on. Nothing to it. It was over a gambling debt a fireman owed me.

Q: How many fist fights have you been in in your whole life?

ALGREN: Not many, very few. A couple of schoolyard fights when I was in school. I've been engaged in a great many threats and counterthreats of extreme violence. I've been engaged in long discussions in front of bars, in which the question is, Did you call me this? I said, Yeah, I called you that. Now what are you going to do? Then it's great for taking off coats, at which time some angel of deliverance would step in and say, "Now, what's all this about? What did he really say?" And, well, I said, he said this, and at this point, the opponent would tighten his shoelaces so he shouldn't slip in this bloody battle and by this time you get quite a crowd. Well, this gives the opponent time to take his coat off and have him hang it on a car, hang it on the car, because you want to be stripped down, see. Well, then the other one has a chance to loosen his collar. And then you resume the discussion. You can lose two or three crowds this way. Then finally some intermediary will come in and say, "Aw, look, he's a good guy and he's really a good guy," and the idea is how can you, how can you keep a thing going without backing down. The only way, the only way you can save your dignity is to say, "Well, he asked me, see." You're not there voluntarily but you are prepared to defend yourself to the death if he will make an aggressive move. It takes a third person to get you both back in the bar, see, and have a drink together. And it creates some very solid friendships based on a recognition of that mutual cowardice.

Q: So, while your life has been closely connected with violence, you have not personally, you are not a violent person?

ALGREN: No, I don't react very quickly. I've known men who do spontaneously know whether to knock somebody cold. But I'm afraid I have to go home and think about it for three days and decide it was justified and say now if you would stand exactly in the same position you were when you said that, now I'm going to give it to you, see. But the occasion is gone. This can leave a little rankling. You asked me before, you know, did I believe in killing, or did I ever kill anybody? Well, I have killed somebody in the heart. In the Army there was a sergeant that I knew should be dead and I would wake up every morning thinking how to make this man now alive be dead forever. I wanted to kill him. I couldn't. When I saw him it was red. I saw him in colors of red, and he knew this, and in fact he was using me. He knew more about drilling and about the Army than anybody in the outfit. He sent me down to the mess hall and I was burning up, and he made a point when he got to the mess hall and tells the mess hall staff, "Give him the works." Then he threw this in. He said, "Now, if you don't like it, we'll go outside, just me and you, we'll go outside to finish this out, see." And I just had this rankling thing about that. I didn't take it up, I just stood there, see. This, this is not what should have been done.

Q: What should have happened?

ALGREN: Well, I should have gone outside. I suppose I was scared. Whatever could have happened I would have hurt him as much as he hurt me. There wouldn't have been much to it. In a thing like this you should always take it up. You should never stand still, you know, because you're going to get a kickback on that. Since you're going to have to live with yourself for a long time, you shouldn't let this come back. But, unless you do, it does come back.

Q: And did it come back?

ALGREN: Oh, yes, yes, it still comes back and I can't get out of it by saying, well, he was a sergeant and I would have got court-martialed for hitting a sergeant. He was willing to take off his coat. He was willing to assume the man-to-man thing. I don't know where he lives now. He'd be awful surprised if (*laughter*) I showed up someday and just clobbered him one, but I don't know whether that would do it now or not.

Q: And in Wales you ended up as a private.

ALGREN: Well, I stayed a private. I came to Wales, I mean, I ended up in the war as a private, which was not bad since I started as a private.

Q: And then you went to Liverpool?

ALGREN: Yeah. We took a train to Liverpool and a channel boat across the Channel, then we switched. The name of the next boat we switched to to go up the Seine was the *President Warfield*. Not Garfield but Warfield. I looked over the side of this big tug and there is the name *President Warfield*. I don't know who Warfield was but it was a curious boat because years later it became the *Exodus*. I saw it in the description of the book *Exodus*. It was this American boat— just a big tub and no can on it, nothing, it was just jammed with us and we didn't have far to go. So I was on the *Exodus* but I wasn't going to Israel.

Q: Were you ever wounded?

ALGREN: (*Laughter*)

Q: I mean were you ever hit?

ALGREN: (*Prolonged laughter*) I got hit with a shoe in Marseilles after the war was over. But it hurt. I got hit in the back of the head right here (*indicating*).

Q: Who threw the shoe at you?

ALGREN: I don't know but I have a suspicion that it was a man who was working for the same people I was. He denies it. No,

I didn't get hit. That was the only wound I suffered. Other guys around me got killed but not through gunfire.

Q: Then how did they get killed?

ALGREN: They were called "industrial accidents." It was a medical outfit and we were always pitching these big tents. Everybody would jump out and there would be some big hillbilly who'd grab this huge pole in the middle. He'd want to do the whole thing himself and then everybody else would run and tie things down. Big squad tents. We were always setting up hospitals wherever we went and guys were always running around putting on tourniquets. Nobody was bleeding, but some of these guys had been bandaging things for three or four years. They could bandage *any*thing. The American Army—there never was such an army in the world where you have thousands to train one guy into being a good medic. A lot of these guys were good. They could do anything. They had a medical education before they went overseas—thousands of them. They could do anything for anybody who was wounded. They could prepare guys for operations. There was nobody to operate on them. Finally we went to one of these cigarette camps in the woods in France. "Twenty Grand" is the one I went to. We took this *President Warfield* ship up the Seine and got off and went into the woods, pitched a tent, and we never saw France. It was not near any city. Thousands of soldiers. We walked guard every night. There were Italian prisoners. But there was no war near there. Then, after two or three weeks, we got on trucks and went right through Belgium into Germany to a great big Catholic hospital, München-Gladbach, gee, absolutely a wonderful hospital. The sisters were there. The medical help had gone. We took over that hospital and we began getting people and then we went further. Nobody wanted to leave that place—we lived in comfort. They had German girls waiting on us, everything. A big mess hall, fresh eggs, everything. But we had to leave. We went to Düsseldorf on the Rhine. That was the only time we saw artillery fire—it was something called the Ruhr Pocket, I don't know what they call it now. The Germans were being surrounded in the woods. My medical outfit was a detached unit. It wasn't attached to any particular army. We just went around, and if we saw any infantryman bleeding, somebody was supposed to bring him in. We set up a hospital and had casualties then, and we had casualties too among Russians and Ukrainians. That was the time the Germans were using, as I wrote you in that letter, the Germans were using what was called "hazardous fire." I mean every once in a while they'd set fire to something and throw it. They were firing everything they could lay their hands on—rocks, old bedsprings, everything.

Q: How did you feel under fire in war?

ALGREN: Well, literally, when the fire was overhead, it didn't disconcert me. The outfit I was in was never fired at. It was a medical outfit and it had no strategic importance. It was unattached. So we never ran into German fire. The only fire we heard was overhead when we were in the wrong place, when we were ten miles ahead of some infantry outfit that we were supposed to be serving instead of ten miles behind. If anything had landed it would have been saddening on the Germans' part as well as ours because it would have been a waste of ammunition. Actually, as I recall, I paid no particular attention to it.

Q: Did you ever think you were going to get killed?

ALGREN: I never thought I was going to get killed by the Germans. I could very well fancy getting killed by our MP's or by our own guards. I think that was the only risk. I took some precautions against that. My total preoccupation was divided between gambling and getting wine and getting out around the countryside. This entailed a kind of danger, but from our own men, possibly because this wasn't an infantry outfit and legally we weren't permitted to bear arms, being medics. But our guards, who never had any experience with small arms, were allowed to have them or had picked them up from the Germans. On duty, some of them wanted to get into the war. They wanted to shoot somebody; it didn't particularly matter, so that what you had to watch was when you went out to get wine—we were limited to that company area, of course, but we did sneak out—and when you did sneak out, you had to watch out sneaking back because our own guards were half inclined to shoot somebody. The only danger I ever had of getting shot was coming in late, not knowing which one of the guards was on. We went back to another camp and had it very easy near Paris. I went to Paris. I was in Paris when the war was over. And when the war with Japan was over I was in Paris. Then everybody thought we were going home. We went to Marseilles, took the whole outfit down to Marseilles, and, aw, those guys—I suppose it happened to every outfit—they were so homesick and then they found out that the outfit had to go back to Germany. But I got separated. I was thirty-six. They took every man who had been overseas a year who was over thirty-five. I didn't have enough points to get home, but I had enough age. I got separated. A couple of other guys got separated. They put us in tents above Marseilles. I mean but *tens* of *thousands*. There was nothing you could see but tents, tents, tents, and that's all but tents. There were three huge camps in the mountains there. And I was a private citizen in uniform. I mean I just had no outfit to attach myself to. I just had a cot and my belongings and in the morning the sergeant would come and tell me what outfit I belonged to. Every morning it would be a different outfit. They were trying. He'd say, "Now you're tank corps." Next day he'd say, "Now you're field artillery." They tried everything to get us on that boat. It took months. But when I got into Marseilles I wasn't even anxious to get on the boat.

Q: You liked Marseilles?

ALGREN: Oh yeah. I practically lived out of bounds. It's a little different now, but it was kind of a Wild West town then. There simply wasn't enough military police to cover all the different troops—American troops and Senegalese troops and the Canadians and the British. The town was full, full of guys with arms. Parachute guys with German guns, trading them off. When you'd go into a whorehouse there, all the signs said, "Out-of-bounds to British and American Personnel," so the joint would always get raided. One joint I remember used to get raided every half-hour. The American MP's would raid it. In between raids the guys would be just running up the stairs, thousands of guys. They must have had twenty-five or thirty women in there, available all the time. And a lot of the French people living around there had nothing to do then and so they would sit outside just to see the place get raided. They liked to see the GI's coming down fixing their pants, and the MP's pulling them in. This little crowd of Frenchies had nothing to do but just stand in front of the door watching the MP's come in, "It's a raid, it's a raid," pull everything down, catch guys in the sack with their pants down. But if they had a pass, they let them go. So that's the sort of town it was then. I used to go to a pizza joint not as wide as this room—about ten feet wide—with the oven in the back and I used to go back there and sit there with this load of black-market stuff, cigarettes, Eisenhower jackets, sit there and eat pizza with Chianti all day. I used to sit there because it was warm, and I'd make some deal. Somebody would come in and you'd make a few bucks, enough to buy wine. I never drank too much because I used to like to go by myself and there were too many industrial accidents that way. I didn't want to go that far. Too many guys got killed that way.

Q: Killed for what?

ALGREN: Well, there wasn't any *reason* for it. Among soldiers who are used to killing, there wasn't any *reason* for it. If you see a GI who is drunk and you can use his shoes, then it's very easy to push him in the river. I mean the Senegalese were great. They had huge round bank rolls. But nobody is going to bother you if you're not staggering. They ain't going to bother you. I had a lot of deals with these Senegalese guys. They liked to pull tricks on you, see. They'd say, "Hey, Joe!" They'd want the jacket, you know, the Eisenhower jacket, "How much?" they'd say, quibbling at the twenty bucks. "Well," they'd say, "let's go in here." What they've got is a bar you can walk right into and the first half of the bar is all right for Americans, but in the back end of the bar where there is another door to another street, that's out-of-bounds to Americans. They'd say, "Well, come on—let's see what you've got." Then you lay all the stuff out—cigarettes, razor blades, jackets—you've got all this stuff they're picking out. Then one of them hollers, "Hey, Joe! MP! MP! MP! Run, Joe! Run!" It's supposed to be a raid and I'm supposed to run. Oh they had a lot of tricks. One Senegalese got me in a hallway. He wanted one of these jackets—they just loved these Eisenhower jackets—so I'd say, "Do you have any dough?" And he said, "Not here, not here, Joe. Let's get in this hallway." He is a big pinheaded kid with blue marks on him, a huge kid. He wants the jacket. "Where's the dough?" "Oh," he says, "I've got the dough." I give him the jacket and he was going to give me the equivalent of twenty bucks. He gives me a couple of paper francs and I take the coat off in the hall. As he goes on paying me, he begins to drop money on the floor. The idea is that I'm supposed to bend over and then he's got the coat almost free, see. So I won't bend over. I'm holding onto the coat and he chokes, "Get the money! Get the money!" Now he is pulling on the coat in the hall and I'm pulling on the coat pulling him out into the street. He's a big tall guy, but I have a pretty good grip on the coat. Then a little Frenchman comes by with a little cap on him—he was a mailman or something, something official— and *he* says, "You should be ashamed. Give him the jacket. He's poor and you're rich." I said, "How do you know *what* I am, you son-of-a-bitch." There I am fighting with both these guys, but I saved the jacket. He was a big guy but he couldn't hold on that long and I knew if I could hold on long enough, then law-and-order would see whose jacket it was because he was in the wrong uniform to have that jacket.

Q: I want to ask you a naïve question. Why did you have any- thing to do with the black market while you were in the Army?

ALGREN: The reason I was in the black market was to get rich because I didn't have enough money to gamble. As a private I had a very little amount of money and the stakes in gam- bling were very big there. I was operating as a private. But I was playing for stakes which would have interested generals. A lot of privates were. But in order to support that gambling habit, if I had a bad night, I'd have to make it good by peddling cigarettes, contraband jackets, shoes, and anything else. Money was very easy. It was very easy to get money. It was a seller's market. Anything that you could bring in from the camp was in demand in town.

Q: Did you do any writing in the Army? Did you want to?

ALGREN: No. Nothing but letter writing.

Q: Did you think that the whole of society was falling apart?

ALGREN: No. So long as I was holding together, it couldn't.

Q: You knew it would be over and it would be all right?

ALGREN: Overseas I knew it would be over, but when I was in the States I remember one afternoon I resigned myself to the fact that this thing was never going to end, that it was just going to go on.

Q: Before the war, in the thirties, were you a Socialist, a left-winger?

ALGREN: Oh not a Socialist, no. I might have started out as a Socialist, but I'd say I was a Communist.

Q: Did you ever join the Communist Party?

ALGREN: No, I never joined the Party, but I did a lot of work for them.

Q: When did you stop doing that? When did that cool off?

ALGREN: During the Civil War in Spain.

Q: O.K. You say the disenchantment with the Communists came during the Civil War in Spain. Why? What happened?

ALGREN: Well, my disenchantment wasn't, I didn't share the disenchantment that some Communists felt when they swung to the Trotskyists' or Anarchists' line. My disenchantment was not an ideological one. I had gone into the Communist Party because I believed the world was changing and I wanted to help change it.

Q: Now what do you mean when you say that you went into the Communist Party. You were not a member?

ALGREN: I went into the Communist movement; that is, everybody I knew was a Communist and I worked knowingly with Communists and I belonged to a Writers' League in which there were many leading Communists. I worked with them and whenever there was a demonstration organized by the Communists against the Italian invasion, the Italian bombing of Ethiopia, I marched with the Communists. I thought they were right on that issue. I thought they were right on many issues and I thought they were right on the issue in Spain. What I did run into was a certain kind of rigidity, and a kind of authoritarian attitude toward people who, like myself, were doing the leg work, for the League of American Writers of Chicago, as Chairman of the Chicago Chapter or something, which meant that I got money for Spain and attended and organized meetings around here. But I didn't like being told by the Secretary of the New York Chapter, through a letter, that he heard, that he'd been informed that I and another member of the League of American Writers had been drunk and disorderly. He felt it was his duty to remind me that, with my present responsibilities, it would look better if I'd try to be a little bit more austere in my conduct. My reaction to this was simply to tell him that my conduct was no concern of his and he could find somebody else to do this work because if he was going to interfere with my drinking and disorderliness, I wasn't going to let that interfere. I put it in a way that would offend him because he didn't answer the question of "How do you know?" I mean, what kind of operation is it when somebody will write to New York and say somebody else was drunk? This went against me. There wasn't anybody I knew who wasn't friendly, but obviously I was with people who had a higher obligation than a personal one; that is, the personal obligation to inform, to keep the other people thinking the same as they did, which I thought was what we were fighting the war against. A meeting of writers was organized, of artists and writers, and I was expected to be there and I didn't go there because I didn't want to go through a lot of bureaucratic parliamentarianism, and then I was told by one of the organizers of the meeting, very abruptly, "Where were you Thursday night?" Well, I wanted to know what concern it was of his where I was Thursday night. I said, "Where were you *Tuesday* night?" So my disenchantment was based on the purely personal thing that there was something morally wrong to me about being at anybody's behest. They were simply little bureaucratic functionaries so I simply moved away from them and got started thinking more about writing.

Q: But the Communist activities in Spain, or even earlier in Germany against the Socialists, didn't bother you?

ALGREN: Oh, no, no. In fact, the reason I was associated so closely with the Communists here was because the Communists in Germany and the Communists in Spain were of a breed that I admired very much. I mean, they were real revolutionaries. These were people who laid down their lives against Fascism. They were the only ones and this kind of—

Q: You know that there are a lot of people who would argue with you about that.

ALGREN: Well, they died, they died there. They went there, they got killed. The Italians and the Germans and the Moors killed them. And they believed in what they were doing, that there was a way of stopping Fascism. I was not talking about the interweaving of Party politics in the American Party that could say black is white today and white is black tomorrow and either you switch or else we'll excommunicate you. That isn't what I'm talking about. I'm talking about the individual, the individual American who believed strongly enough in the threat of Fascism to fight it personally. And a lot of Communists did this, a lot of men did this and lost their lives.

Q: Did the Stalin-Hitler pact bother you at all?

ALGREN: Well, it bothered me. It bothered me. I still didn't believe that Fascism and Communism are the same thing. I still don't believe that Fascism is the same thing. It looked to me like a deal had been made, an opportunistic deal. But I wasn't so concerned about that. I was more concerned about the local scene. I was more concerned about what was going on in the United States than what was going on between Hitler and Stalin. I wasn't deeply, I was not closely involved emotionally, politically at all. It was an incidental thing. What I was involved in in that period was the same thing I'd been involved in in the early days of the decade; that is, I was just going around Chicago—

Q: But you weren't writing any books between 1936 and 1939?

ALGREN: Between 1936 and 1939, I think I turned out some short stories and a couple of poems, but about the city. It was all Chicago stuff. It was about the old-time Black Sox, and I started a whole series of stories about the cheap hotels on South State Street and I went to a Walkathon, one of these three-day, I mean, everlasting dance marathons. I spent a couple days there. What my real interest was was in the dance marathons and the whorehouses and the old-time ballplayers and it wasn't in what was happening inside the Communist Party at all. I never sustained any interest in the different lines in the *Daily Worker*. I did contribute, I think, to the *New Masses* to a special literary section or something: "Black and white, unite and fight" and so forth, which became purely a mechanical pattern.

Q: Have you written much about the Army?

ALGREN: I wrote one short story about the black market. It touched on the black market.

Q: Is that included in *Neon Wilderness?*

ALGREN: Yeah. It was called "He Couldn't Boogie-Woogie Worth a Damn." A very bad title. It was not a satisfactory story.

Q: Isn't there a big book about that, about the war, you and the war? I feel there is a big book there.

ALGREN: Well I don't know. It was too long ago for a big book. Oh there certainly *was* a big book there, but I think it's too long ago. The time for that big book was right at the end of the war. The theme would have been about an A.W.O.L. American guy, you see, playing and living on the black market before he gets home, living with a French woman as a lot of them did. In one place in Italy A.W.O.L. Americans had their own camp. They set up their own little outlaw army there. It was quite an operation—they had food and guns and trucks and their own women. Outlaws from every army came in. It was a very dramatic thing and if you could get into the files of the GI's who were caught, who they lived with, what they did, it would be a very interesting thing. Reading my story later in *Neon Wilderness,* I felt I had missed a chance there to sharpen it, to make it topical. But the girl in the story never really comes quite true.

Q: How did you feel about writing when you got *out* of the Army?

ALGREN: I just wanted a place to write, I was kind of serious, I thought it was about time to get serious about writing.

Q: In 1945. You say it was about time to get serious about writing. Why?

ALGREN: Well, this was just a natural reaction to having been gypsying so long. It was 1931 when I got out of the University with the idea of doing some writing. Here it was 1945 and I had been doing nothing but gypsying so—

Q: But you had written some good books.

ALGREN: Yeah, but in mid-air, as it were—always while working at another job. Now I had an opportunity to stay in one place and do nothing but write and, what's more, I had more to write about. So I simply settled down to doing nothing but write for a number of years, several years.

Q: And that's why you decided to get serious? How old were you when you decided this?

ALGREN: I got out of the Army when I was thirty-six. It seemed like it was time. It's simply unnatural to keep flying around from one part of the world, one part of the country. I'd spent the years in jumping, first riding the rails and then jumping around, then after that, jumping around with the Army from place to place. While with the Army I always had the feeling wouldn't it be great, after we'd made a move by convoy, if we just stayed here a while. Not knowing whether you're going to stay in a place eight hours or eight years gave me a certain longing: If I ever get out of here, I want to stay in one place the rest of my life. And there were also other things I wanted to do. I just wanted to do one thing the rest of my life and live in one place and that would be to write and simply not be preoccupied either with politics or with anything that wasn't pertinent to myself. It seemed to me that I had perpetually been involved in things that pertained seriously to other people but didn't pertain to me at all and I wanted to do something that pertained to myself. So I did. I got a room on Wabansia and Bosworth in Chicago. Ten dollars a month.

Q: That was in 1945?

ALGREN: Yeah. That was the rent ceiling then, partly because of the area it was in and because there was no heating or lighting or anything. I put in a fuel oil stove and got the lights connected and later the rent was raised to thirteen dollars a month. But it was a very good place, it was an ideal place for me. It was a very clean little place.

Q: One room?

ALGREN: Two rooms. Bedroom. John but no shower. I went to the YMCA to wash.

Q: You've spent a lot of time in YMCA's.

ALGREN: I went every day.

Q: Throughout your life you've spent a lot of time in YMCA's.

ALGREN: Well I've spent a lot of time exercising. I always go to the YMCA. I've always had the exercising thing. I always do something.

Q: What do you do these days?

ALGREN: I swim about an hour a day. But at that time on Wabansia I was on a heavy and light bag and jump rope kick. I don't know what that bug was, but I did it faithfully.

Q: Did you ever do any fighting, any boxing?

ALGREN: Not seriously, no. Just clowning around gyms. This Wabansia place was a very good little writer's workshop because it had nothing in it but a bed, a typewriter, books— many of those—and a stove, a table, and a sink with one faucet. That was all. To me it was luxury because after three years in the Army the idea of having a place to yourself just becomes a passion. The fact that you can actually have privacy, that you can get up or go to bed as you wish—this is a wonderful thing. Just to wake up slowly. I was free to make my own choice as to what I wanted to do.

Q: What did you write?

ALGREN: I put that *Neon Wilderness* together, which I had started before the war. I finished it then and then I wrote *The Man with the Golden Arm.*

Q: Writing *The Man with the Golden Arm* took you up to 1950— what did you write then?

ALGREN: I wrote that *Chicago: City on the Make* thing.

Q: When did you write *Walk on the Wild Side?*

ALGREN: From 1954 through 1955.

Q: Why have you written the books you've written?

ALGREN: Well, I wrote the books I wrote because, because I was living in the middle of these books when, before they were books, when they were merely scenes in which human beings were involved in conflict, I was in the middle of them and simply recorded my own reactions and tried to catch the emotional ebb and flow and something of the fear and the terror and the dangers and the kind of life that multitudes of people had been forced into with no recognition that such a world existed. They lived in a world which is very plain, which anybody could see, which is lived in the streets of the city, but which the people who didn't live in this world said, "It doesn't exist, they aren't there, we know that they aren't there, and if they are there, it doesn't matter, because we're here and we don't live in that sort of world." And in this, although I was confident at the time of making a dent in this, by writing books about it, books which were accepted and spoken of in reviews and even honored one way or another—I thought I'd make a dent—I didn't make the least dent, because there is no way of convincing or even making the slightest impression on the American middle class that there are people who have no alternative, that there are people who live in horror, that there are people whose lives are nightmares. This is not accepted. The world of the drug addict doesn't exist. The world of the criminal doesn't exist. The world of the murderer doesn't exist. Nothing that does not touch the person individually exists.

Q: At the time you thought you could make a dent?

ALGREN: I thought that there was a certain sentience. I thought there was something you could reach. Now I don't think it can be reached. When such a book comes along more recently, such as *The Naked Lunch,* which I don't think is a great book or anything, but it does tell what a mess a man's life can be, an American life, just a nightmare—I've seen many people live through this nightmare—it immediately becomes a literary confection of some kind. Nobody really believes that this is so. It *is* so. Mary McCarthy says it's a great book and somebody else will say it's not even reviewable, but it simply is a literary event, something that sells for six bucks a copy. It isn't going to change much.

Q: Yeah, but I was primarily interested in why you wrote it at the time.

ALGREN: Well, because, uh . . .

Q: Weren't you doing something new? Was that important to you?

ALGREN: Of course there's a tradition, Dreiser, and certainly at the turn of the century Stephen Crane. He said it does exist in *Maggie: A Girl of the Streets*. He broke out of the middle-class world into the world that the book reviewers largely panned him for and he persisted in it.

Q: Who else besides Dreiser and Crane? Of your day—

ALGREN: Céline.

Q: —of the thirties? Who else was doing what you wanted to do in the thirties?

ALGREN: Well, just Dick Wright, that's all. That's the only one I know of in the thirties who was writing, who wrote anything that was not just from the bottom of American society but a bottom where a tremendous number of people lived inarticulately and I had known Wright and had seen that he had made these multitudes articulate to himself. They had become articulate to him and, well, even before I knew Wright I had this source. I had already established quite a sort of wellspring with the people who didn't belong to American civilization: to the people of the underworld, to the outcasts.

Q: Why have you stayed in Chicago?

ALGREN: Well, one reason I suppose is that I'm identified with the city. Chicago literally has become my trade. I'm a little reluctant to leave. I'm certainly never going to become a professional New Yorker or a professional Parisian, although I'd rather live in Paris than Chicago. I'd rather live in New York than Chicago. I'm quite uncertain about staying on. I'm not as confident as I was ten years ago that it makes any sense to stay on in Chicago. It's very difficult to stay in communication with people who are interested in what's going on in the world in Chicago. You have to do it by reading the papers and by subscribing to magazines. You don't see anybody directly. Chicago is, ah—

Q: *What* is Chicago?

ALGREN: What is Chicago? Chicago is a place where a great deal of people have come together to occupy an industrial area on the shore of Lake Michigan in the hope of getting enough money to move to the suburbs before they get caught and thrown into the can trying to make it, you know. I mean it's not the kind of a city where it is important whether a certain actor or actress gets a certain part in New York. It's of no importance. Nobody in Chicago is going to get excited whether Bette Davis or Margaret Leighton has the lead in a play by Tennessee Williams. To me this is important. It's much more important than who's the precinct captain.

Q: But there are good people in Chicago, aren't there? You know I spent ten years in that town, then I left Chicago.

ALGREN: (*Standing*) I stand for you. (*Sitting*) Well, I will say I have friends in Chicago. I have one friend who identifies himself as a disk jockey and I identify him as a disk mule, that is, he's been hauling human communication uphill for an hour each morning tirelessly every morning. *Nothing* discourages him.

Q: You mean Studs? Studs Terkel? On WFMT?

ALGREN: That's what he *calls* himself. Actually he's Marlon Brando.

Q: Listen: tell me some of your feelings about New York.

ALGREN: Why I think the buildings are high and I think there's rivers on two sides. I think the thing has spirit, a European spirit. It's a place where you get responses from people and it's an infinitely more human city than Chicago.

Q: You keep mentioning the theatre. What's this about you and the theatre?

ALGREN: I like the theatre. I like the whole idea of make-believe. I believe most people who fool around with fiction, whether writing or painting or by any other means, I believe that they believe there's only one real world and that's the make-believe world, the world that Tennessee Williams created in *Streetcar Named Desire,* a world a lot more real than the real world. I think the important thing is the make-believe world. *Alice in Wonderland* is much more real than, say, a report on Europe's resources.

Q: It is certainly *not* more real than a day at the races.

ALGREN: Well, a day at the races is pure make-believe.

Q: You think it is all fiction?

ALGREN: A day at the races is just a kind of a fantasy.

Q: When are you going to the races again?

ALGREN: Tuesday or Wednesday. Closer to Wednesday. I would like to finish a certain book review by Wednesday. That would be the best day. Are you interested in going that day?

Q: Thursday would be a good day for me.

ALGREN: Well, let's go Thursday then. We can get to Aqueduct by subway.

Q: I have to ask you some more questions. Could I see you again Thursday morning here?

ALGREN: Yeah. All right. Then we'll go to the track from here.

PART II

ALGREN VS. HOLLYWOOD

4   *The Con Within the Con*

QUESTION: How much money did you make from Hollywood on the film version of your book *The Man with the Golden Arm?*

ALGREN: Hardly nothing. Altogether about fifteen thousand bucks.

Q: And how much were you paid for *Walk on the Wild Side* when it was made into a movie?

ALGREN: Not much. About twenty-five thousand bucks.

Q: But many people, including many in the literary world, think you are a rich man because of Hollywood.

ALGREN: I know they do. But I'm not. As a matter of fact, I'm still a little in debt.

Q: Do you mind talking about this? Will you tell us how this happened?

ALGREN: Sure. I'll be glad to talk to you about my war with the United States as represented by Kim Novak.

Q: First of all—do you like movies?

ALGREN: Oh, I love movies.

Q: Which ones? What do you think are some good, some great films, films made from books.

ALGREN: Oh, I liked *The Grapes of Wrath* and *The Ox-Bow Incident* and *The Lost Weekend* and *From Here to Eternity.* Those last two—*Weekend* and *Eternity*—were better films than they were books. And I liked *An American Tragedy.* I also liked *The Asphalt Jungle* and *Rififi.* Then there's *La Dolce Vita,* which I like very much. The first movie that ever moved me deeply was *Anna Christie* with Greta Garbo. I like Garbo. And I like Brando. I'll go see anything Brando does.

Q: You seem like a man who takes his fantasies seriously. Do you think that movies are an art form, or merely a cultural throwaway on our cultural scene?

ALGREN: Oh no, no, not at all. I mean I don't think anyone could have told the story of *Rififi* so well—how safecracking is a trade, like any trade, a business, it's work, without any moral implications. The movie is an art form as much as anything can be. The framework, the possibility, is limitless, enormous. It is like asking, "Can a mirror reflect?" The films can show you the way we live—

Q: Do you consider yourself as a writer to be an artist?

ALGREN: I consider myself a free-lance journalist. But I can occasionally get into something more lasting than just day-to-day journalism.

Q: But you write short stories, novels, and poetry, too?

ALGREN: Yeah.

Q: Haven't you written lyrics for a musical version of *Walk on the Wild Side?*

ALGREN: Yes.

Q: And you still want to make movies?

ALGREN: I want to see good movies made. I'm not primarily interested myself in making movies.

Q: But you once were, weren't you?

ALGREN: Never primarily, no.

Q: When you had finished *The Man with the Golden Arm* as a book, did it appear to you that it would make a good movie?

ALGREN: From what I knew about the taboos that the Johnson office, or whatever office it was, put out, I did not think that there was any serious possibility of it being a movie. Because of the taboo, I didn't think the movie could be produced.

Q: What did you think when you heard that someone in Hollywood wanted to make a movie from your taboo book? How did you hear about it?

ALGREN: I heard about it through my agent, my *former* agent. I have a *new* agent now. But my former agent saw a note in *Variety* saying a guy was negotiating for the book. The former agent wanted to know if I knew anything about it. That's the way they do things.

Q: Who was the guy?

ALGREN: An insurance man by the name of Moxon, who was also John Garfield's producer. He had produced *Body and Soul* for Garfield. He got in touch with my former agent first, and then when he came through Chicago he called me up and said he was interested in making a movie. He asked me to come down. I think he was staying at the Blackstone. I'd been expecting him to call so I alerted this local guy who was using narcotics, not a big habit or anything, but a guy who was very troubled by it, a guy named Acker—he was about the first addict I ever knew. I said to him, "I think this guy will put up transportation to California." And he said, "Sure, I'll go."

Q: Why did you want to take this man to California with you?

ALGREN: Well, I heard nothing from him but that he was very, very troubled by using the stuff. He'd be off two or three weeks. Everybody who's on, who uses narcotics, always has a way of getting off. One guy'll come and say, "If you let me have dough, I can break the habit by getting a driver's license to get this job driving a truck. Then I'll be driving cross-country and I won't have any chance to use the stuff. That's how I'll beat it, so can you let me have fifty bucks to join the union?" Then he doesn't join the union, of course. The fifty bucks will go for junk. You know he's conning you, but because of the possibility that he will go off the stuff, you still have to let him have the fifty. There's always a solution that they themselves believe in. Acker's solution was to get to California where he did not know anybody. And he is a photogenic guy. He probably resembles the guy physically in the book a little bit. He's a very dramatic-looking guy.

Q: Acker resembles Frankie?

ALGREN: Yeah. Frankie Machine in *The Arm,* not Frank Sinatra. And Acker was a very, very fast-moving, very resourceful, very incriminating guy. When I asked him what he used the stuff for, he said, "Well, you gotta belong to somebody." The idea was: it is better to be a drug addict than a nobody. So I told Acker I was conning Moxon. I had the idea, which was right, that Moxon was a con guy, so when Moxon called I was conning him and I said, "I don't

have any firsthand acquaintance with drugs, but I know a
guy who has. He could be a technical adviser."

Q: Why haven't you had any firsthand acquaintance with drugs?

ALGREN: I don't like people sticking needles into me. I respect
myself too much for that. And it's unhealthy. It knocks you
out. My idea was to get Acker to California, and Moxon
said, "Bring him out. Sure, I'll make him a technical adviser."

Q: Who paid for the trip out?

ALGREN: Moxon. Ultimately I paid for it, but at that time he paid:
He included that in the tab later.

Q: How did you go out?

ALGREN: On the Super Chief. We had dough for the tickets from
Moxon the night before and Acker scolded me first because
I got tickets for some other train, just a train that went out to
California. Acker said, "You can't do that. They'll throw
rocks at you. You gotta go on the Super Chief." So I think
it was about five hundred bucks.

Q: How did Acker know these things, this sociology?

ALGREN: Oh, I don't know. He picked up a lot. He was a very
alert guy. He would just pick up everything. He was in his
thirties and this was in 1950. But he almost did not get to go.
The day before we were supposed to leave from the La Salle
Street Station, about four o'clock a guy called and said, "This
is your brother." And I said, "Well, I don't have a brother."
And he said, "Well, I'm talking *for* your brother." And then
I realized Acker is in the can. He had told this guy, "Call my
brother." That simplifies it. It is very seldom guys will do that
when they are getting out, will actually make good and call
up. But he called up for Acker. Acker was in the can and

scared to death. He was always getting picked up like that because he had a small record. They knew he was an addict. So I went down there. I don't know what they picked him up for, but he was in a cell down there just scared to death. Oh, he was *scared*.

Q: Why was he *that* upset?

ALGREN: Oh, he was just scared to death of that jail thing. He was just terrified, just terrified. He took it as though he were going to be executed. Well, anyhow, I had this letter or contract or document. They know Acker for vagrancy. One of the cops who was always picking him up went to grammar school with him. He picks him up every time he sees him, a cop named Smickles. Acker hasn't been able to get away from him for twenty years. So I go down there and I talk to Smickles who says, "Well, that son-of-a-bitch is no good. He's a junkie. . . ." And all that. And they didn't want him particularly. I said, "No, he's John Garfield's technical adviser." So the guy looks at me. He says, "You've got the wrong guy." I said, "No, he's going to take a part in this play. You know, he might take the lead." I've got his name on the contract Moxon gave me.

Q: At the time did you think it was a real contract?

ALGREN: Oh, I didn't think Acker would really get a job out there. I didn't really think he was going to get on the payroll. I was very dubious about the whole thing.

Q: Is this merely retrospective knowledge? How did you feel at the time?

ALGREN: I felt that Moxon was a con guy. His action was phony.

Q: What happened to Acker?

ALGREN: I showed them the contract and they let him out. We caught the train. About a dozen addicts came down and saw us off at the La Salle Street Station and we got out of there all right. Acker looked very sporty. And we really stayed at John Garfield's joint.

Q: Where was Garfield?

ALGREN: He was at some other joint, I guess. He used to come by from some place nearby.

Q: How was Garfield?

ALGREN: Oh, I liked Garfield. He was a very friendly little guy. He always had his shirt out and he always had that sweat shirt tied around his middle and the arms of the sweat shirt tied around him. He played tennis like mad. In fact he dropped once—he had an attack while playing tennis. His shirttails would be out and he always had that sweat shirt somewhere.

Q: Tied around his waist? Like kids in school?

ALGREN: Yeah, yeah. A little, little, tightly built guy, always with a wide smile and a masculine handshake: "How *are* you?" He worked very hard at that. He worked very hard at being who he was supposed to be. He knew he wasn't who he was. I mean the screen image. He was trying to be like the screen image. I mean this little New York East Side guy and—

Q: Was he a good actor?

ALGREN: Oh, I think he was a good actor. I still see reruns. He was a good actor. He was a serious actor. And he might have got better.

Q: Were you interested in him for the role, the role of Frankie Machine in *The Golden Arm?*

ALGREN: Oh, yeah. That was a real, that was a big attraction.

Q: Is that why you went to Hollywood?

ALGREN: I didn't go out there for any particular reason.

Q: Had you ever been out there before?

ALGREN: No. There were two or three reasons. The idea of getting a movie was attractive. The idea I was going to get ten thousand dollars was attractive.

Q: Who told you you were going to get ten thousand dollars?

ALGREN: The contract called it five thousand and then ten later. There really wasn't any reason not to take it.

Q: Which contract? The one you signed in Chicago?

ALGREN: I didn't sign a contract in Chicago. I ultimately signed one out there. Fifteen thousand and five per cent of the film's profits.

Q: Is that why you went out there? For the money?

ALGREN: There were half a dozen reasons to go out there.

Q: Well, let me talk a minute.

ALGREN: Yeah.

Q: The tradition of the American writer going out to Hollywood is almost a cliché: the more serious he is as a writer, the more trouble he's going to have out in Hollywood.

ALGREN: Yeah.

Q: This you knew about. Did you know anything about Dreiser in Hollywood, or about F. Scott Fitzgerald out there?

ALGREN: I didn't know about them at the time. I knew the general setup, that nobody goes near Hollywood.

Q: So you knew that. And you thought really deep down that your book never had a chance to be made into a film because of the film code. And you did not like Moxon from the start? So why did you go out to Hollywood at all?

ALGREN: In the first place, as an adventure. Just the idea of getting on the train, of taking a free ride and having a ball in Hollywood was attractive. I had an ex-wife out there. I wasn't going to go that far to see her, but it was somebody you knew out there, you know? I'd never been to California. I'd like to see Hollywood. I can't lose by it and I thought it was a good idea. Part of the reason was to get Acker out of the way, to give him a free ride. I get a free ride myself and I wanted to see the thing through. I actually thought that if they made a movie out of *The Arm* this guy would be usable. I didn't know that they didn't work that way.

Q: Did you at that time *want* to make movies?

ALGREN: I would have liked to have seen a movie out of the book. Naturally you write a story, you'd like to have a lot of people see it. Very few people get to read a book or pay three and a half dollars for a book. I half bought Moxon's story that he'd be able to stay somewhere within the book. I really didn't believe the guy, but still I felt like going along with him. I didn't seen any harm in it. After all, I was getting paid five thousand dollars in front. It looked like a lot.

Q: What was the five thousand dollars?

ALGREN: Option money.

Q: And the ten thousand?

ALGREN: If he picked up the option. I bought a little house with the money in Gary.

Q: How did that kind of money rate those days?

ALGREN: Oh, fantastic. I don't know of one single serious writer in Chicago who was financially independent at that time [1950].

Q: No, I mean how did it rate as movie money?

ALGREN: Oh, not well. I'm sure I could have gotten more.

Q: *The Man with the Golden Arm* was a best-seller, wasn't it?

ALGREN: Yes. Other agents said they could have made it at least twenty-five or fifty thousand. But I bought Moxon's story that nobody else but him would try to make the movie because of the taboo. I bought that. And I did not know what the market was. I had no idea. I wasn't supposed to. I wasn't even supposed to deal with Moxon. I'm not equipped to deal with this guy. I'm not in his field. My agent should have been dealing with the guy. That's what I was paying her for.

Q: At the time, did you know that your former agent was not dealing with him?

ALGREN: No, I didn't know that.

Q: But then you did find out about it and didn't you cover up for her, covering up the cold hard facts?

ALGREN: I covered up for her at the time. . . . Now I feel that dealing with talent is a hazardous occupation. I feel there ought to be some limitation, some qualification for somebody setting up as agent to handle situations like this. The writer isn't supposed to know what's going on. He can only give his attention to one thing. I was giving my attention to the dialogue of drug addicts, to watching the drug traffic, and I can't give attention at the same time to the value of a property. I did not know it was of value as a "property." I know its value as a book. But my agent is supposed to know its other values. I'm in Hollywood trying to handle that deal and I get a call from Ken McCormick at Doubleday. He wants me to fly to New York for the National Book Award and to make it very secretive because it was the first time, the first award. It was important because it was the first award. Even at that, I just went up and got the award and thanked Clifton Fadiman for being so nice to me. What am I thanking *him* for? I'm going around thanking the hanger-on for hanging on! When you write the best novel of a given year, you've done everybody, chiefly publishers, a favor. I'm acting like they're doing *me* a favor! You don't get to write the best novel of the year every year. When you do, and you're dealing with people whose passion is investment in books, in films, in every aspect of the entertainment world that yields profit, but people who are themselves talentless, you need somebody to wise you up. There wasn't anybody. The book went out the window and I went back to Los Angeles, where the rye bread grows on trees. I didn't even know that—if you sell the movie rights right off—you lose interest in the possibility of the book becoming a play. The book was a play, not a movie. Who wants a movie? I wanted a play. I don't think *anybody* should be a literary agent just because he or she *wants* to be.

Q: When you went back to California was Moxon impressed with the fact that the book had won the award?

ALGREN: No. He had to protect himself. He could not let any of it have any value. I mean he wouldn't, he couldn't acknowledge the literary world at all.

Q: What did Garfield think about the award?

ALGREN: Garfield never got into questions of value. He'd just pop in and say things like he liked the humor of the book and he wanted to do it on the stage. He talked in clichés. He was almost a totally mindless guy. He could only repeat phrases he had heard, that's all.

Q: What did Moxon want from you then?

ALGREN: He wanted a script. I told him I would give him one if he gave me a collaborator. I'd never written a film script so I wanted to work with someone who had. And I said I would write it in Chicago, but not out there.

Q: What happened then?

ALGREN: Well, we insulted each other.

Q: How come?

ALGREN: His whole manner was insulting. It was one of absolute confidence that he was talking to an idiot. You could not, you could not ever dent that, that self-satisfaction. Everything was condescending. He says, "Look, I would rather give you the money than to the lawyers." And I said, "What lawyers?" He said, "Well, you are committed you know. I can just drag you through the courts." That kind of stuff. Like sending in the superior fan.

Q: The what?

ALGREN: The superior fan. Moxon and I are talking about my legal commitments to him one night and he says I am such a good guy I can have a whole bottle of whiskey, which he shoves under my armpit like a baton. And the doorbell rings. Moxon answers the door and it is a little guy who says something to Moxon. Moxon turns and says, "Hey, Algren, here is a fan of yours, a *superior* fan." I don't know what it is all about. "A *what?*" I say. And the little guy says, "Am I speaking to Nelson Algren who writes books?" And I told him he was, so he serves me with all the summonses. He shoves it up under my *other* armpit. I think it was under my right armpit. The whiskey was under the other one, under the left. Then the little one leaves and Moxon starts running around the room as if I am going to start chasing him. But to tell you the truth I am still worried about the bottle of whiskey under my armpit. I wanted to look at the subpoenas, but I did not try to reach for them because I would have to reach for them with the hand connected to the arm holding up the bottle of whiskey, and I did not want to reach for the whiskey because I was suddenly afraid the pieces of paper would float away if I let it go. So I walked around the room like a spastic with my arms up tight against my body and my hands hanging up as if both wrists were broken. All this time, Moxon was running around saying things like, "Why do you make me act like such a shit?" And I was following him around with the whiskey and the paper saying, "I *don't* know. Why *do* I make you act like such a shit?" Finally I put the whiskey down by grabbing the neck of the bottle with the same hand—I twisted up the hand, you know, and I began to read each summons. There were about seven of them. None of them made any sense. And nothing happened about them. But that was when he said, "I'd rather give the money to you than to the lawyers." That's pretty insulting. I mean, you know, the assumption is that you're really idiotic.

Q: What did you do?

ALGREN: We moved. He had the landlord ask for the rent. First he said not to worry about the rent. But then when I wouldn't sign, he called up the landlord and told him to throw us out. So I paid a week's rent, about one hundred and fifty bucks, and we moved out. Acker found a place. A crummy little Hollywood furnished joint.

Q: Were they ever interested in Acker?

ALGREN: They were nice to Acker. I don't think they ever actually intended to spend money on Acker. But even then the
idea was that Acker had gotten away from Chicago. In
Chicago Acker's claim was that every time he got two dollars
he went down to Madison Street and got a shot in the arm.
Well, he had no place to score in California. So from that
point of view it worked. He did not go back on the stuff.
When I saw him out there some years later, he was still off
the junk. So that's what he said he wanted; that's what he got.

Q: When did you leave Hollywood?

ALGREN: Soon after that. The book award was in the middle of
March, 1950. I suppose I went back to Chicago about the
first of April. I came back with Trivers.

Q: With whom?

ALGREN: With Paul Trivers, the collaborator Moxon found for me.

Q: Then you did sign a contract?

ALGREN: Yeah. I signed one out there finally.

Q: Was it the contract Moxon wanted you to sign all along?

ALGREN: No. It was the contract I wanted to sign. I was holding
out for five per cent of the net, which he wouldn't go for.

Q: But which you got?

ALGREN: Yeah.

Q: And you got the other ten thousand, making fifteen?

ALGREN: Yeah.

Q: What did you and Trivers do?

ALGREN: He went with me back to Chicago and we took three
months working on the script, which we completed and which
I still have.

Q: Did you get any money for that work?

ALGREN: Yes. I think I got forty-five hundred bucks. It was
Garfield's money; the company was called Moxon Productions.

Q: So you got nineteen thousand five hundred dollars for the
book and for the film script work on *The Man with the
Golden Arm,* right?

ALGREN: Just about. Less the agent's fees and other expenses.

Q: Then what happened?

ALGREN: That's all. We finished the script. Trivers took it back
to Hollywood and I heard no more of it. Then I read that
Garfield had dropped dead.

Q: When? When was that?

ALGREN: About a year later, I think. I don't remember. Then
there was silence for two or three years. Nothing happened.
The property was just lying there. Nobody bothered with it.
Moxon was black-listed and went off to England, where he
is still and where I guess he'll stay, and I guess he met Preminger there, my guess is, and they made some sort of deal. I
don't know. What it was I don't know except that Preminger
sat on the thing for a long time, the property, and then he
started making the film.

Q: You said Moxon was black-listed. Was he a card-carrying man?

ALGREN: I don't know, but he always professed to be very liberal.

Q: Would that have mattered to you?

ALGREN: Oh, no, I would have preferred to work with a left-wing man.

Q: Why?

ALGREN: Because I'm a left-winger.

Q: Was he a left-winger?

ALGREN: Well, actually no. That's what he professed to be. There was an economic advantage for him to get work from black-listed guys. He could get their services for next to nothing.

Q: Did Otto Preminger get all the literary properties in John Garfield's estate when John Garfield died?

ALGREN: I don't know what he got.

Q: But the movie rights you had signed over to Moxon?

ALGREN: Yeah.

Q: And you had no script control rights?

ALGREN: No.

Q: And the next thing you knew, Otto Preminger was going to make a movie of your book?

ALGREN: Yes.

Q: When was that?

ALGREN: Why, 1955, I believe.

Q: Did you get in touch with Preminger, or did he get in touch with you?

ALGREN: Neither. An agency out there got in touch with my agent.

Q: Which agent? Your former agent or your present agent?

ALGREN: My former agent. They said a producer was making *The Man with the Golden Arm* and they wanted to know whether I was available to do the script for it.

Q: Did anybody mention the script you had already done?

ALGREN: Preminger later commented that he had seen that script and that wasn't what he wanted. He didn't want anything to do with that script.

Q: Did he say why?

ALGREN: No, he didn't say why. It was just not the story he wanted.

Q: But you thought it was a pretty good script?

ALGREN: I don't know now whether it was good or not. I still have it, but I haven't reread it for years.

Q: What did you reply to your former agent?

ALGREN: I told her I would go out to Hollywood because I was concerned about it, you see, and not so far as getting any writing done goes. I didn't know what my rights were and I thought I still had a voice. I didn't see how it could be anybody else's property, you know. I didn't see how the guy could have a right to it. I didn't understand how somebody I'd never heard of could be just going ahead and making the movie. So I went out there. The second time I went out there, I went out because I thought I should see what's going on.

Q: And what happened?

ALGREN: The film agency out there told me to be nice to Otto. They wanted me to be nice. They were very concerned that Otto might get mad at me for something. They offered me a thousand a week before I got out there. Then when I got out there the agency said, "Well, now he only wants to make it seven-fifty." I said, "Well, the telegram said a thousand."

Q: Who paid your way out there?

ALGREN: I paid my way out there. The telegram said he was to take care of the thousand dollars a week and expenses. I mean I advanced myself my own fare.

Q: Did you have the telegram?

ALGREN: Yeah, yeah. Then when I got out there it wasn't a thousand, it was only seven-fifty, and before the first day was over, it was only five hundred. My relationship with Preminger didn't last as long as mine did with Moxon. This lasted about three days. I only saw him twice and I didn't even take the expense money. I didn't even take the thousand a week. I came into town on a Sunday and I saw him on a Monday and then again the following Wednesday. They put me up at a place called the Carleton Arms or something and the first morning there his secretary called and said, "Mr. Preminger is coming by in his car. Would you mind being outside so he doesn't have to get out of the car or park the car. Be on the curb." Well, when the call came to my room that a gentleman was waiting for me in the lobby, I went down and met Preminger, and we got into his red Caddy. He kept playing with the windows much of the ride to the studio.

Q: How do you mean?

ALGREN: Oh, as soon as I got into the car, he said, "You want *opp?*" and all the car windows went up by themselves. Then he said, "Or you want *donn?*" And all the windows went down. *Opp. Donn. Opp. Donn.* He was playing with the windows as we drove along. Then he handed me the *Los Angeles Mirror* with the headline that one Serge Rubenstein had been murdered in New York City. "Old friend," he said. *"Terrible* man," he said. "How you like *ho*-tell?" We talked about that for a while and then he said, "How come you know such terrible people you write about?" I did not ask him then how come he knows such terrible people as Serge Rubenstein. So we went to his office and he showed me around the studio and we talked and met his help. I remember one guy came in smoking a pipe and Preminger said, "Pipe *oudt!*" So the guy emptied his pipe into his weskit. He was a publicity man, I think. Pretty soon Otto said to him, "Now you *and* pipe *oudt!*" The guy went. After that conference I saw him once again at his place in Malibu, and I handed him my treatment.

Q: You did a treatment for Preminger?

ALGREN: Oh, sure. He wanted a treatment from me he said. So I went to a movie in Los Angeles. I was stopped by a movie poster that showed a girl in a leopard skin saying, "White Goddess say not go that part of forest." So I went in. Then I went to the Carleton Arms and wrote the treatment. A few days later when I saw him again I handed him the twelve-page treatment and all he could say at first was, "So little pages?" Then when he came to the part where I had Frankie Machine say, "White Goddess say not go that part of forest," he put the treatment down and said that this was not the story he would pay money for.

Q: Did you offer him that kind of treatment because you felt things had just broken down completely?

ALGREN: Oh, I saw no chance of having a relationship with this guy at all.

Q: But you offered him a treatment which from his point of view was completely fantastic?

ALGREN: Yeah, yeah. His reaction, according to the agent who reported it to me, was that Otto says you don't take this thing seriously, and then I got hot about it. I said, "Well, I came from Chicago. I came more than two thousand miles. That shows I do take it seriously. What he means is I don't take *him* seriously." I mean this guy—I think he's the most ridiculous man I ever saw. I said I thought *he* was kidding. "But," I said, "I don't take *him* seriously and *I can't* do that. If I took *him* seriously," I said, "then I couldn't take *myself* seriously." And they said, "Oh, be nice to Otto, be nice to Otto." But we saw eye to eye, that is, Preminger and I. He just picked up the phone and told the agent, "Mr. Algren and I have agreed that he doesn't care to do the sort of script I want, so . . ."

Q: What about the letter and your check for forty dollars?

ALGREN: Oh, I wrote him later. His last gesture to me was very insulting. He said something like, "Thank you for letting me meet a very interesting person." So I sent him a letter saying that I found him a very *un*interesting person. In turning down his thousand dollars and expenses I wasn't being heroic. I had the idea that if I took any money from him, then I couldn't legally kick about the movie. I figured I had a claim to the movie, a legal claim. I just didn't think his claim to the movie was legally sound. The small check I sent *to* him, the idea there, was that I wanted to give him small change.

Q: Did you check soon after that on whether or not he had film rights to your book?

ALGREN: Yes. When I told my agent I didn't want to let this thing go with Preminger, she was very passive about it like she didn't want to touch it, but when I insisted, she got me an attorney from a big law firm that deals with magazines and books, a woman attorney. And I made another mistake there. I should have done it on a contingency basis.

Q: You paid the lawyer a fee?

ALGREN: Yes. I rushed through, I hurried through on that *Walk on the Wild Side* book. I turned it out fast because I wanted some legal money.

Q: How much did you pay the lawyer?

ALGREN: About five thousand dollars I think. It wasn't put out in cash. I didn't have the money. I'd thought she was working on contingency, but the only contingency that came up was when she involved me in legal difficulties. I'd paid seven thousand five hundred dollars for the house several years before and thought it was mine. It wasn't. After it was lost, it dawned on me that what the producers, the Hollywood agents, and the New York lawyers had been going at each other for, fang and claw, while I was standing aside wondering what the bloodshed was about, was money. Somebody was going to *get* it. Preminger got it, the law firm got their fee, and—later—I got a new agent. There's no battle so bitter as when it is about money that somebody else has earned. Preminger finally got it. The law firm got their fee. I got a new agent.

Q: What had your lawyer told you?

ALGREN: That I had a wonderful case. She wasn't lying. It *was* a wonderful case. For *her*.

Q: How long after you had retained her did you find out you did not own the film rights any more?

ALGREN: I never did find out. I might very well still have rights on paper. I never did find out that I do not have rights to it.

Q: What *happened?* Did people just stop talking to you about it? Your former agent? Your lawyer?

ALGREN: The lawyer carried on with it for a while. She summoned Preminger and she summoned Moxon and she went through a lot of legal things, but nothing happened and then she didn't pursue it any further because I didn't have any more money, so she dropped it. That was all there was to that case.

Q: When did the legal proceedings stop?

ALGREN: They started in 1955. I guess they were still dragging on up to 1958.

Q: When did you get a new agent?

ALGREN: About that time.

Q: How did you find her?

ALGREN: I went to New York with a photographer I know who took me to meet the new agent. She gets good prices and sells things. She does these things very well and she does things to protect properties.

Q: Which agent sold *Walk on the Wild Side* to Hollywood for twenty-five thousand?

ALGREN: The former agent.

Q: Did you try at all to have anything to do with the film script of *Walk on the Wild Side?*

ALGREN: No. Not after what happened with *The Arm.*

Q: Have you seen the movie made from *Wild Side?*

ALGREN: No.

Q: Why not?

ALGREN: Well, there's no point to it. It can't be anything like the book and I don't want to see it for the same reason I don't want to go down to the corner if I hear somebody's been hit by a car. It's a mess. It's got to be a mess and there's nothing I can do about it. I don't want to go and look at the remains laid in the middle of the street.

Q: Did you see *The Man with the Golden Arm*?

ALGREN: Yeah.

Q: How did you like it?

ALGREN: I wasn't deeply disturbed, but I didn't like it. I thought it was sort of comical. It had nothing to do with drug addiction. I thought it was cheap. It was better than most movies. I liked the music. Sinatra looked dramatic. I was sorry that it was a Chicago story that had nothing to do with Chicago. Some of the people were dressed like old Vienna and some like old San Francisco. The book very specifically took place at a certain time, at a certain locale, and the movie took place nowhere. It was unframed, it was very murky, and there were just plain idiotic things in it. About ten guys crowding over a poker game as though it were championship chess, following the movies. And the girl, Kim Novak, collecting, picking up all the sharp instruments, all the knives, all the houseware, because he might start stabbing people. You know, real nutty.

Q: What was the matter with that?

ALGREN: Well, because addicts don't stab people. They just go to sleep. A guy on morphine is not a murderous guy; he doesn't have the strength to hurt anybody in the first place. In the second place, he's scared of everybody and he isn't going to rape anybody because he can't function that well. I

mean the idea, you know, of a drug addict going around mur-
dering and raping just ain't so. All he does is crawl up in
some flophouse and lock the door and go to sleep. It seems to
me if you'd make a movie, you'd at least check up on some
judge, just call in a doctor and ask him—just *any* doc—you
just pick up the phone and say, "What does morphine do?"
And he'd tell you. Morphine is like it says: it puts you on the
nod. But they did the same thing in *Hatful of Rain*. The guy
takes a shot, so he runs all over. He comes tearing out of
the bathroom about ninety miles an hour and he jumps on
the bed and starts giving his Army serial number over and
over. What the hell is this? What's happening? If he took a
shot, you know, then he ought to be kind of sleepy. He would
just sit there and say something like, "Whaddiya know?"
That's all. Everything slows up, like in *The Connection*.
They've got one good scene in *The Connection* where the guy
starts looking at that little light bulb. He can't get his eyes off
that little Mazda up there and he says, "Light travels a hundred eighty-seven thousand miles per second, per second—
per second." That's all. I mean you'd think that the guy would
find out that morphine is a depressant. It's not a stimulant.
Heroin is essentially the same as morphine. It may be harder
to break, I guess. But it is not a stimulant. Cocaine is a stimulant, but that was not mentioned in the story or the film.
But they could have some sense of *responsibility*. I mean
they might just find out what Chicago looks like. The reason
Preminger gave for not making the movie in the neighborhood—I think they took one shot in Lincoln Park nowhere
near the neighborhood—he said, "Oh, that neighborhood's all
built up now; there are no slums left." But the neighborhood's in worse—it is more depressed than it ever was. So
there was no particular honesty about it. There's just that one
thing: Get the Dough into the Bank. That's what I mean when

I said that the whole thing was done out of contempt for the book and the people in it. There's no respect for the book or the people in it. It's just a chance to make a fast buck. That's what I felt about the movie.

Q: Do you want to make any more attempts to make a movie out of any of your writings?

ALGREN: Yes, if I had another book that made a good stage play, that said something essential and true in an original way and I succeeded in getting it on the stage.

Q: Why do you like that sequence—the play and then the movie?

ALGREN: For the same reason everybody else does. Once you sell the movie rights, nobody's going to back a play. But if you have a play going and then sell the movie rights, then you can get your money back on the play. But nobody is going to invest in a play if the movie rights are already gone.

Q: Why have a play at all?

ALGREN: Because a play is truer. You can get the thing over. You can tell the story better. You have a better chance on the stage to say the same thing you said in the book.

Q: After the film version of *The Man with the Golden Arm* came out, a stage play was produced off-Broadway, right? Who did that?

ALGREN: Jack Kirkland, the guy who did *Tobacco Road.*

Q: What did you think of that?

ALGREN: Well, it didn't last, the play. But I liked it better than the movie. It wasn't a bad production, and Kirkland did try to keep it going, but it soon closed.

Q: Does it matter to you that Preminger's production of *The Man with the Golden Arm* was the first film to ignore the taboo against dealing with drug addiction?

ALGREN: No.

Q: What about the question of the breakthrough? Preminger has the reputation for being a pioneer by making *The Arm,* which, from your point of view, from the author's point of view, is a terrible film. But Preminger did act like a hero and a liberal and a man fighting against censorship. How do you feel about this?

ALGREN: I am against censorship. I don't think there is anything more stupid than censorship. But I am not happy about being used as the spearhead of a producer's publicity drive. That man is not interested at all in drug addiction or anything else. It was just personal publicity. While I'm glad to see that censorship broken, I'm sorry that I was used to break it for a man whose social interest has nothing whatsoever to do with the problem which was dealt with in the book.

Q: What other books of yours could be made into movies after being made into plays? How about *Never Come Morning?*

ALGREN: Yes, that could be a very good play. A writer named Paul Herr—he wrote the novel *Journey Not to End*—is doing a play of it now.

Q: Have you ever written a play?

ALGREN: I worked with a collaborator, with David Peltz, on a musical version of *Walk on the Wild Side.* Peltz really put it together. I didn't do much. He organized the play and put it on the stage. A guy named Tommy Wolfe wrote the music. I'd like to see it produced again. It ran in St. Louis at the Crystal Palace for about sixty performances. I think it is a hell of a play, with really good music and a completely original kind of production.

Q: Would you like to see a good movie made out of *Never Come Morning?*

ALGREN: I'd like to see a good play. Then I'd think about the movie.

Q: But you respect movie men like George Stevens, don't you, and Stanley Kramer?

ALGREN: Oh, yeah, yeah.

Q: They make good movies?

ALGREN: Yeah. Stevens made that *Place in the Sun.*

Q: What if one of these men, a man you respect, were to buy *Never Come Morning* and wanted you to go out to Hollywood again? Would you go out there again?

ALGREN: I wouldn't go out there. No, I wouldn't go out there. I mean, I wouldn't go out there under the idiotic kind of circumstances I went out before, without any guarantee or anything. I would go out to make a movie after the thing was on the stage if a contract was signed beforehand which would give me script approval. Everything would have to be in the bag. I wouldn't get on that train again and go there and then have them tell me what they were going to do. It would have to be the way my new agent wanted it. Then I'd go.

Q: But you still like movies?

ALGREN: Yeah. I still like movies. There's no reason to give up this idea of getting to millions of people who don't read books and never see plays. To say I don't believe in movies would be like saying I don't believe millions of people go to them.

Q: But it is more affirmative than that, isn't it?

ALGREN: The more people you move, the better. When you write something, you want more than this. If you write something and you believe in it, you'd like to see sixty million people moved by it. But not in a perverted way. Naturally you want to reach as many people as you can and the movie is how you do it. But there's no use doing it when the thing that you say is turned exactly around.

Q: O.K. Now I'm going to ask you specific questions about the writer, about innocence, about failure, and about money. O.K.?

ALGREN: Yeah, yeah.

5 *A Question of Innocence*

QUESTION: From the things you said in the conversations we've
had, Nelson Algren, and from our correspondence, I've got
the feeling that when you went out to Hollywood the first
time, to see Moxon, that you were just looking around and
that you learned some things. When you went out the second
time, though, I have the feeling you thought you were going
to fail; almost as if you expected to fail in what you set out
to do—that is, to try to write a usable film treatment of what
was then your major novel, *The Man with the Golden Arm.*
Am I wrong in thinking that?

ALGREN: Oh, I didn't have any belief any longer that Hollywood
would seriously make a movie that was true to a book that it
took. I went out to see if I could get some of the money that I
knew they were going to make, that was all. Preminger had
some money coming.

Q: Preminger made millions on that, didn't he?

ALGREN: Yeah.

Q: But you went out there with an opinion about Hollywood much
like William Carlos Williams' opinion of Broadway. He was

convinced you can't do a serious play on Broadway. Do you agree with him about Broadway?

ALGREN: No, not at all. No, I don't.

Q: But do you feel that way about Hollywood?

ALGREN: Yeah.

Q: So you actually did not fail when you went out to Hollywood because you did not expect to succeed, right? Or is that too—

ALGREN: I didn't expect any real belief in the book, but somebody had gotten hold of a property that had much more value than I thought and I wanted to save some of it if I could.

Q: But if it had just been left to you and your agent, nothing would have been done in Hollywood to get *any* part of your book into a movie, right?

ALGREN: Yeah, that's right.

Q: But a man whom you dislike and distrust, a series of men you dislike and distrust, got something of your book onto the screen.

ALGREN: Yeah.

Q: So weren't you wrong about the capacity of Hollywood to produce anything good?

ALGREN: Oh, I know Hollywood can. There are producers in Hollywood who have produced good movies.

Q: Those are the heroes, those are your heroes. But even men for whom you have no respect saw more in your work than you did. They saw a greater possibility of producing it.

ALGREN: They saw more than I did the possibilities of making money out of it.

Q: But in order to make money out of it, Preminger, for instance, did have to break the rules of the code. No matter what his motives were, he did do what people said would be a good thing if he could do it—that is, to get dope addiction on the screen, to treat addiction as a sickness. It was a perverted view of your book, but he did present dope addiction on film. What I'm trying to get at is this question of innocence and being misused by the public, by the businessmen, by the entrepreneurs. Did you think you were particularly innocent when you went out to Hollywood to talk to Preminger? Who was the innocent of the two: Algren or Preminger? Which was the innocent one as far as money and works of art, movies and personality go?

ALGREN: Oh, well, I was as innocent as possible on his territory—in his field. I'm as innocent there—if innocence is the right word—as I would be playing the stock market when I don't know what is bearish and what is bullish, when I don't even know the first thing about stocks and I'm talking to a stockbroker. In dealing with that movie I'm challenging a man to a duel who is a professional duelist. There's no question about it. I mean we weren't talking about literature, we weren't talking about human values; we were talking about how you go about borrowing money from a bank and getting somebody to write the script, and about how you get an organization together—about how you make a production using the title of a book and how you get the money. I was totally innocent of all this. I mean, I've never given it any attention. It wasn't where my attention was focused.

Q: Can an innocent also be contemptuous of the people who are not innocent?

ALGREN: They don't let you feel anything else *but* contempt. I would have liked to—I reached around to *find* some way of

respecting the man. I mean you much prefer to respect somebody. It's a lot more trouble to feel contempt.

Q: But can an innocent feel contempt about anything? Isn't that
a rather uninnocent human thing?

ALGREN: No, I don't think so. Of course, you've got to put some
limitations on innocence. We're not talking about the kind of
innocence you have from not coming into contact with
the world, the sort of innocence of a recluse or of someone
who's taken monastic vows. I'm not talking about that
kind of innocence. I'm talking about the innocence that comes
through contact. Innocence is not just the *lack* of something.
Innocence is an achieved thing. You can't be unworldly without first being worldly. I mean anybody can be unworldly,
I mean just duck the world. But to be an innocent in the best
sense is to have the kind of *un*worldliness that comes out of
worldliness, to be able to see that the worldly thing is just
make-believe, to be able to dispense with the ordinary com-
pulsions that people have, to be able to see how people waste
their whole lives just to have security, to get a lot of
security to protect themselves and then there's nothing to
protect—they are sloughed off into their graves. What good is
security? I mean, nobody in his right mind gives his life
that way. Which is as much as saying most people are out
of their minds, because that's what we do.

Q: There's a third kind of innocence, too, isn't there, which
may be closer to the one we're discussing? That is the
one where the professionals of movie-making call in the
writer and present certain requests of him, and he tries to
supply them, innocent of their motivations, so he is left
holding an empty bag financially and a sorrowful bag emotionally. That's the innocence I'm talking about. Insofar as

you went out there to try to help make money for yourself, you were not innocent financially.

ALGREN: I was also concerned about the book itself. I mean I don't know who Preminger is. Maybe, for all I know, he's a man who would actually do the book. I'm still fond of the man of the book, Frankie Machine, and so I would like to see Frankie Machine done in a sympathetic way. For all I know, maybe Preminger is a man who really, really likes Frankie Machine, too. I don't know. I'd never heard of Preminger.

Q: That's why you went out. But you did go out innocent in a sense, and I don't mean ignorant.

ALGREN: I went out innocent in the sense that my attention had been given to just one aspect of society and there's no more time to be more than one person, and that absorbed me. So far as what is going on in the business world or in the financial industry—well and good, but I'm not interested in it.

Q: Don't you have to be interested insofar as these things affect your work?

ALGREN: No. That's what you have an agent for. We're back on that—

Q: Yes, but we have to talk about that. As a writer you were innocent about the requirements of an agent representing you. You are no longer innocent about certain of those aspects. But you were. Give me your opinion about the innocence of a writer who picks an agent to represent him in the business world and the agent doesn't do a good job. He has been innocent in his choice of agents then, right?

ALGREN: I thought all agents were the same. I suppose that shows a kind of innocence, or unawareness anyhow.

Q: But innocence for most writers and for you is something to be nourished and maintained, isn't it?

ALGREN: I think there's a distinction between a creative writer and a journalist because the journalist is conscious of what he's doing. He knows just what he's up to and proceeds to express it in an orderly way, because he simply is working out of a conscious plan and this never comes to anything more than most journalism because the only things that last are the things that are done when the writer doesn't know what he's doing—that kind of innocence. Faulkner didn't really know what he was doing. He didn't know what he was doing because he was working out of a compulsion. He didn't know and he certainly would have defended himself against having it broken down. He knew that much about it. He had a drive. Certainly Hemingway, in this sense, never knew what he was doing.

Q: Yes, but a writer must keep himself in condition, must he not, to always write?

ALGREN: Yes.

Q: If he kept himself innocent about maintaining his physical health and was always ill so that he could not write, he could not maintain *that* kind of innocence, right?

ALGREN: I don't mean a total innocence. But so far as knowing what he's doing—a writer who knows what he is doing isn't doing very much.

Q: But when a writer doesn't know what he's doing and places himself or his work in the hands of other people to the detriment of his work—and if we call that action a form of innocence—then we have to ask if that innocence should be maintained and nourished. It hasn't been in your case.

ALGREN: No. I just—

Q: You've changed, haven't you? How have you changed?

ALGREN: I don't think anybody ever really changes.

Q: With respect to Hollywood you've changed.

ALGREN: Oh, well, I'm at least wary. But you don't really basically change.

Q: I'm not talking about basic changes, I'm talking about the change in attitude.

ALGREN: In that sense, sure I've changed.

Q: When asked if you'd go out to Hollywood again to make a *good* movie you said yes under certain conditions—

ALGREN: I'd go out there under conditions that nobody would think of meeting, I mean because—

Q: But isn't that the same attitude you had when you first went out to talk to Preminger?

ALGREN: No. I had more hope then of getting something of the book onto the screen. I was much more gullible then. I'm much less gullible now, yet I don't think that there's any real chance of having what I hoped for then. I don't think that'll ever be.

Q: Now how much of a childlike attitude is that? That one, in order not to be disappointed, convinces oneself that the nice things won't possibly happen, or that the good thing can't possibly turn out?

ALGREN: It's the rules of the game. I'm not making the rules. Rules are made by the producers. I wouldn't sign a contract unless I had script approval and I just don't think any producer would give script approval.

Q: But you did not ask for this the first two times you went out to Hollywood?

ALGREN: No.

Q: So this change in you is actually, is it not, a loss of a kind of innocence about how the business world in Hollywood works?

ALGREN: Sure.

Q: Now is this a good loss?

ALGREN: It's a bad loss.

Q: Are you not better able to take care of your written work in its potential cinematic form by this loss of innocence?

ALGREN: Yeah, yeah, yeah.

Q: Then insofar as taking care of your written work, it is a good loss?

ALGREN: But insofar as writing goes, it is a bad loss.

Q: Why?

ALGREN: Because it's a loss in belief. It's a loss in belief. My assumption was that if this is a good book, then the man I talked to, he wants to make a good movie. My assumption is that if I'm sympathetic toward Frankie Machine, then this guy who wants to make the movie will like Frankie Machine, too. But I know, immediately, as soon as I talk to him that this guy, Preminger, wouldn't touch Frankie Machine. He wouldn't say hello to him. One of the first questions Preminger asked me was, "How do you know such people?" You know? Such animals, you know? I said, "I've known them all my life." But he says, "But it's unfathomable why anybody should even talk to people like this." This wasn't my basic assumption. My basic assumption was, well, I like these people in my book and those who want to film my book must like them too. If you are undisturbed in this attitude, if you really believe that other people are fortunate to have compassion going toward people in need of compassion, if that's undisturbed, and if you really believe in that compassion, it's a very useful thing, because you are a much better writer if you're compassionate without any distrust.

Q: You are not a man who trusts everyone. Why should you have trusted Preminger without meeting him, simply because he liked your work?

ALGREN: I know the guy's a producer. I'm just talking about a personal thing. I know what this guy is, just a producer. I know before I see him what his function is. He's a man who can't do anything himself. There are many like that. He can't act, he can't use a camera, he can't write a story. But he knows how to borrow money from a bank. He's always on that end. He arranges things. But all the same, this kind of man *can* personally be sympathetic. I mean, I *know* he's organizing a thing so that he can get a million dollars, but that doesn't necessarily mean that he can't produce a compassionate picture or that he might not himself be interested. He might *him*self even be a man like Frankie Machine, a more skillful one. I mean there are people who have wanted to make a million dollars out of movies and who are still able to make good movies. (Look at the way the shadows look on the buildings. Purple shadows. Isn't that fantastic?)

Q: I hadn't noticed that—it looks like a phony set.

ALGREN: Yeah—it's a strange world out there.

Q: Name some men who make good movies and millions of dollars.

ALGREN: Whoever did *The Grapes of Wrath* was good. That was certainly successful.

Q: Then why didn't you go to one of these people?

ALGREN: I don't know who they were. I knew of certain names. I know, for instance, of John Huston. I know of him but I didn't know the guy. I can't go knocking at the door and say, "Will you make a movie of my book?" If a moviemaker wants to make a movie of your book, he has to express an interest. You can't go from studio to studio.

Q: Why not?

ALGREN: Because you're not supposed to be out there. You're supposed to be writing, to be working. You can't be running around out there any more than you can run from publisher to publisher saying, "Will you publish my book?" You're dead as soon as you present yourself and say you want something. Somebody has to come to you. He has to say he wants to see a book and is willing to take a chance on you. The same thing with a producer. He has to say, "I like it and I want it." He has to want it. I was edified that Garfield was so personal about it. His feeling was so personal about it. He liked this guy, Frankie Machine. He wanted to be Frankie Machine. He genuinely liked this guy and the part. I was influenced by that. I mean I was very gratified that a good actor should want to be the guy that I created. So—

Q: But Garfield died.

ALGREN: Yeah, well—

Q: And Garfield was not a producer really.

ALGREN: I didn't even know there was such a thing as Moxon Productions. Moxon Productions took the property, and I wasn't primarily interested in a movie. The book wasn't aimed at Hollywood in the first place. I didn't expect that anybody in Hollywood would be interested in that kind of a book.

Q: This is a kind of innocence, isn't it?

ALGREN: It's a safe assumption. Hollywood up to that time in 1949 wasn't interested in serious books. They weren't making them.

Q: All I have to do is just mention one book, one serious book, that they had already filmed before that time, and we have a kind of blank contradiction. You have already mentioned one.

ALGREN: Yeah. There were what you called heroes who did do some. They made *Wuthering Heights*. And they made *The Informer*. And they made a dozen other good things. But as a general thing, Hollywood wasn't primarily interested in serious writing.

Q: You have never dealt with yourself as a general thing in general situations. Why should you treat yourself any differently in Hollywood? I am trying to find out whether or not you feel that at that time you were nourishing, if not enforcing, a kind of innocence about how the real world out there worked, how it functioned insofar as getting something on film is concerned. I want to know how much you think anger is involved under that façade of innocence. Do you know what I'm talking about?

ALGREN: No, I don't.

Q: If some of the things you wrote about in *The Arm*, some of the bad things, some of the things you did not think were good, if these things were also operative out in Hollywood and if you could make a movie of *The Arm* only under these conditions, thereby supporting these conditions, you'd have to be angry about that, wouldn't you?

ALGREN: Yeah.

Q: So you would have to, in a way, sabotage any effort to make the movie at that time. What I want to know is, how much did you sabotage your own effort to get your book into a film? Did you think you did at all? Did you do any of that at all? Was it all Hollywood's fault?

ALGREN: The only way I could have sabotaged it would be just to not have made any move at all. That would have sabotaged it. If I'd wanted to sabotage the movie, I didn't have to do anything.

Q: And that's what you did with *Walk on the Wild Side.* You had absolutely nothing to do with it. But you made an attempt to get something good out of *The Man with the Golden Arm,* and you failed. I want to know whether or not you think you should have failed, and whether or not you wanted to fail.

ALGREN: I have no doubts about it: I've never had *any* desire to *fail.* I have a strong desire to *succeed.*

Q: And you've written to me that you begrudge every penny made by others from your written work.

ALGREN: Yeah.

Q: Well, what about going out there and being fooled by these people, twice? Didn't you once tell me that your friend John Ciardi, the poet, asked you, "How come you're back in that same box?"

ALGREN: Ciardi said, "Why don't you protect yourself?" He said I've been in the world long enough to know that it's full of people like Preminger and that they're going to take you, that the world is full of people who want something for nothing and if you expose yourself, they are going to take you. His mild reproach was, "You're a man; you've got to take care of yourself." And my story is that you can't do two things, that you're entitled to protection if, in writing a book, you're preoccupied. I mean you should be entitled to have a total preoccupation, you should be entitled to innocence. Let me put it a different way. About ten years ago I am talking to two addicts about *The Man with the Golden Arm.* They had both read the book. There were two schools of thought going. The addict sitting on the right-hand side says, "It's a hell of a book, it's a good book." The other addict isn't enthusiastic about it. I said, "What's the matter with it?" And the guy on the right-hand side asks the other junkie, "Why don't you think it's a good book?" The other junkie says, "Well," talking about me, "he's a square." He can't understand talking to me. He knows I can't understand him. But he'll talk to the other junkie on the right-hand side because the other guy can understand him. He says to the other guy, "You know it isn't like that," he says. "I come on and I read three or four pages of the book this guy is telling what it's like." You know the part where the junkie in the book, Frankie Machine, is talking, dramatizing the thing. This guy says, "Well, you know it isn't like that. We don't talk like that about junk." The other guy, the guy who liked the book, agrees that the junkie in the book was a phony. "Yeah," he says, "that's right. But if this guy knew what it was really like, he couldn't have written a book. He'd be out in the county jail. He'd be on junk. You can't write a book when you're on junk. It is the best thing that a square can do." And the other guy says, "Oh, is that what you mean? For a square. All right. It's a good book for a square." And that settled the argument. But in the same way, if you have enough guile, enough distrust, to deal on an equal plane with Preminger or any of them, I just use Preminger as a name, with this whole pack of make-believe people, if you could deal with them, then you wouldn't be able to write the book.

Q: Any book?

ALGREN: You wouldn't be able to write a particular kind of book which is based on, which has innocence. I mean, if you really had any real distrust, if you really didn't believe in the world, if you didn't believe in people, if you thought basically people are shit, if you wouldn't sit down and knock yourself out for two or two and a half years to write a book like that, or to write any book. As *you* know, you work on it every day and you work out of belief. Nobody is going to sit down in a society where he can do something else and write a serious book about people unless he had a really deep belief in people. You can't stop that. A belief carries over from the book. I mean you develop innocence.

Q: Are you saying that this developed innocence should be maintained for the sake of your work?

ALGREN: I say *entitled* to innocence because not everybody makes it. You are very fortunate if you come along that far and can develop a belief in people. It's something that happens.

Q: But you are less innocent about Hollywood now, aren't you?

ALGREN: Yeah, yeah.

Q: And it has not detracted from your work. As a matter of fact, you can now do a little writing about Hollywood, can't you.

ALGREN: Yes, I suppose. But it certainly detracted from my will to work because I would never sit down now and work for two and a half or three years. As a matter of fact, at the time I finished *The Man with the Golden Arm* I thought, well, now I know how to write a book and I've got enough of an economic foundation—I can work at my own pace— and I'll spend five years, that's what I figured, working on a particular novel about a woman. I wanted to do it just line by line, day by day, just making every sentence count. I believe I would have been very happy to do that. It means a pretty rigid life, but no more rigid than the things that actors do when they do just nothing else but try to learn how to act. It's a very, very rare opportunity when somebody is given by accident, by a hundred different accidents, a chance really to do something that is serious, when everybody else is doing something they don't believe in at all. I can say that at the time I was the only person I know of in Chicago who was doing something that was actually worth while. I didn't know anybody else. I'm sure that later in Paris and New York, too, you do find people who are totally preoccupied with something important, with something that has something to do with people. They're plugged into our society. You go around now and see somebody knock himself out with a public relations outfit or something—all this advertising and all the hokum that people use to get by—they don't believe in it themselves—they don't believe that it has any importance—they have to do it to survive. But once in a while somebody's extremely fortunate and gets his work all cut out for him. And there's really nothing else for him to do. It can be sculpting or acting or singing or something, but that is a really privileged person. So, in that sense, in losing that opportunity, I think the experience with Hollywood was very distracting. I don't think it was good for me.

Q: Why not?

ALGREN: I think it's a lost opportunity because I would never do that now. I would never put in the three, four, five years to turn out a book that has a chance of enduring.

Q: Why not?

ALGREN: Because I'd get nothing out of it.

Q: I don't understand that.

ALGREN: I mean you have to have a reward. You have to believe your work is *wanted*. After all, *The Man with the Golden Arm* wasn't my first book—it was about my sixth. I was willing to go through that.

Q: Aren't you going to go through that again?

ALGREN: No, no. I wouldn't do that again. You don't have to do this to get money. And you've lost two or three years. There's a lot of money. You can get money much faster than by doing it this way. There's no point in doing it for money. You'd do it for the real satisfaction—you'd assume— that it's wanted. But the real deception, the real disappointment is that actually it's not wanted. The work is not wanted. Maybe this goes along with that innocence we were speaking of, but I really believed that *Never Come Morning* and *Neon Wilderness* and *The Arm* and that story you liked, "A Bottle of Milk for Mother"—I believed that these were close enough to our society. I mean if total strangers write to you and say that they got something out of this, then the money thing is secondary. I think anybody, anybody, if given the choice, would always take the privilege of having his work wanted by other people rather than the privilege of having more money than anybody.

Q: But haven't you received letters about your work from people?

ALGREN: I receive a letter now and then.

Q: And a million people bought the old paperback edition of *Never Come Morning,* right? Why did those million people buy it—just to pass the time on a train?

ALGREN: Yeah.

Q: They could have selected many other things. How do you know your work isn't wanted?

ALGREN: That doesn't mean it's wanted. People buy Mickey Spillane by the seven millions, by the ten millions.

Q: How do you know when your work is wanted?

ALGREN: You feel that.

Q: Are there any other indications besides your feelings?

ALGREN: Nobody's work is absolutely wanted. But the point is—do you *believe* it's wanted, or not.

Q: Do you believe your work is wanted?

ALGREN: No, no. I don't know. I certainly did then.

Q: When?

ALGREN: Oh, up until the time and for a short time after I finished that *Man with the Golden Arm.* The fact that it may not be wanted isn't important. The fact is you believe it.

Q: And your Hollywood experience made you feel that it was not wanted?

ALGREN: As one aspect of the whole experience. All I'm saying is I don't have the belief.

Q: But did the Hollywood experience lessen your belief that your work wasn't wanted?

ALGREN: Oh, sure. The Hollywood experience and the New York experience, too.

Q: What New York experience?

ALGREN: Because I didn't find any real difference in the values of the publishing world than in the values of the studios. It's the same thing. Their values are: get something that sells; get books into the presses and then promote them.

Q: Do you agree with Robert Louis Stevenson that everyone lives by selling something?

ALGREN: Well, yeah, but—

Q: Then what's the matter with Hollywood and Madison Avenue?

ALGREN: Hemingway was selling something. Hemingway was selling vitality.

Q: Why shouldn't Hollywood and Madison Avenue sell?

ALGREN: They sell sterility.

Q: So it is the product they sell that bothers you, not the process?

ALGREN: It's what you sell. Sure, everybody sells.

Q: What about you and money? Do you know the value of a dollar?

ALGREN: I am very good with one dollar.

Q: Do you know the value of two dollars?

ALGREN: Yeah. Oh, the questions are getting harder now. That was a tough one. What's the next one? You're leading up to three, *four*, FIVE!

Q: How about a million dollars?

ALGREN: That's a real head-scratcher! That's a *lot* of money.

Q: Is it too much?

ALGREN: No. It ain't enough.

Q: Do you want a million dollars? What would you do with it?

ALGREN: Oh, I tell you that isn't too much. It's not unmanageable. I could use that and not even be conspicuous, not even be dropping money at the dice or the horses. It'd all be essential. The thing to do would be to keep the mint. Put it away and get a hundred thousand a year. And a hundred thousand a year isn't too much. I'd buy a home. I'd buy a place, possibly in some area like Cape Cod. It would have an ocean close and I don't think that's a luxury. I don't think you could get a place big enough to entertain people in for less than fifty thousand dollars. That is not a very grand place. Just a roomy place with a breakwater and a view of the ocean. And then I'd want a boat out there. I don't mean a luxury boat. Something I could go out on the ocean with. And I would want books. There's at least ten thousand dollars' worth of books I should have. There's all kinds of books. I don't even have a set of Dickens. Now what the hell kind of writer is that? I should have a Dickens. I should have a library. That ten thousand dollars in a library wouldn't be much. It shouldn't be paperbacks. It shouldn't be cheap editions. I want a set of leather Dickens. And I want

Alice in Wonderland. I don't have a copy of that. Then you should have, you've got to have a family. I mean if you're living you can't go it alone. You're nothing, you're nothing alone. I mean what are you going to write about if you're not attached anywhere. There should be a family and there's got to be room in the house for the family. You don't want to marry a broad for her domestic things. I want to take her in the boat. I want to talk to her. So that means kitchen help. There should be a women who likes to cook there and there should be somebody to bring it out. Neither of us should have to be making a beef stew or peeling potatoes if we've got something better to do. And there should be liquor. You shouldn't have to share a six-pack of beer if ten people come in, you know. There should be cases. There should be cases. There should be Scotch and bourbon and somebody to mix a martini. You don't have to have a party every night, but you got to see people. There are people you should meet. You are living in the world. I mean, the way I'm living I never see anybody. That's *no*where, you know? Oh, once in a while I meet people like Zero Mostel and Gerry Page and so forth. But you should have enough to go around. You know when I give a party it's hopeless. It's a hopeless bunch of horses' asses. Terkel and the Kogans come around and they're lively people, but, by and large, at my parties there are just stolid people. One had a barber-shop and one has a real-estate office and all that. I like them but I am not going to talk about Algiers with them. They'll just look at you. But I want to know about that, I want to talk to anybody who has been there. I want to talk to a Fascist, an O.A.S. guy, I want to know what it's like. Oh, you got to have a place. Anybody would come around, you know, if I had a place in New York. I could get the best pickpocket in New York to come every night and I'd get to meet real interesting people. Oh, people will come around any place if it's pleasant. All I'm saying is I want to entertain, with my broad, somebody presentable in a dress. I don't want some dog there, you know. I want somebody that's real, you know, someone who reflects credit on me. Somebody sharp.

Q: So you could say, "That's my girl."

ALGREN: *That's* it.

Q: You'd travel, too?

ALGREN: Then I want to travel. When I'd worked a year, then I'd say, "Well, pack up your things." We would travel for three or four months. While we are gone, we'll send the kids to a school for the retarded.

Q: Are you worried about selling out?

ALGREN: Selling out?

Q: I know some young writers who are worried.

ALGREN: I don't know if I'm in a position to worry.

Q: By young, I mean under thirty.

ALGREN: Maybe they are flattering themselves that they've *got* something to sell out.

Q: But you are worried about it, too, aren't you? In your Hemingway article you wrote: "The hard-bought American belief that literature can be made only by a willingness to take one's own chances was sold piecemeal by individual surrender. . . . Honesty among writers had meant a willingness to take the kind of personal risk by which, if it fails, one fails alone; yet if it succeeds, succeeds for all. Now the writers began to subserve, rather than to stand against, the businessman's world." That sounds to me, Nelson Algren, like the protest of a writer who's worried about selling out. How much did you fear, if you have a fear of selling out, how much did that fear figure in your work when you went out to Hollywood or when you talked to publishers?

ALGREN: I've never been afraid of the accusation of selling out. Nobody makes it but those with nothing left to sell and I'm not accountable to them.

Q: No one has ever accused you of selling out. But have you ever been *afraid* of selling out?

ALGREN: Well, you see, I'm trying to think of just what it means.

Q: It means what you accused most other writers of doing.

ALGREN: If you don't keep producing, it's kind of a sellout.

Q: I don't mean that. I mean a sellout to the bourgeois, square, moneyed world. Can our culture produce writers who make a million dollars who have not sold out?

ALGREN: Sure.

Q: Is it conceivable that you'll make a million dollars sometime?

ALGREN: I don't think so.

Q: What if *Never Come Morning* as a play runs for a year on Broadway and you sell it to Hollywood for a couple of hundred grand plus a percentage and your script approval condition is met and the film makes a lot of money? Is that conceivable?

ALGREN: It's conceivable but a little dubious because everybody carries a certain price tag on them immediately and it doesn't necessarily have much to do with his worth. The price tag is what his agent sets. To be more specific, Irwin Shaw put himself down as a *very* unavailable, *very* high-priced writer *immediately.* I give him full credit for that. Irwin Shaw is always extremely hard to get. He's very high-priced. He did this way back in the thirties and he stuck to it. I happen to have had an agent who hung a very low price tag on herself— which was appropriate for herself—but she wrapped me into her crackerjack box. I'm the tin whistle of American letters.

Q: You're speaking now of the past?

ALGREN: The past still pertains. James Jones gets three-quarters of a million dollars, Algren gets a free train-ride to New York. They know what the price is. This is the price category I happen to have been put in. That's why I mention my present agent, my new agent, because she understood right away and saw that the problem was how to get me out of this free train-ride league.

Q: But *you* got the new agent, which means you were no longer willing to put up with the old price standard?

ALGREN: The world of those standards doesn't exist any more.

Q: Yet, in terms of a senior high school psychology course, your evaluation of yourself has gone up because you got yourself a better agent.

ALGREN: My evaluation of myself has never varied. It's very high. I'm a solid-gold whistle. I'm a platinum saxophone.

Q: Then your own estimate of your own *monetary* worth has increased?

ALGREN: Oh, yeah, yeah. Just look around me. I know that if James Jones, who is a fourth-rate writer, if Jones is worth three-quarter of a million dollars, then I must be worth Fort Knox.

Q: But how come the time that you are taking better care of yourself financially is the same time that you feel your work is not wanted?

ALGREN: Well, the work that is wanted is not very well paid, and the stuff that is not wanted gets paid very high.

Q: Isn't that a pretty good definition of a writer's innocence?

ALGREN: I don't know what you mean by that. What *I* mean is the highest price goes to the most useless stuff, the most unwanted stuff.

Q: Do you *really* feel that?

ALGREN: Well, I don't know.

Q: Is your best work behind you?

ALGREN: I'm not prepared to answer that because I don't know what's coming.

(The next day, after listening to the taped recording of this whole conversation, Algren made the following comments.)

ALGREN: In listening to this discussion about money, I remembered our last conversation in Riccardo's when you quoted Camus to me, to the effect that a man is what he does. And then, of course, five minutes later I took exception to that because it could be that a man turns out to be not what he does but what somebody else does.

Q: To him?

ALGREN: To the world. I think you have more of a belief in Camus than I have.

Q: I mentioned him only as a bona fide representative of an idea I thought you also held—that it doesn't matter what a man says he'd like to do, nor what he hopes he can do, but what he actually does.

ALGREN: I agree with that, but I don't share the common reverence for Camus. I believe he was a man of conscience, but I don't believe he was at all a profound man. Leo Durocher said, and I am *not* trying to be funny here, Leo Durocher said the thing just as profound and he's not the man of conscience Camus was, but he did say the classic thing, you know, when he said, "Nice guys finish second." He said, you know, "I like my mother, but if I'm playing second and she's trying for third, she goes down." In other words, either you win or you lose. You come to bat in the last of the ninth with one out and two men on and you're two runs behind, and you hit a drive over the third baseman's head—a direct smash into the left-field seats. Both runners start moving home. But the ball ricochets off the flagpole into the outfielder's glove. He throws it to second, doubling the guy off there and catches you coming into second. The game's over. You didn't win four to three. You lost three to one. You hit into a double play, that's all. You hit a flagpole, that's all. So as far as these movies go, especially *The Man with the Golden Arm,* it turns out that it is not important what was in the book, because this is what was done to it, and according to the reviews you showed me about *Walk on the Wild Side,* both of these books I did turned out on film to be flagpole shots. How many times did I say that? Shall I proceed?

Q: Yes.

ALGREN: In the same way that a thing turns out depending on whether you hit the flagpole or not, the same thing happens with money. We spoke a great deal about money. Well,

CONVERSATIONS WITH NELSON ALGREN

money is what whoever has it is. Money is no specific thing. To one man, money is safety, his total security, but to somebody else money is music. It depends whose hands it's in. My identification with money is almost identical with writing. I've never believed in writing directly from imagination. If I had the imagination maybe I would. But this kind of work is good for Immanuel Kant or Marcel Proust, who stay in one room, you know. This kind of writing can be done very rarely. My kind of writing is just a form of reportage, you might call it emotionalized reportage, but—as *you* know—the data has to be there. Compassion has no use without a setting. I mean you have to know how do the law courts work. You have to know how many bars there are in a jail cell. You can't just say, "The guy's in jail." You've got to *know*. You've got to know there are different doors—there are solid doors, doors without bars. Some cells have one bar left out in the middle for a little shelf there. You have to know what that shelf is for. Actually it is used to put coffee on, or a little Lily cup of milk or something when the prisoner gives money to the matron or the screw—they go out and get coffee or milk and put it on that little shelf. Or if the prisoner comes in late at night, it is a little pantry. They use that. And you have to know do they get blankets or not. You're talking about a jail in Texas—well, how do you know if the cot is iron or not, or if the blankets are cotton, or whether you get blankets, or whether you get a mattress or not. Some jails have mattresses. The reason I've never read Jack Kerouac is because the first book of his I picked up says in the first sentence that the guy was lying in a gondola. Well, I stopped to think: a gondola is a coal car and the bottom opens. You can't lie in a gondola; you'll hit the track. He doesn't know. He doesn't know what he talks about, so why read him? But if you read one sentence, if you read the first sentence of John

Cheever, then you know Cheever knows. If you are a serious writer, you have to find out more than anybody else. For me this takes money, a little money so I can move around for the data, for the stuff you make books out of. I'm just trying to explain what I consider money to be. For instance, I remember a morning, about four in the morning, when I was with an addict, a guy, a six-and-a-half-foot drummer from Arkansas. He's an addict. I wanted to go home. It was getting late. I was broke. He wanted to make a stop somewhere. He wanted to go into some little restaurant and just wait. I was tired of it and he said, "Well, you don't know what it's like to have a monkey on your back." This is pretty stale stuff by now, this phrase. It's been used in a dozen hundred paperbacks. It's common language now. But at that time in 1949 I don't believe this phrase had come into the language of articulate people. It was something that musicians, that drug addicts said. I happened to be there and I repeated it. I knew it was good. I used many things like that. If I found something like that, I'd go home. That's what you make books out of.

Q: Where did the title *The Man with the Golden Arm* come from?

ALGREN: Oh, there was a dice-player in the Army who always wanted to roll the dice, and when somebody else would say, "Gimme the dice! Gimme the dice!" he would say, "Naw, naw, I have a golden arm." But I wanted you to know that my idea of money is the stuff you use to get around to pick up things for books. See what I mean? So this way I don't think in terms of a hundred thousand or a million bucks.

Q: Yet, yesterday when I asked you what you would do with a million dollars, you gave me a rather beautiful description of a civilized man being a compassionate, free human being.

ALGREN: But the possibility didn't exist in 1949. That was for other people.

Q: Does the possibility exist for you now?

ALGREN: Yes, it exists, and I'd accept it, but only as a secondary thing. Now the best reward is the kind of reward that Dickens got, regardless of whether he made any money. People followed him around. They wanted to thank him for enriching them. The characters were more real to them than the people they knew.

Q: But Dickens *did* make money?

ALGREN: Yeah, he did happen to make money.

Q: In your writings you say you think a lot of Mark Twain— and Mark Twain made money.

ALGREN: Sure, so did Jack London. But Twain lost money.

Q: He did not lose it in writing. He lost it because he went into another league.

ALGREN: What I'm saying is that I don't believe Twain or Dickens were primarily concerned with money.

Q: My point here is that the good writer, in certain cultures, makes good money, and I wonder what you thought about yourself, Nelson Algren, in that context?

ALGREN: Well, I would accept money and I think money's good, but it is not the main thing. I would take it now because there has to be *some* reward, even if it is the secondary reward. If you don't get the real reward, then you take the secondary thing. I'm reflecting on the society we live in. This isn't a peculiar situation, peculiar to me. I recall at least two writers of the thirties I met briefly—Ignazio Silone and Albert

Maltz. At that time there were many writers who were merely writing out of an intellectual pattern, but these two guys, my feeling about these two guys was that they were writing out of an almost Christlike feeling, out of a real heartfelt concern, really concerned with the world. And I don't think they needed any monetary reward for that, although later Maltz made a lot of money.

Q: Where?

ALGREN: In Hollywood.

Q: Did he sell out?

ALGREN: No, he never sold out.

Q: Did Silone make any money?

ALGREN: I think he made money.

Q: Did Silone sell out?

ALGREN: No, I don't think so.

Q: In this unpublished manuscript which you were kind enough to let me see, as you have been kind enough to let me see a number of things, a manuscript called *Things of the Earth: A Groundhog View,* you wrote: "Thinking of Melville, thinking of Poe, thinking of Mark Twain and Vachel Lindsay, thinking of Jack London and Tom Wolfe, one begins to feel there is almost no way of becoming a creative writer in America without being a loser." You wrote this in 1950 about the time you were dealing with Roberts out in Hollywood. Now you do think this is true today? Do you have to be a loser in order to be a creative writer in America today?

ALGREN: No. We have examples of good creative writers who aren't losers. It can happen.

Q: Do you think that Nelson Algren must be a loser?

ALGREN: Oh, yeah, yeah. Yeah.

Q: Why?

ALGREN: I'm trying to connect this with your question before when we talked about the loss in Hollywood. That was a bad loss because you have to take money for your purpose. The loss is that there isn't any place now to do what guys like Silone and Maltz were doing—they were working out of straight compassion. This don't work. The loss is the loss to make the connection with humanity. I mean, take Camus: think of a guy being a conscience for millions and millions of people! American kids are still crazy about Camus, more than Sartre or De Beauvoir. Camus represented something and there are people in every field like that. Our friend Gerry Page I think is like that.

Q: You mean that our unintellectual, anticultural, poorly educated American youth are interested in a man like Camus?

ALGREN: Yeah, they love Camus. I don't know whether they know what he means, but he stands for something for them. How many men are there like that? Camus, Albert Schweitzer to a lesser degree. I feel the same sort of thing when Gerry Page gets on a stage. Maybe there's a hundred women in the audience who feel the same things she feels, but it doesn't make any difference with them because they aren't plugged into anything except their immediate families. Page is plugged in to them; she represents them. She represents as many people as can see her or hear about her. This is a very big thing. And Gerry Page makes all sorts of money, but I don't think she started acting in the hope that she'd be a millionaire.

Q: If she makes a million, will getting all that money make her feel she's done something wrong with her art?

ALGREN: That's Miss Page's problem. It can be done.

Q: So the presence of money is not an indication of having sold out?

ALGREN: No. Of course not. Jack London made money. Stephen Crane made money. Dreiser made money. Dick Wright made money. What the hell—Hemingway made money. Rocky Marciano made money and he never threw a fight. . . . But the loss I am speaking of is in the shifting of a writer who's plugged in one way, the good way, to our society. Now the only way I can be plugged in again is on this money thing. That's the only thing by which you can get respect.

Q: Consider something which may sound quite high-flown. What do you think of the possibility that a writer, because of his job, because he must pay close attention to the triumphs and tragedy of life, very often is tempted to blame the unhappy truths, the problems, which he uncovers, on the very thing he is studying?

ALGREN: I don't think I follow you.

Q: Doesn't a creative writer very often feel that he must be a loser because he's paying close attention to a losing proposition—life? You are an atheist, aren't you?

ALGREN: Yeah.

Q: So am I. So we can't count on any afterlife—this is it, and we have to pay attention to it now.

ALGREN: Yeah.

Q: But it is a losing proposition. We can either go like that fighter, Paret, in front of millions of people, or we can get it quietly all alone and eighty, in our sleep. But we are going to go. Writers pay close attention to this process which is, as Malraux wrote, man's fate. Don't you find writers often can't cope with the very truths they say they want to study, and so they blame their plight on something else, on part of what they are studying—the system, the economy, the culture, money, women. "My mother loved me," Steig said. "But she died." Or something else?

ALGREN: I don't think it's any commoner among writers.

Q: But shouldn't writers do *less* of that kind of blaming, less than other people?

ALGREN: Well, they're just as much people as other people. They're no stronger.

Q: What about innocence and anger? Many people think of you as a terribly angry man. They do not know any other side of you. You have a reputation for being a very tough guy and a very angry one. Are you angry? Do you express your anger as anger or as innocence?

ALGREN: Oh, I don't go around being angry. Nobody who is *really* angry goes around *being* angry. As for innocence, I think it is a very lucky thing if it's an achieved innocence, if it's something that happens to you. I think Brendan Behan had innocence. I think Dylan Thomas was an innocent. You have to go through the world to get to that sort of innocence. I mean there's no trouble for a woman to be chaste if she's never been tempted to sleep with anybody. The really chaste woman is the whore. There is nothing less whorish than an old whore who hasn't gone down the drain. She's not a whorish person. The whorish ones are the prick-teasers, the middle-class prick-teasers, who run in and out, who play with sex. There's much more whorishness there.

Q: You've made other notes there. Do any of them still interest you?

ALGREN: Well, for some reason I wrote down something of Henry Miller's where he says the writer's got to go all out. That hooks up with something I said before about how the only good writing is done by people who don't know what they're doing. They just go all out. Like Hemingway and Faulkner, they were working out of a compulsion. There were things they had to do for their own survival which was expressed in their writing. But it had to be total. It goes all the way.

Q: What about your comment that "there is almost no way of becoming a creative writer in America without being a loser?"

ALGREN: I don't think the American writer is necessarily damned.

Q: But you also keep quoting that thing by Scott Fitzgerald. Over and over again you quote it: "Why was I identified with the very objects of my horror and compassion?" Consider, if you will, the possibility that a writer must *always* identify himself with the objects of his horror and compassion, and that this is one of the things that F. Scott Fitzgerald never found out. It was too late when he started asking himself that question. He couldn't cope with it. Do you believe that?

ALGREN: It just jives with what I was saying—that it takes a total commitment. Fitzgerald identifies himself. He was as good a writer as he was because he identified himself so closely.

Q: But did he? He didn't say "Why did I identify myself . . . ?" He said, "Why was I identified with the very objects of my horror and compassion?" Implying that he did not wish to be so identified.

ALGREN: He was a writer despite himself. He didn't want to—

Q: But haven't you identified yourself with the objects of your horror and compassion?

ALGREN: I hope so. I don't know, but I hope so. If you lose that identification, well, then you're just a journalist.

Q: What about the possibility that because Fitzgerald could not identify himself with the objects of his horror and compassion—

ALGREN: He didn't want to, but he did.

Q: You think he did?

ALGREN: Well, he felt something had been done to him, but actually he did it himself, out of his compulsion.

Q: Do you do these things to *your*self? Much of your critical writing sounds as if you do, but I have been talking to you and—

ALGREN: If I did it, I would be identifying myself.

Q: It would be under your control, though, wouldn't it? Under your commitment and your wish?

ALGREN: I think that's important. I don't think anything has been done *to* me.

Q: This makes you and Fitzgerald different then.

ALGREN: Well, I can see there's a difference.

Q: When he speaks of a writer being a loser or how a culture doesn't understand the writer, you would have to feel then that this didn't apply to you. Now you've written about Wolfe and his troubles, and Lindsay. But you are no Wolfe, nor a Lindsay. You are different there, too. You write often about Chekhov. What about you and Chekhov?

ALGREN: I have a liking for the guy's personality, what little I know of it.

Q: You keep quoting him about how when he was at home all by himself, everything was fine, but as soon as he walked outside his door, life became horrible.

ALGREN: That's not exactly it: "When one is peacefully at home, life seems ordinary, but as soon as one walks into the street and begins to observe, then life becomes terrible."

Q: But do you agree with that? Why should he be surprised by what was outside his door? Do you think life is *that* hard?

ALGREN: Oh, yeah. It's the same thing that Tennessee Williams knows, or that Sherwood Anderson knew about. There is no such thing as a normal life. It's never lived that way. A critic in Chicago once got tired of Tennessee and wrote, "Why can't we get back to writing about plain old workaday Sunday folks?" Or that other critic saying, "But why don't we ever read about happy marriages?" Because there are none.

Q: Has Hollywood stuck pretty close to what Tennessee Williams intended?

ALGREN: They made a better movie out of *Streetcar* than it was on the stage. I found it more moving than the play.

Q: Did you like *Summer and Smoke?*

ALGREN: It was good to see because Page was in it, but this guy, this guy Laurence Harvey, he's deadly. But it was worth seeing because of her.

Q: Why aren't you going to work as hard on a big book as you did on *The Man with the Golden Arm?*

ALGREN: That hooks up with a question you asked before when you said there was a loss and you said it's a good loss, and I said it's a bad loss because the fact is I value my time more now. It also hooks up with what I was saying about the reward. I could take out three years and do the book. To do a solid book, you couldn't do it in less. But it means you couldn't do it in less.

Q: Are you going to do that?

ALGREN: No, I'm not going to do that. I wouldn't do that again. The book you asked me to be specific about would be called *Entrapment* and one part of it has already been published in *Playboy*. I guess I've got a stack of stuff this high. It would mean going to court. It would mean living exclusively for that. It would mean taking three years. And it would be absolutely pointless.

Q: Did Hollywood make you feel really pointless?

ALGREN: Not just Hollywood. Nobody wants it. Nobody wants this sort of slow, line-by-line writing.

Q: You do, don't you? You want this kind of writing, don't you? You know I'm working on my *first* book, line by line, day by day. I've been on it for five years and it's going to take me at least another—

ALGREN: How old are you?

Q: Thirty-seven [1962]. But when I finish this goddamn book you will care about it. Studs will care about it. You may not think it is any good, but you are going to care about it.

ALGREN: That's two people.

Q: That's two people, and my family. There are a couple of others. But we don't have to pull "Kafkas" and write the stuff only to throw it into a trunk. I have to throw a statement back at you. Earlier you said that if a writer does not keep producing, it is a kind of a sellout. Now, since there is no finger of God telling you that you should write something, and because you do not have to do it to avoid starvation, consider the possibility that you should do it because you are an artist, that you should spend three years doing the work, but that you decided not to because you feel your work isn't wanted. Isn't that kind of a sellout?

ALGREN: It's a sellout only if you consider me an artist with a capital A and not a person, because I must turn it around and put it another way: it would be a sellout of myself.

Q: But you must keep producing, mustn't you?

ALGREN: I'll produce what I like to produce in my own time, but I won't extend myself. I won't commit myself to this all-out thing that Henry Miller prescribes.

Q: Why not? You write poetry, don't you?

ALGREN: Sometimes.

Q: Is your poetry wanted?

ALGREN: No.

Q: Then why do you do it?

ALGREN: Because I want to and I like to and it's fun.

Q: Isn't poetry the hardest kind of writing?

ALGREN: No, no. Novel writing is the hardest because it's drudgery. Poetry is fun. To write a novel, you have to just do this single-minded thing.

Q: Are you taken seriously as a novelist?

ALGREN: I don't think anybody is taken seriously. When you go to a book-and-authors' luncheon, who's the main speaker? Milton Berle. Ann Landers. Max Shulman.

Q: *Nobody* is taken seriously?

ALGREN: Well, sure, I've got my friend Geismar, you know. I respect his opinion. Sandburg used to come around now and then. Malcolm Cowley.

Q: A bunch of finks?

ALGREN: No. And Martha Gellhorn. I got very serious appraisals from them.

Q: Let me ask one more hypothetical question and then we'll wrap this up, O.K.? You went out to Hollywood twice to try to help make a good movie out of a book you thought was pretty good, and you didn't do it. And you sold another of your books to Hollywood for small change and it and the other book, *The Arm,* made a lot of money for other people. Two things are evident. One, you write books that can be made into movies; and, two, everybody thinks you're rich.

ALGREN: I know that.

Q: Do you want to try again to do a good film script of, say, *Never Come Morning,* for Hollywood?

ALGREN: I can't add to the answer I gave then—I would be open to a Hollywood offer to film that book only if it had first been dramatized on the stage, and then if a Hollywood producer was interested in making a movie I would have no objection to him going to my agent and making a deal with him, but I would advise her beforehand that I would want script approval. On those conditions I would take the money.

. . . I don't think anybody has the right to be without money at this point. . . . (*Laughter*) You know, Bodenheim's day is over. . . . I mean it was just an affectation, you know. Bodenheim could have had money. It was just pure posture. . . . (*Laughter*) . . . That is why (*laughter*) I try to keep up (*laughter*) the pretense of having money (*laughter*). . . .

(*Voices of friends sing,* "Happy birthday to you," *etc.*)

ALGREN: Oh, don't sing that song.

VOICES: Happy birthday to you . . .

ALGREN: Sing "Where have all the good girls gone?" That's my birthday song.

VOICES: "Happy birthday, dear Nelson!"

ALGREN: (*Singing*) "Where have all the good girls gone? Where have all the good girls gone? . . .

PART **III**

THE INNOCENT ABROAD

6 · *The Far East*

QUESTION: How long was your last trip, the boat trip to the Far East?

ALGREN: The ship took three months and seventeen days to go from Seattle to Korea, then down the coast of China to Hong Kong and around India, Bombay—from Hong Kong to Singapore and then from Singapore up around India to Bombay, Calcutta, one stop in Pakistan, with stops at little places such as Fiesta de Cantina and Iloilo, and some of the most incredible out-of-the-way places without even docks. Back to Singapore where I'd already made friends, then to the Philippine Islands—those blue-mist Philippines—beautiful country and very likable little people. They're sort of retarded Japanese. They look like people who were shipped there because they were likable but weren't quite bright enough to be Japanese. And they certainly wouldn't be flattered to be called Japanese because of their war experience.

Q: Are you going to do a book on that trip?

ALGREN: Yeah, yeah. I will do a kind of a reinspection of the ports of Korea, Bombay, Calcutta, and the Philippines, and then from the Philippines back to Long Beach, and then Los Angeles.

Q: It was a tramp steamer?

ALGREN: I was on it, wasn't I?

Q: You were the only passenger?

ALGREN: Yeah. There were other passengers very briefly. I was the only passenger who made the whole trip, which astonished the seamen because they could see why somebody might pay to get to Japan, but to get to India became a standard joke among them.

Q: Can you say anything about that trip that would not detract from the book that you ultimately write?

ALGREN: Oh, I'd love to talk about it. It, it won't detract from the book at all so far as I can see. I even wrote a couple poems, which I don't have. . . .

Q: How was that trip?

ALGREN: It was tedious, largely tedious.

Q: When did you sail?

ALGREN: June 28th of 1962, and came back in October, June, July, August, September. The last two weeks coming back from the Philippines was incredibly tedious, simply unrelieved, and I was very glad to get back.

Q: How'd you find that part of the world?

ALGREN: Well, I find it isn't nearly so benighted as you might think and not far away at all in human terms. It would be very easy to live in that part of the world.

Q: Certainly you were struck by the poverty in India?

ALGREN: Well, it was too much to be struck by. I mean, it's a place where humanity comes in such numbers that it's a kind of affliction. Something like fourteen million people are in the area of Calcutta now, so that they are no longer people. You have the feeling when you go stepping along the street— you know, carefully, in order not to step in somebody's face —that it might be a more imminent danger than any bomb. I think if there were four more cities in the world like that, it would really be ominous because there you learn very quickly not to respect humanity at all. You can't, you can't take the time. I mean, there's throngs.

Q: How would it be easy for you to live there under those conditions?

ALGREN: I wouldn't want to live in India. When I said I would like to live in the East, I was thinking, perhaps, of a city like Hong Kong or Singapore, which is quite something else, which are cities under control. The cities that are run by the Chinese that I saw, Hong Kong and Singapore, are very controlled cities.

Q: They're not run by the British? They're run by the Chinese?

ALGREN: Oh, they're run by the Chinese. I mean the Chinese own them and the Chinese run Singapore. I mean they're not totally Chinese cities but the Chinese conduct the economy, and when you have the Chinese conducting the economy, why, you certainly get a more joyous life than you get in India, where it's given over to the drabbest, most medieval sense of sin and an ominous kind of piety over all, over every kind of double-dealing. When you come into Bombay, the first thing you're told is this is Prohibition, you can't get a drink here. And then you go through all the corruption, all the corruption of getting a drink, all the people that have to be paid off, just in order to get a drink. The Chinese don't put up that huge paper structure. They don't seem to have this awful Indian thing of imposing a morality on you. The Indians seem very quick to be contemptuous of you since you come from a country that goes to war, especially coming from a city like Chicago where they assume you believe in violence. And yet you find out that they have their own kind of violence in their own way. So far as I could see through my personal contact, what they mean by nonviolence is simply that if somebody is bigger and stronger than you and you're not in very good shape, it's best to plead nonviolence. I mean, if you're in a world of stronger people, than God help you if they are stronger. In short, I would rather have somebody put a gun on me and take my money than have somebody simply follow me and follow and follow, clawing and begging, and pleading and putting himself in the most abject position in order to get it. This is nonviolence, too, but there's also an emotional violence.

Q: How did they respond to the attack by China?

ALGREN: All I know is what I read in the papers. They responded violently, according to the papers, in a very strong, nationalistic way. But my impression is that if they went to war with China, they'd bungle it. So far as I've seen, they don't do anything very well. Even their thieves—they don't even have good pickpockets. When a guy tries to stick his hand in your pocket, you know, if I can catch a guy with his hand in my pocket, he must be awful slow. You know, when you're looking the other way and you can catch him—I hollered after him and he just kept on walking. I said, "What a lousy pickpocket you are!" I didn't see a good pickpocket in India.

Q: Were there good pickpockets in Singapore?

ALGREN: I didn't run into any. When I came out of the bank with a lot of money and very thoughtlessly put it in my top pocket, it was about ready to fall out, and a young Chinese guy came by and just tapped me. He tapped me on the shirt pocket and said, "Watch your money." He could as well have taken it as not, the way it was hanging, but it was not his, my money was not his concern. He happened to notice it and said, "Watch it, you're either going to drop it or somebody will take it."

Q: Why did you take that kind of boat? You were primarily interested in the land areas, weren't you?

ALGREN: It wasn't a boat, it was a ship.

Q: Why did you take that kind of a ship?

ALGREN: I ran into a very cold attitude from the crew when I mentioned that I was on a boat. This was not a boat, it was a ship. Later I mentioned I was going to go up the stairs and close the windows in my stateroom. They said, "No, there are no stairs here, that's a ladder, and there are no windows, those are portholes. I found out a boat is something much smaller. It's what you take to shore from the ship.

Q: Why did you take that kind of ship?

ALGREN: I took it simply because I didn't have any experience in going, and didn't know anybody who knew anything, so I simply wrote to an agency in Indiana and some agent arranged it.

Q: But why did you put yourself in a ship where you'd be at sea for weeks at a time?

ALGREN: But where could I go? I can't take a special trip and look at the thing. This is what should be done. You find out the ship, you go on the ship, and look at it. I just took a chance. I took a chance on where the thing was going.

Q: I don't understand, though, why you didn't go from city to city the quickest way you could. You were primarily interested in the cities, weren't you?

ALGREN: It would have cost a great deal, I think, to go from city to city. This way, for twelve hundred dollars, I could cover three months at sea, room and board, and have the whole thing covered. What it would cost me to go from city to city, I don't know. I just decided to take a ship at that price, and with the contract that said it would get me back, and take a chance on what it was and, as it turned out, my original idea of taking a ship to Japan was a good idea. It didn't happen to go there. It went to India. (*Laughter*) They changed their minds.

Q: It was not a good trip, was it?

ALGREN: I'm not sorry I took it, but it could have been a better trip. There were some places there that I'm very sorry today that I saw, but I am glad that I saw Calcutta. By the time you got to Calcutta, you have been locked up in the ship for nine weeks. Oh yeah, it was like a traveling prison. I mean, these are, they are very submerged men. I mean, they're like men in prison. They don't talk either. No, if I did it again, I'd take another kind of a line that I'd take either to Japan or to the west coast of South America, where you get into a new port every day. But this I didn't know until I got on, and there were men on that ship who never got off. It represented very closely what the, what the United States is like. I think it was a small—

Q: What the United States is like? Not the world?

ALGREN: It was an American ship. I mean, what was wrong with the ship was, I think, what is wrong with the United States.

Q: What's that?

ALGREN: Well, a kind of isolation, I mean, among the men, the confidence that these other people were inferior to them—the people of these countries, the Japanese, the Koreans, the Indians, and Filipinos. They only looked at them with a contempt, but they don't want to see them or deal with them. It's a buyer's market. The ports were always crowded, the docks were crowded with people waiting for an American ship to come in. One Mama-San at a Filipino port came up with girls in one of these things. They row out and she said, "We wait, it's been a month." She said, "When a ship doesn't dock here for a month we have to sell our clothes." I mean, a total dependence. And then when the Americans come off the ship, the women of the ports and all the hustlers wait for this American ship, for the crew—for the crew to spend. Their lives depend on the crew, so the crew is too used to having it their own way. They can't say no to a member of the crew because he's got the money. I think this is why I say the ship represents in a way what is wrong with the United States because in our dealings with a lot of the smaller countries they can't say no. Underneath that is a lot of resentment toward Americans. . . .

7 *Paris and Friends*

QUESTION: What about your other trips, Nelson? How many trips did you make to Europe?

ALGREN: I've been to Europe three times: While I was in the Army in 1945, then as a tourist in forty-nine, and again as a tourist in 1960.

Q: Now you had not been back to Paris for four years. How did the place seem to you? Had it changed much?

ALGREN: Of course it had changed a great deal. I only saw it on half a dozen passes when we were at one of the cigarette camps near Paris during the war. So my recollection of Paris was simply wandering around on the Rue Pigalle, and I never got to see Paris. I mean, just the throngs of GI's and the black market and then grab the truck back. So I really didn't get a look at Paris.

Q: Well, then, how did you like Paris? This was your first time at actually seeing it then? How did you meet Miss de Beauvoir?

ALGREN: She came through Chicago in 1947 and in 1948 we went down the Mississippi. We took a train to Cincinnati, caught one of the Green Line stern-wheelers. She wanted to see the Mississippi and we took about five or six days to get to New Orleans, another city she wanted to see, which I wanted to see again too, because I had seen it in the thirties. And from there we flew to Guatemala, Yucatan, and saw the old Mayan, the ruins of the old Mayan civilization outside of Mérida and then we flew back to Mexico City. We had a week or so in Mexico City and then we flew from Mexico City to the Tavern-on-the-Green, here in Central Park. It was a long trip. I remember it chiefly because I hadn't realized that Mexico was cooler than the United States. When we left Mexico City, it was very pleasant weather, and got into Houston—I didn't realize that Houston was lower down—it was stifling hot. It was like coming into a tropical country and then hotter than that, the next stop, Washington, which was like coming into an oven, and then we hit New York.

Q: How was she introduced to you in 1947?

ALGREN: Well, she introduced herself, in a manner of speaking, because when she came to New York she didn't know anybody. The only name she knew was something called "Partisan Review." Somebody had told her that there were people called "Partisan Review" and she called them because she wanted to see New York and she got to meet them. But chiefly she got to meet Mary McCarthy, who is still after all these years trying to figure that one out. Mary McCarthy still makes references to this bewildering situation, this bewildering woman, because De Beauvoir has a remarkable traveler's sense of what she wants to see. She can go into a strange city and look around and find the right restaurant. She'll say, "Don't go there, go up this street and down this street," and she's always right. It's an infuriating thing. After I got to know her, I could see it would have infuriated

Miss McCarthy, because when she got here she didn't have
much time and she has a furious curiosity. Her time, time,
time, her sense of time—she can't waste a minute, and she'd
never been here before. She wanted to see the Automat and
it seems there was a discussion. So far as I can reconstruct
the situation, it would be all right to see the Automat, but if
Miss McCarthy and friends went to the Automat, it would
give the impression that they were slumming, which would
be an artificial move. So de Beauvoir simply walked off and
went to the Automat by herself. She somehow sensed that she
wouldn't get to see New York their way. She knew the intellectual life of Paris, and this sort of washed-out New York
intellectual life which depended so much on Paris became
uninteresting to her in no time at all. She walked away not
even knowing anybody's name, and not even caring to meet
them again. This was breach of courtesy that the McCarthy
gal keeps referring to: like where did she go and why did
she do this? But she *does* do this. It can't be done, but she
does do it. She had asked who could she see in Chicago. I
recall very clearly. I had a little ten-dollar-a-month couple of
rooms. They had a ceiling on rents at that time so you could
get a reasonably clean little place for that little, really that
little.

Q: Was this on Wabansia?

ALGREN: Yeah. Wabansia and Bosworth. I was fussing around the
stove, trying to cook something, and the telephone rang, and
the telephone, often when it rang it'd be somebody with a
strong, very strong Polish accent who had never used a telephone before and they would holler into the phone, and so
this time the phone rang and somebody hollered into the
phone, screeched something, and I hung up. I said, "Wrong
number." I had something cooking. No soon than I got back

to the stove, the phone rang again and I got that same hoarse screech and I did this three times. I hung up. The last time I hung up I just said, "Wrong number," and bang! About half an hour later the phone rang and a very clear voice said, "Would you mind holding the phone for a minute, don't hang up for just a minute, there's a party here would like to speak to you." So then I listened and next a heavily accented French voice was saying that her name was, ah, ah, something. I didn't quite catch it. I said, "Where are you at, I'll come down." "Leetle Café," she told me, in "Palmer House." I'd never heard of it. I'd heard of the Palmer House all right, but not of the Leetle Café. When I got down there all I saw was *"Le Petite Café."* She wasn't taking any chances on my understanding French it looked like. Then I saw this woman coming wiz copy of leetle magazine—*Partisan Review.* That threw me off. I leaped to the conclusion she'd been sent by Mary McCarthy. I don't want a date with Mary McCarthy even by surrogate. I decided to think this over.

Q: You're kidding about that.

ALGREN: I deal in *facts,* man. The hard terrible *facts,* the iron truth.

Q: What did you do?

ALGREN: I just sat there and waited to find out what her next move was going to be. As long as I didn't make a move, I was still free to go home. She went in and out that door four times before I decided in her favor. I bought her a drink. I had no idea what she was talking about. She seemed to be trying to tell me something. I didn't know who she was but the accent was French, so I told her about the war. *All* about the war. Where I thought *she'd* been while I was fighting it I didn't stop to think.

Q: How long did she stay in Chicago?

ALGREN: Three days. I showed her the electric chair, the psychiatric wards, neighborhood bars where I told her everyone sitting around was a sinister character. She looked around a while and then told me, "I think you are the only sinister thing around here." Then I took her to a midnight mission. I thought it was time to SAVE HER SOUL. I took her to cheap burlesques, Maxwell Street, a police line-up, and the zoo. I explained American literature, how the police operate, the Loeb-Leopold case, the Heirens case, the Haymarket riots, and why I was the only serious writer in Chicago since Dick Wright left in the 1930's. Later she told me she hadn't understood a single word I'd said in three days of self-perpetuating conversation.

Q: And how long, how many trips did she make to Chicago?

ALGREN: Oh, well, let's see. This must have been forty-six she came. Then she came in forty-seven and forty-eight and in forty-nine I went to Paris.

Q: On your trip down the Mississippi and to the Yucatan and back, how long were you together?

ALGREN: Oh, let's see, two months at least.

Q: It was a good trip?

ALGREN: Oh, yeah, yeah, it was a very successful trip.

Q: And then you went to Paris in 1949?

ALGREN: Right.

Q: Then you saw something of her there?

ALGREN: Oh yeah. We stayed in the Rue Boucherie. I stayed with her there in the Rue Boucherie, which was a little tenement street. It's the fifth floor—the building's still there. And my friend Clancy Sigal later moved in there. I don't know how he happened to move in but he moved into the same place later. It was just a little place under the roof where, as in the good French tradition, when it rained you put buckets to catch the water. There was an Algerian café right below. You could hear the music. And a little tenement street, which is still there, still an Algerian street, and you could see Notre Dame and that was a very good summer.

Q: Tell me what you remember about Paris in the 1949 trip. Did you meet Sartre?

ALGREN: Yeah, I got to know Sartre and a number of other people. Greco was there. Juliette Greco, who was just beginning to sing then, and a young French novelist, still a friend of Sartre's, and still a friend of mine. Jean Cau, who was Sartre's secretary at the time and recently the author of something called *The Mercy of God,* Prix Goncourt. One of the worst books that I've ever read. It doesn't seem so much a secondhand Sartre as a secondhand Camus. And I knew Cau then and the actor Mouloudji. I knew people whose names are not so familiar. We went to fights.

Q: How are the Paris fights?

ALGREN: Well, the Paris fights are very poor fights. I saw Marseilles again. I wanted very much to see Marseilles again. I had become very fond of it. . . .

Q: How did that compare with the town you knew while you were still in the Army?

ALGREN: Well, it hadn't yet had time to make the big change. The big change I saw in Marseilles was in 1960. The old Marseilles, the Marseilles I saw in the war, in the last months of the war, was an outlaw town, a knocked-out outlaw town, very ancient. I had never been in an old, old city before, very old. I guess older than Paris. And I was out-of-bounds most of the time, uh, on the Rue Phocéens, street of the Phoenicians, which really *was* the street of the Pheonicians, and I liked this city. I liked the smell of it and it was an adventurous city.

Q: And did you like it when you saw it in 1949?

ALGREN: In 1949 it was different. I was a tourist. I went around to one or two of the pizza joints I'd hung around in in forty-five, but it was different. The black market was gone. It was a law-and-order town and I was a tourist. It wasn't Wild West any more. By 1960, it had settled down to being just a fairly prosperous city with a real-estate development around the harbor. The whole harbor is encircled now with buildings you might see in the Bronx. You know: very dull-looking. It's lost some of its color.

Q: Your 1960 trip—one of the results of that was your most recent book, *Who Lost an American?* right?

ALGREN: Yeah, I wrote part of it. I began it there. I left here, let's see, late February, March, of 1960. I had a week or so in England, about five days in Ireland, then flew to Paris and was in Paris seven months. I worked on the book there.

Q: Then you went to Spain.

ALGREN: Went to Spain, Greece, and Turkey.

Q: Did Miss de Beauvoir go on some of these trips with you?

ALGREN: Oh, yeah, yeah. I met her in Spain. I went to Formentor and then I went to Barcelona, and picked her up in Seville. I didn't see her in Barcelona. We went back and we made one more trip to Marseilles. We took this jet thing that goes, you know, in no time at all. You pass Athens and then you're in Istanbul, and then from Istanbul to Crete. We had about a week down in a little fishing port, Herakleion, as old as Troy, just a very old, old port, older than Greece. Then back to Paris and then a short trip down to Marseilles and back, and by that time it was October and I went back to England and then got the S.S. *Hanseatic* home with about seventeen hundred South Bavarians, you know.

Q: Do I know what?

ALGREN: Well, I say do you know, do you know what that can be like? It was a mob scene, it was a mob scene. Everyone moved in a mob. Nobody moved by himself. If one put a little feather in his hat, in his hat, his little green hat, everybody did. They were already Americans. They were new American citizens, displaced persons. They didn't look displaced. They were quite prosperous. They were coming to live in the United States, and I'm sure we need South Bavarians but I was a little disconcerted by this inability for any one of them to move in any direction. Everybody went in the soup line at the same time, whether they wanted soup or not. Everybody had their photographs. Nobody had their individual photographs taken. Photographs were taken en masse and then your face is circled in it. Nobody would think of having an individual picture taken, because they didn't have any individual feeling. Their sense of individuality is with this mob. Somebody buys a beer and then they all hold up the beer. The the guy on the platform with the accordion, he plays something like *bloomp-da-da-da, bloomp-da-da-da,* then they all pop at once and then they all drink the beer, and ah, it's, it's really quite a sight, you know. It's one of the most terrifying things you ever saw. (*Laughter*) I mean, at least it explained to me my own preference for the French, because you couldn't get two French people together to do the same thing in the same room like that at all. They simply wouldn't do it.

Q: Were there periods of time when the three of you, Miss de Beauvoir, Sartre, and you, were traveling together?

ALGREN: Oh, no, no, we never traveled together. I just traveled with her. She and Sartre haven't been together since, I guess, the twenties, something like that. They've lived separately since he was a professor at the Sorbonne. He was twenty-three, she was nineteen or something, but they'd been separated, at that time, for twenty years, I guess. Well, they saw each other every day, as far as that goes, but they lived separately and still do.

Q: When is your next trip to Paris?

ALGREN: Oh, I have no plans for another trip. I've no plans at all.

Q: Now, what parts of the world have you not seen? They're getting fewer and fewer. You've seen Africa?

ALGREN: (*Laughter*) I haven't seen Iceland, haven't seen the Gobi Desert.

Q: How about Africa?

ALGREN: I haven't seen Africa. I haven't seen South America. I saw Central America. I'd like to see Africa. I would like to see the Soviet Union. I haven't seen Poland. I don't have an active curiosity about Russia. I don't have any acute desire to see Russia; it's more of a political curiosity than anything, but if I travel I really want to—

Q: What do you mean, "political curiosity"?

ALGREN: Well, I think people go to the Soviet Union to see what it's really like economically and what it looks like, but I don't know. From the few Russians I've seen, they're not as interesting as the Latin people as individuals. I don't know. I would rather see Spain again than see Russia. I'd like to go down the west coast of South America. I mean, that'd be an exciting trip.

Q: And China?

ALGREN: That's another great big brute of a thing. I wouldn't know what to do with a visit to China, any more than I'd know what to do with a visit to Russia. I mean, it's such a massive thing. I think in the smaller countries you can cut into it, like in British Guiana, stay there a week, and have some idea of the country.

Q: How about Rome?

ALGREN: Well, if I was going to go to Italy, I'd rather go to Naples. I have the same feeling about Rome as I have about Madrid or about Washington, D.C. It's kind of a showcase. Just as Barcelona is so much more interesting than Madrid, so is Naples, to me, much more interesting than Rome.

Q: What parts of the United States do you find interesting, in different ways?

ALGREN: Well, of course New York. There's no use talking about New York. It's a perpetual, perpetual city, perpetual wonder. Next to that, there's San Francisco. I don't know what New Orleans is like now. It was a beautiful city. I imagine it still is. Louisville is a very nice town. And of course that Cape Cod area. I was invited up there by some friends and just got a view of it, walked around the dunes, and got a whiff of that salt air—the same whiff as I got in San Francisco. Seattle is another beauty. That Northwest country is spacious.

Q: You have no plans for travel right now?

ALGREN: No immediate plans. I'd like to live outside Chicago. I have no means of doing it now, so I don't have any plans.

Q: Any time you do travel or make a move, you have to pay your own way at the time, right? Somehow.

ALGREN: Right, right, right.

Q: You've never gone in for any of these fellowships?

ALGREN: No, no, I haven't scored there.

Q: Have you tried?

ALGREN: Oh, I tried. I think I hold the world's record for Guggenheim applications. I began trying in—I had a book out in 1936, and I think I tried in thirty-six, thirty-seven, thirty-eight, thirty-nine, and forty, forty-one. I was still undiscouraged and overseas, forty-three, forty-four. They had some kind of a special Guggenheim for people in the Armed Services, who had been in the war zone a year and had published a novel and, since I'd published a novel that had been favorably reviewed and had been in the war zone a year, I thought I must be about the only application. This thing seemed to be made to order for me. So just to make sure, as my sponsors I got Carl Sandburg, Ernest Hemingway, several editors who had influence, and then I waited for them to send me the Guggenheim. But it didn't work. I was going to do a war novel on the Guggenheim. I didn't make it, but I continued to apply until *The Man with the Golden Arm* came out. Since that got the National Book Award, I applied again for a Guggenheim, to do research on the traffic in narcotics. Uh, this was, this would—I made application on different bases before, but this was the soundest because at that time I had connections with people who were involved in the traffic to whom I had access. Nobody else had access. The only other people who had access to them were the police. I think this would have been worth a Guggenheim. But I didn't get it, so after that I just made the applications out of frivolity and applied for fellowships because I wanted to be a jockey or anything. Since I knew I wouldn't get it, I just filled it out that I wanted to be a boy author and study. I just filled out the applications as a joke.

Q: How many times?

ALGREN: Oh, just once or twice, you know, until the joke wore out.

Q: How many times in all have you applied for a Guggenheim?

ALGREN: Well, I don't know. It went on for a decade and a half— I'd say fifteen times.

Q: You've written seven books, you're a National Book Award winner and you've never received a Guggenheim?

ALGREN: I haven't applied lately. I haven't applied since, ah, I would say since 1952. But meanwhile I've acted as a reference for a number people who applied for Guggenheims. I'm proud to say nobody I ever sponsored got one. I have a sort of kiss of death for Guggenheim, you know.

Q: You say—

ALGREN: Joe Heller. I told Joe Heller after he wrote *Catch-22* that he had a very good chance to get one if he didn't involve me. But he involved me. He didn't get it. Terry Southern wrote a very good book, *The Magic Christian,* that I will remember to put on you, and he might have made it except I sponsored him. There's quite a list of people who would be well-to-do now if I hadn't sponsored them.

Q: You said that Hemingway was one of your sponsors. When did you first get to know Hemingway?

ALGREN: I never knew him very well. The woman he was married to at the time, Martha Gellhorn, came through Chicago in forty-two because she liked that *Never Come Morning* book very much. She liked it and he also wrote me about it, a friendly letter, and gave a quote, unasked for, to the publisher which they used—

Q: That's where he calls—

ALGREN: —and used and used, over and over and over again.

Q: That's where he calls you one of our best writers.

ALGREN: Yeah.

Q: How did you and he get along?

ALGREN: Oh, I got along very nicely with him. I saw him after his crash about the time of that picture [*indicating wall of the interviewer's study*]. He was in about that shape in 1955, Christmas of 1955. I was in Florida so I took the Miami-Havana steamer over there to Cuba.

Q: How long were you in Cuba?

ALGREN: Oh, hardly three days, I guess. I saw him. I called up and his wife Mary invited me out. I saw him that day and then the next day was Christmas and I spent Christmas Day with him, then talked to him for some time. Very friendly. I liked him.

Q: Did you know Faulkner?

ALGREN: No, no. Not even remotely.

Q: In all your travels—you've been traveling now for thirty years and you know this country pretty well and you know a lot of the world—what have you found out? Have you seen the world change much? Or is it still the same? What's it like out there?

ALGREN: Oh, it's rough out there. (*Laugh*) Yeah, it changes. My story, my latest story on the thing is that we have changed— I say this every time we talk—we've changed from a first-person to a third-person country.

Q: How about the world? How about the world?

ALGREN: Well, the rest of the world is changing from a third-person to a first. The African, the detached African house-boys are becoming aware that they're people. The people in Caracas, Venezuela, are beginning to want a name and an address and so on. What we should do is all get together and have a second-person world, you know. Everybody calls everybody "you" . . .

Q: I and thou.

ALGREN: Have an "I" and "thou" world.

Q: Have you read Buber's *I and Thou?*

ALGREN: No.

Q: I haven't either yet. I think that's enough for now.

ALGREN: Yeah. I'm going to see you tonight.

Q: Yeah, you're going to see me tonight to go out to that literary party. Come up about eleven, ten-thirty.

PART IV

CONTROVERSIES

8   *Where Is the American Radical?*

QUESTION: What do you think of these conversations?

ALGREN: I have no idea what it'll come to—how relevant it is. But it gives me a chance to say things.

Q: Why do you like to say things? Why do people write?

ALGREN: I like to say things on the chance that somebody might be listening.

Q: What if they are? Why don't you paint instead? Why do you write?

ALGREN: I would just as soon paint, just as I'd just as soon act. I'd just as soon play a cello. But I can't. I would like to play the cello differently than anybody else and I would like to be an actor like the world has never seen. I'd like to paint something that's never been painted before, too.

Q: Why do *any* of these things?

ALGREN: Well, because there's nobody else like me. I'm the only one and there never was one like me before and there's never

[195

going to be one like me after me. Since I can't be around for more than forty or fifty more years, I think it's only fair to the world to leave something of me. I mean I have so much, you know, that it's a shame to take it *all* away from the generations to come.

Q: You are unique. But don't you believe that everyone is unique, and, if so, should then everyone be an artist?

ALGREN: Everybody's unique, but I'm uniquer.

Q: All right—

ALGREN: Everybody is different. Everybody who walks down the street has a different personality and shape and way of expressing himself, but to nine hundred and ninety-nine out of a thousand this fact does not make anything different.

Q: Why doesn't it?

ALGREN: Because they're not connected with anything except the clothing business or some other kind of selling.

Q: What are you connected with?

ALGREN: I'm connected with an odd group called the human race.

Q: Every human is connected with the human race.

ALGREN: But I'm articulate about it, more or less.

Q: But what makes you the artist while some other man, as unique as you, is not?

ALGREN: I don't know. You shake up a kaleidoscope: it turns out different patterns. At a show—say, with Geraldine Page —there's no qualitative difference between her and a hundred other women sitting in the audience, but she's connected with something that expresses millions of women. The women in the audience who are not connected with anything beyond their own immediate families have no real effect, but somebody like Page—or to name another: Simone Signoret in that *Room at the Top* thing—affects millions the way Hemingway affected people.

Q: Who decides to affect people—the artist?

ALGREN: There isn't any decision. It just happens.

Q: What *just* happens? You don't believe anything *just* happens, do you?

ALGREN: I don't know. I don't know. It's a mystery. It's certainly a mystery why Page—and since I picked on Page, I'll stick to her—it's a mystery why Page can impersonate, and can make her personality on stage impersonate and come true, whether she's playing a nineteen-year-old virgin or a fifty-year-old beat-up actress. I'm sure Page doesn't know why it happens.

Q: Let's talk about you. We know Page is a very good actress, but we're trying to find out from Nelson Algren—your name *is* Nelson Algren, isn't it?

ALGREN: No, I'm impersonating him. My real name is Leslie Fiedler.

Q: We're trying to find out from Nelson Algren why he writes, why he thinks people write and why he thinks people read. If there were no readers, there would be no writers, right?

ALGREN: Oh I wouldn't say that. Look at the people in the Middle Ages, the monks. Who was reading when they were doing all that illuminated writing?

Q: They were doing it for readers.

ALGREN: There were very *few* readers.

Q: But there *were* readers.

ALGREN: Well, they'd read it themselves. Each had one reader: himself.

Q: Do you think of yourself as a monk in a kind of Middle Ages?

ALGREN: No. I just think of myself as somebody middle-aged. But I don't live a cloistered life and I don't believe in a cloistered life.

Q: Do you think we're living in a kind of emotional Dark Ages?

ALGREN: No darker than in other ages. I believe we're living in an age of light, also. I think the events of the present century show we're certainly no further away from the kind of barbarism with which the Romans were involved, and the Greeks were involved.

Q: When do you think there were better times for the average man?

ALGREN: The average man?

Q: Where and when?

ALGREN: I can only give a vague romantic answer to that because I wasn't there, but I think to be Parisian in the 1880's, from 1880 to 1890—I mean, to be a member of the French bourgeoisie—I'm not talking about the French working class —to be a member of the French upper classes at that time; it was an enlightened time—there was great affluence and they explored themselves as human beings. That was, of course, the modern French—there was so much great writing and painting—they were extremely civilized people. That was one good time. I think that in the United States before the Civil War when they first started moving west, that was a good time—between the Revolutionary War and the Civil

War, when the country was new, I think that it was a very good thing to be there. You can get an idea that those people had an awful lot of dignity and clarity. It was a little simpler then. They saw things. I guess it was a simpler world. I think there were more people having contented lives, full lives, than now. I don't see anybody having a full life now. I think it's very rare now. I think in those times that some New England families, and maybe in the South, there was a culture, before the Civil War, that it was very good to grow up in. The old plantation culture brought up some very good lives.

Q: Who?

ALGREN: Oh, now you've got me. But I could look it up. There were some. It was a very rich life.

Q: For the average man?

ALGREN: No. When you're talking about average, I say there never was a time when life was as good, when it leveled out for the working people as now, but what I was talking about is the culture flowering in France in the nineteenth century, the flowering of New England, the flowering of the Greek culture, the Athenian culture, and the flowering of the culture of the pre-Civil War South, even though it was always based on thousands of people who lived—

Q: Slaves?

ALGREN: Yeah. In Greece it was the slaves. In the South it was the slaves. And in New England it was the mill hands who weren't technically slaves but were—

Q: And in France it was the Empire.

ALGREN: Yeah.

Q: Émile Zola about that time, about the time you mention as being a good time, was writing things like *Nana*.

ALGREN: Yeah.

Q: And Shaw in England was also doing similar work. Certainly you don't want those times to return?

ALGREN: No.

Q: And had you been alive and in the Paris of 1890, you would have been violently opposed to all the comforts you now nostalgically speak about—particularly those comforts which were had at the expense of other people.

ALGREN: They've always had them at the expense of others.

Q: Aren't you against comforts that are gained largely at the expense of other people?

ALGREN: All comforts are gained at the expense of others.

Q: What do you think of America today and our materialistic culture? Isn't the average man in America more comfortable now than any other so-called average man in the history of man?

ALGREN: No. He's not more comfortable; he has more comforts. He's more uneasy.

Q: Is this a good thing, having more comforts?

ALGREN: No, because it's made him so uneasy. He can't take any comfort from his comforts. His dependence on the comforts has made him uneasy. Certainly it's a good thing to have a refrigerator instead of having the food get spoiled and all that, but comforts have become items of prestige. A man who doesn't have a refrigerator or a television is considered to be a failure.

Q: Nelson Algren, I do not understand you. Everybody has a refrigerator and a TV set these days. There are more TV sets and radios than there are bathtubs.

ALGREN: I believe in bathtubs and refrigerators.

Q: But if it is easy for most men to get these things how can the fear of not getting them be a source of uneasiness?

ALGREN: It is a source of unease because we've come to judge a man's success by how many gadgets he has.

Q: If *every*one has gadgets, how can you use that as a basis for judgment?

ALGREN: Some people have more gadgets than others. Naturally you consider a man with a fin-tailed car more successful than the man who's driving a model five years old. It's false to judge people that way.

Q: But it is no longer fashionable to have a fin-tailed car. And you can rent a limousine for fifteen dollars a day.

ALGREN: If it's fashionable to have a split-level floor, then it's false to consider a man who owns a split-level floor a superior person to the man who doesn't have a split-level floor. Our values are based on who has got what.

Q: Do you actually know people who think that people with split-level floors or duplex apartments or fin-tailed cars are superior to other people?

ALGREN: I think if there was a painter painting something original and important, and he lived in a cheap flat, and he was having an exhibition, nobody would come. Nobody wants to walk up three or four floors to a crummy place and see a guy who may not have washed himself recently and who may not have enough heat in the place. But if you take those same paintings and put them in a Lake Shore Drive or Park Avenue apartment, where the apartment owner is a man who is known to be on the board of directors of a dozen companies, if he has a party, if he opens his apartment for an exhibition of those paintings, then people will be fighting to get up there, and it won't be because of the paintings. It will be because those paintings are in that man's apartment.

Q: If you painted or had a friend who painted and it was up to you to decide where to hang those paintings, would you hang them in an expensive apartment or in a slum tenement?

ALGREN: I would just hang them on an open street.

Q: Say that it's winter and it's raining. Where would you hang the paintings?

ALGREN: Oh I'd hang them in the better apartment.

Q: Do you really think that the American public thinks respectability goes along with affluence?

ALGREN: Oh sure, I most certainly do. The rich man gets attention: he gets more than respect. He gets attention to himself.

Q: Have *you* gotten any attention?

ALGREN: Occasionally I've had some attention. I haven't been able to hold American culture in a fixed stare on me. The gaze wanders off now and then.

Q: Have you ever done anything you haven't wanted to do as far as your work is concerned?

ALGREN: I review a lot of books I'd rather not review.

Q: Why do you review them?

ALGREN: I get paid for them.

Q: Money or attention?

ALGREN: Well, they don't give me muskrat skins.

Q: There are people who review books for attention in the literary journals.

ALGREN: I don't review books for attention. The thirty-five or fifty or seventy-five dollars I get for a review is a very convenient little item. Otherwise I might let the review go.

Q: But you don't *want* to review books?

ALGREN: I don't want to review all books. Sometimes I take a book and I won't want to review it and I review it anyhow.

Q: Why? Aren't there enough good books published for you to be able to review the books you want to review?

ALGREN: I don't always get the books I want to review. Sometimes I'm asked to review a book that's a little dull and a little long and a little unnecessary. I have to read it even though I don't want to read it.

Q: I'm surprised. You agree then, with Vance Packard, that there are such things as status symbols?

ALGREN: Well, yeah. I said our values are confused. The point about hanging the paintings in the warm apartment or in a slum is that nobody really cares whether the paintings are good or bad. The point is to get them into a millionaire's house.

Q: How can you say nobody cares? Do you care?

ALGREN: There are people who care. There are always people who care. I'm talking in generalities.

Q: Do you know of a good painter in America who is not getting paid for his work?

ALGREN: I don't know him, but I would take even money there are a hundred in this city who aren't.

Q: How about writers? Do you know of any good writer who isn't making money?

ALGREN: I don't know any real good writers who are making any money. I don't know any good writers who aren't having a struggle. I know writers who are extremely affluent, but they are the guys who have a knack for turning things out on a conveyor—the more mediocre it is, the better paying.

Q: You do nothing else but write to earn a living?

ALGREN: That's all I do.

Q: Do you earn a living writing?

ALGREN: I'm self-sustaining. I'm self-sustaining. I don't live in want.

Q: Do you know of any other culture outside of America that has been better to its artists, particularly its writers, than America?

ALGREN: Uh-huh.

Q: Which? When? And where?

ALGREN: Well, the French are better. The French have a national theatre. The Scandinavian countries sponsor writers. They have a state theatre. In England they do not pay their writers as much, but they do protect writers. I don't know of a culture that is harder on its writers and its actors and its painters than ours. The much poorer countries are much better to their artists than we are. The reasons I think these poorer countries spend more and make life more tolerable for their writers is that there is a basic respect among Europeans

toward the artist. The shoemaker or the woman who sells
you the newspaper—if she knows you are a writer or an
artist of any kind, she has more respect for you than a
writer can get from the hollow men of Madison Avenue.
You go into a publishing house on Madison Avenue and
you can feel the friendly contempt, the tolerance. They are
superior people—the *Time* boys, the junior editors. One of
them once said to me—and it seems like it could have been
said by the whole strata, right off the campus—he said,
with sort of a little derisive smile, "How can you walk down
the street with all this stuff going on inside you?" I said,
"I don't know how you can walk down the street with nothing going on inside you." Which is the great advantage of
being one of the present hollow men. This is also the reason
I say that there is less respect for the creative man from these
guys who run our culture than you find from the waiter in a
French restaurant. This also goes along with the economic
situation. There's no use, you know, in pointing out that
James Jones got three-quarters of a million, or that some
other guy's got a million from writing, any more than there is
anything said when you say that among fighters: look how
much Sugar Ray Robinson has made, or that Patterson gets a
million or so every time he fights. These big gates are not
representative, and the percentage of writers who make it big
is about the same, I imagine, as the percentage of actors who
make it. There are plenty of actors working for the minimum
each week, and there are plenty of fighters who pick up
twenty-five or thirty-five bucks a fight. That's the average
status of the writer.

Q: Do you think most fighters should get more than that?

ALGREN: If the guy is going to risk a beating-up, he should get
more protection than thirty-five bucks.

Q: Why? He has to be good enough first of all, doesn't he? Do you think all fighters should be supported by the fight game simply because they want to fight?

ALGREN: No.

Q: Then why should all who just want to write be supported as writers simply because they want to write?

ALGREN: That's your idea. I haven't said anything like it. I say that if you're a good fighter you should get as much out of it as a man who writes good advertising script. If you're a good writer or a good painter or a good actor, you should get out of it as much as a good barber. How many actors make as much as barbers? Which is easier to do: to get on a stage and express an entirely different personality—to give something original—or to cut hair?

Q: It is harder to cut hair.

ALGREN: All right—hanging wallpaper, fixing electricity, fixing a sewer?

Q: It's all hard. It's all harder than acting.

ALGREN: Well, you know goddamn well that ain't true. You know there's nothing harder than acting. You know that ninety-nine guys out of a hundred are good mechanics. They can fix a machine, they can fix a tire, they can do ordinary mechanical work. There isn't one guy in a thousand who can act.

Q: You are not surprised to find out we disagree about this because you know we disagree about almost everything.

ALGREN: Oh no—we disagree on *La Dolce Vita* where I happen to think that it is a great film and you don't. And we disagree on Wayne Bethea. But on the basic thing like this—

Q: I think acting is one of the easiest things in the world.

ALGREN: You know better. I won't argue with it. You are just pulling my leg.

Q: No. You and I disagree about many things.

ALGREN: Then why aren't you an actor?

Q: Because I do not have that talent.

ALGREN: Oh, then it is hard. It isn't easy. You have to have talent.

Q: It's not hard to have talent.

ALGREN: Then most people have talent?

Q: No. Most people don't have that talent.

ALGREN: You are just one of the exceptions who don't have acting talent.

Q: Actors are produced by their childhood experiences which cause them always to wish to perform—Don't drink *that* coffee. It's cold coffee.

ALGREN: It's not cold coffee. I like cold coffee. Only finks drink hot coffee.

Q: Oh my God, there's another thing we disagree about. To get back to acting—acting is much easier than a nine-to-five job where you do the same thing over and over.

ALGREN: Then why are there only about a dozen people in the United States who can act?

Q: There are supposed to be five thousand unemployed actors in the city of New York.

ALGREN: Uh-huh.

Q: Because we don't need that many actors.

ALGREN: Do we need advertising men?

Q: Always, because advertising burns out people quicker than acting. Avertising is much harder than acting. All trades are harder than the arts because the people in the arts are doing things they want to do.

ALGREN: What is hard about advertising? Anybody who is in advertising is always basically ashamed of the fact that he is doing an infantile thing and getting well paid. I don't know of any of these guys who are at ease with themselves.

Q: I do.

ALGREN: Well, I don't. The guy we played poker with the other night was just typical.

Q: I know advertising people who love their work, who do good work. I don't agree with the fashionable liberal opinion that all advertising is a lot of shit.

ALGREN: That's a conservative opinion; it's not necessarily a liberal idea. All you have to do is look at the papers where you can find the complete horseshit of advertising where the ads will try to convince you that you can attract a woman by smoking a cigarette, and that people of distinction use a certain kind of filter, and if you drink a certain coffee in the morning that entitles you to belong to an international coffee set. Anybody who is turning out this stuff, and has to turn it out for a living, has to be basically ashamed of it. Anybody who isn't ashamed of doing it for a living is an idiot and there aren't many idiots in advertising. They're mostly bright boys like the guy we played poker with the other night. They're almost always guys who would like to write or to act or to do something else, but they can't do it and earn a good

living. Advertising and TV give them a good living. So they
live with a sense of corruption, and they give the extra money
to an analyst.

Q: Is it advertising that has given them a sense of corruption?

ALGREN: Oh, yeah. Sure.

Q: Could they have had the sense of corruption *before* they
approached the trade of advertising?

ALGREN: No, no. Not necessarily.

Q: You think Chessman attacking that girl sent her to the nut-
house?

ALGREN: No. Not at all.

Q: She was on her way before she met Chessman?

ALGREN: Uh-huh.

Q: Well, what about the probability that these guys you find in
advertising with a sense of corruption, that they are like that
girl in that they had a sense of corruption of their own, a low
estimate of their own worth *before* they went into advertising?

ALGREN: Everybody has a sense of corruption. An infant has a
sense of corruption.

Q: An *infant?*

ALGREN: Of course. An infant has a sense of shame.

Q: Where does it get it?

ALGREN: People are always born with a sense of shame. As soon
as a kid is articulate he has a sense of shame.

Q: Where does he get it?

ALGREN: Now how would I know where he got it? After I tell you where the infant gets a sense of shame, I'll tell you how the brain is formed before birth. I know a great deal. I practically know everything, but this is one thing I don't have a ready answer for.

Q: You said earlier that money was nothing by itself, that it was what the people who had it were. Is this true for you also in terms of a whole society?

ALGREN: Absolutely, absolutely. What do you do with it, the individual? Take two people, each of whom has a million dollars. One invests and invests and invests. I mean he protects himself. He thinks of nothing but how he can be safer and safer and how his family can be safer. What can be more meaningless? There isn't any total safety. He's going to die and get sick anyhow and what has he done with it? Now take someone else with a million bucks—he makes it move. They put it to use and get more out of it themselves. I don't mean necessarily people who go for charity, but they can make money move around. The Carnegies make their money move around. The Guggenheims make their money move around. I think it's better if a guy just spends it. I think it's better for himself if he just spends it. We've had people who made eight or ten fortunes, but they live while they have it. It makes them a different kind of person than the one who just holds onto it for security. Now, jumping from the specific to the general: you have a country that spends almost uncountable billions on protecting itself, protecting itself, going for a security that doesn't exist, spending billions on carriers that have to be sunk, going for billions in space, out of a fear, a fear that can never be diminished that way. What if the money went for other things? Think of the progress you could make against drug addiction with just a tiny fraction of the money that's going for one carrier, a carrier that's going to be sunk anyhow in a few years, one obsolete carrier. Think of the money for cancer, for teachers. We're not conquering anything in conquering space because we haven't even conquered ourselves. I think there's a comparison to be made between the individual who goes for a false security and a country that goes for a false security.

Q: Do you think we're going to have a war in the near future, the kind of a war that sinks aircraft carriers?

ALGREN: No, I don't think we're going to have that kind of war. We're going to have a different kind of war. We're going to have a war that isn't a war and it isn't peace. We're just going to have a tightening, a continuous tightening of security as the fear grows. We got an intimation of that in Korea. As soon as we lost the war in Korea, they immediately got a reaction here in security measures.

Q: You think we *lost* the war in Korea?

ALGREN: Yeah, I think we lost the war there, and we'll lose the one in Vietnam, and we'll lose the attempt to get back Cuba. We'll lose all our investments as surely as France lost hers in Indochina, as sure as she lost it in Africa.

Q: Do you see *any* similarity between the United States and colonial France?

ALGREN: Oh, I see a very close parallel. The parallel is that we have money invested there in business and if we don't hold down, we lose the profits.

Q: We have money invested in South Vietnam in business?

ALGREN: Oh, we've got money invested all over the world. Since when did Americans go out of business anywhere?

Q: Is that why we are in South Vietnam?

ALGREN: I don't know what else we'd be in South Vietnam for, except to protect American business. What are we doing there?

Q: Why are we involved in the Congo?

ALGREN: *Investments. Investments.* For the same reason.

Q: Then you must think that the United States is an imperialistic country?

ALGREN: It's an imperialist son-of-a-bitch. We still own Guatemala. When I say we own it, I mean we backed the fruit company that owns it, and when things go against us, when an attempt is made to take the country back, we perform our revolutions the same as Theodore Roosevelt did in Panama—we take it back, we put our own man in. The other guy becomes a Communist. He was no Communist. He was a man for land reform, which means taking land from the United Fruit Company. We back it by force. It's an imperialistic country—that is, we send soldiers, we take the country back by force for the United Fruit Company exactly as more recently we attempted to get Cuba back for people who have money invested in it.

Q: Is *that* why we supported the invaders of Cuba?

ALGREN: Sure. Sugar, markets. Markets. Sugar.

Q: Why did we do such a bad job?

ALGREN: I don't know. The CIA is a very clumsy outfit. It was certainly a very bad military job. I and millions of others saw it on TV two weeks before the invasion—the training field in Guatemala where these guys were. It was on a Sunday afternoon. It was a telecast of these guys who were planning to go to Cuba. Then they did and they got shot down, which is proper, the proper thing to do since they were simply mercenaries, hired mercenaries. They put their lives out. They're getting four hundred a month or something. The Cubans have their homes behind them, in their own country. So it was the proper thing to machine-gun them down. It looked even worse when the thing was handled so badly. They were assured, of course—well, you know as much about it as I do.

Q: No. I disagree with you on all this. Do you think Castro was a Communist even before he got into power?

ALGREN: No, and he's not one now.

Q: Now I have to ask you the American Legion question. In another part of this interview you said you would prefer to live in Paris where people are nicer to writers.

ALGREN: Uh-huh.

Q: Yet you continue to live in the United States, and the question is, *Why* do you go on living here?

ALGREN: Well, I'm not looking for a country where people are *nicer* to writers. The word I used was "respect." It's nice to be respected.

Q: All right.

ALGREN: It's nice to be respected.

Q: I don't want to be a hard-nose, but don't talk to me about cutting things fine. All right.

ALGREN: There's a difference. I don't want to go around saying, "Be nice to him, he's a writer." But I would like to get as much respect for what I do as is given to the man who hangs wallpaper, which is very hard to get.

Q: You're sure the writer in France or England or the Scandinavian countries or in Italy gets more respect and will continue to get more respect than he does in America, in the United States?

ALGREN: Oh I'm sure of that.

Q: But if you want this respect and you like these countries anyway, why aren't you living there? Why aren't you an expatriate?

ALGREN: I put up with the disdain. I accept that as part of the creative person's lot in the United States. You must live with the disdain. There's something criminal about being a writer, that is, if you're not a successful writer, that is, if you're not a yes man. There are a lot of yes men who just give a nod to the corruption of business, the corruption of the newspaper world, the corruption of the magazine world, and the hollowness of American life. They give the nod to it. They give approval and they get a pay-off. I'm not talking about these kind of writers. They're regarded with respect. These writers do get respect. But if you go against this, if you point out that the reason Americans are restless is because their lives are empty—that what we have going here isn't a kind of 4-H Club picnic going—that this is a country where there's a great deal of psychological and spiritual anguish, that we live in a nightmare, that the people in Sherwood Anderson's short stories or the plays of Tennessee Williams are closer to actuality than are the pictures we get from Herman Wouk or James Michener, or name whomever you want—the professional approvers—if you go against this Woukian thing, if you don't deal in handouts, then you feel the disdain, then you realize that you are a kind of criminal. You are against society and you have to be against it, it being what it is.

Q: But why stay *here,* under these conditions?

ALGREN: Because English is the only language I speak. I can't communicate in another language. As much as I'd like to live in France, I can't operate on the French level. I'm not going to another country if I can't work this. This is the only country in which I can work at my trade. I'm not ready to give up writing, and the only way I can communicate is on the American level. I couldn't even do it in England. The scene is too unfamiliar. This is the only country where I can work, where I have any sources. So I would rather put up with the disdain and stick it out here, rather than go to a country where I don't have any work to do, where I won't be able to work.

Q: But there are many writers who write about America who do not live in America.

ALGREN: Oh, I know. There are many. There are some expatriate writers who do very well, who go to France and live there fifty years and never come home. They write in English all the time. Unfortunately I'm not one of those.

Q: Why not?

ALGREN: I don't know why not. But I just can't. There are writers who, if they're going to write about Chicago, the best place is the Left Bank. But I happen to be built along different lines. The only place I can write about Chicago is *in* Chicago. If I were going to write about Detroit, I'd have to live in Detroit. Others would have to go to Mexico to write about Detroit.

Q: Well, then is it unfair to say that the practice of your craft is a study in disdain?

ALGREN: A study in disdain? No, I don't feel disdain.

Q: Can it be that because you disdain the culture you feel that the culture disdains you?

ALGREN: Oh, I know the culture disdains me.

Q: And do you disdain the culture?

ALGREN: No, I'm just mad at it.

Q: Have you always been mad at it?

ALGREN: I've been mad at it for some time.

Q: Have you ever been *not* mad at it?

ALGREN: I think I started disliking it about the time I was in high school. I began seeing something wrong. I didn't start writing about it until a long time after that.

Q: I want to know something about this thing that is wrong. Is it something that had *gone* wrong or something that had always *been* wrong?

ALGREN: It's been something that's been going wrong ever since the business interests took over the country, right after our Civil War, I think, when the big-business boom came, when the country was industrialized, and then the industrial middle class took it over from the agricultural interests—when it became a middle-class country, when it became a bourgeois country with the accompanying sense of bourgeois values.

Q: Do you see any other way it could have gone at that time?

ALGREN: Oh, I'm sure it couldn't have gone any other way, but that doesn't mean that I can say the way it's gone is right.

Q: What way *should* it have gone?

ALGREN: Well, there isn't any use in talking about how it should have gone. This is how it *went*.

Q: How would you like it to have gone?

ALGREN: How I would like it to have gone doesn't cut any ice because there was nobody to take over the country but the bourgeois in the 1860's.

Q: How do you want things to improve now in America? What do you want changed?

ALGREN: I would like to see specific changes. I would like to see medicine socialized. I'd like to see more money go for medical research. I'd like to see more money go for schools. I'd like to see a theatre in all these little suburban communities. I can imagine a small theatre going in every town in the United States. There's enough money in every city of fifty to a hundred thousand people to support a theatre, if they got federal help. I would like to see federal help to every community that has a dozen kids to put on Shakespeare. I'd rather see the money go that way than to these nuts in the pressure suits. Who cares? I don't get any bang out of this—I don't really feel any prestige in John Glenn doing an orbit of the thing. I have much more respect for the way the Russians do it. They simply do it for scientific reasons. We do it for prestige. It's like a sporting event. I don't care what Glenn's wife looks like—I mean, we do something with these people and it has nothing to do with the scientific value of the thing. We enhance our prestige just as though we found someone to hit a golf ball longer than a Russian.

Q: You really think the Russians did it just for the scientific value?

ALGREN: Oh, they get much more out of it. In the first place they don't have—they do the thing—who was there when the Russians tossed up a Sputnik? Nobody was there.

Q: Do you think the secrecy was maintained by the Russians because they are diffident and shy, and because they want to do these things just for scientific value?

ALGREN: No, they're shrewder, they're shrewder. How do you know how many times they failed?

Q: Do you think this is good—this kind of secrecy?

ALGREN: Of course it's good. It's good.

Q: Are you aware of the criticism that the Russians spent so much money throwing the Sputniks up instead of increasing their agricultural output?

ALGREN: No, I don't know anything about that. I'm talking about something else. I'm saying that a whole mob, an absolute mob of people who have no idea of what's going on, but who simply want to be there where the excitement is, go down to Cape Canaveral to see this stunt, and it's not supposed to be a stunt—it's a scientific investigation.

Q: Why can't it be both?

ALGREN: Well, I don't know.

Q: Why are you sounding like such a limited person? I think of you as a person who would like everything to be going at once.

ALGREN: I *am* a limited person.

Q: I don't believe that—now maybe I'm all wrong.

ALGREN: I can't consider that John Glenn's going up into space is on the same level as the Liston-Patterson fight, which is where the papers put it. Can you tell me what scientifically, can you tell me what exactly—outside of the prestige thing, outside of the fact that the Russians put up an astronaut and so did we; that enhanced our prestige when Glenn went up—now exactly *what* did we get out of it scientifically? Can you tell me that? I didn't read anything about it.

Q: I have to counter that. I have to counter that question.

ALGREN: I wish you *would* counter that question. I was just going to suggest that you counter it. Yeah.

Q: If it were possible for man to do something absolutely useless —like enabling all people who wanted to fly, to fly simply by flapping their hands—do you think we should spend money finding out about something like that?

ALGREN: Not when it would mean taking money from much more critical situations. I don't measure a country in terms of its technical achievements. I don't care how many nuts in pressure suits we send in orbit. I don't think that makes the country greater than Russia. I would like a country that's more interested in preserving life or improving life than in destroying. I'm very limited that way.

Q: In what country in the world is the average person healthier and better fed?

ALGREN: Probably the Scandinavian countries. Probably in Italy and Spain, the countries that have a better climate. Probably in Germany. Germany's a very healthy country. Contrary to your idea that this is the healthiest country in the world, I would say this is probably the sickest. I'm not talking about how much we eat. Probably the only country in the world that has more suicide than we have is Sweden. I know we don't eat like the Chinese, but I'm certain the Chinese are healthier.

Q: More important than our arguments is the fact that you are a person interested in the "open" society. Am I wrong?

ALGREN: I'm not sure what you mean by an "open" society. If it is what I think you mean, yes, I'm in favor of an "open" society. Do you think we have one?

Q: Of all the countries in the world I think we have the most open society and I think we're headed toward more of an open society faster than any other country in the world.

ALGREN: I would say we're headed toward a closed society faster.

Q: I know you think that and that's why I've been surprised by some of your answers, some of your facts.

ALGREN: I've been surprised by some of your questions.

Q: I think you would agree that the United States is more of an open society than Russia.

ALGREN: This has nothing to do with anything. It's as though I were in a flood in Mississippi and the water is up to my waist and you're saying, "It really isn't serious, because there are people who are drowning in the Volga." Russians' premise and our premise are different, and the fact that we don't have as much wire tapping as Russia doesn't mean we are heading for an open society. So to say that we are not as conformist as Russia doesn't give me any ease at all.

Q: So when you talk about the United States then, you are not comparing the United States to any other country, you are comparing the United States to an ideal you have?

ALGREN: I'm comparing what we have now in the United States with what it was intended to be, that is, an open society and not a closed one. It was a society that in its one stage knew its own name. That's one way of putting it. That is, it was a society that knew what it stood for. It stood for the principles of the French Revolution.

Q: How about the principles of our *own* Revolution?

ALGREN: They were the same principles. I think the French took from us as much as we took from the French. We took principles from the French philosophers but we put them into effect before the French did: Liberty, Equality, Fraternity.

Q: Was our Revolution French?

ALGREN: It was basically French. Surely it was basically French. The principle of equality came out of the French, not the English. The English philosophers were much more caste thinkers.

Q: How about the American philosophers?

ALGREN: It depends upon which ones you mean. Certainly Hamilton was closer to the English philosophers, to the distrust of democracy, whereas Jefferson took from the French philosophers the belief that there could be an open society.

Q: What about our American Revolution was indigenous to America, and *not* to France, and *not* to England?

ALGREN: Without pretending to be an authority on the American Revolution, the indigenous thing about the American Revolution was simply that people refused to be taxed without representation. They refused to be told what they should produce in precisely the same way that the Cubans decided that they would not be told by us what to do. We were told we could not produce this or we could not produce that— although we had a very fertile soil—because the English were turning out these products and we had to buy from the English, so in precisely the same way Cuba furnished a market for our southern states that grew tomatoes and melons and beans and potatoes, and in this way we got back the money that we paid them for sugar. Just as England wanted to keep us a one-crop country, so we succeeded for a half century and more in keeping Cuba a sugar country. And of course it cost us nothing.

Q: What is astonishing is that you will try to convince yourself or anybody else that what went on in the Thirteen Colonies here in the 1770's is the same as what went on in Cuba in 1958.

ALGREN: I didn't say it was the same. I said there was a great similarity.

Q: The question was: What was indigenous to the American Revolution? And you said the same thing that happened in Cuba.

ALGREN: Yeah, I got back to the crops. What this country has always stood for, the premise on which the Monroe Doctrine is based, is that every country is self-determining. The Colonies fought for the right to determine for themselves what they could produce. England forbade it. They sent soldiers over here to forbid it. Now this has become a monstrous hypocrisy because we have said that the principle is true for us but not for Cuba. We say, "Cubans cannot determine what they shall grow; they can only grow sugar." But now let me finish, let me finish the question. Again we say we're for self-determination in Guatemala, but if they do anything more than grow bananas for the United Fruit Company, we use force, as Britain tried to use force against us, as we tried to use force against Cuba.

Q: I can only feel that you are not interested in my question.

ALGREN: I just answered it.

Q: I'm trying to find out what you think happened in the American Revolution that had never happened before in the history of man, and you are talking about crops.

ALGREN: This had never happened before: in what country was any people able to act independently? This was the great thing about the United States. It was the first country in the world in which the individual was able to act individually. This had never been heard of before. Even in the freest of European societies, such as England, if you were born a servant, you stayed a servant. There was a rigid caste system in all of Europe. There was an ancient, an ancient caste system, almost unbreakable, in the East, in the Asiatic countries. And in America for the first time the idea that a man had a right to his own life was actually put into effect. It was an amazing thing. This never happened before. I don't think this happened even in the Athenian democracy.

Q: Was this a French philosophy?

ALGREN: Yes, this came out of the French, out of Rousseau, out of the French philosophers.

Q: It didn't come out of a guy named Jefferson or Thomas Paine?

ALGREN: They certainly didn't originate it. Jefferson and Paine were derived from the French philosophers. They didn't begin this. The French were thinking for several hundred years. Jefferson was a believer in the French Revolution, but the French Revolution was certainly centuries in the making. I mean it came up from the Dark Ages, the idea that a man was free.

Q: Why did it *happen* in America?

ALGREN: It was a new country. A system hadn't been formalized. There was room for the idea. That was why the great liberals—Pulaski and Lafayette—the great liberals from all over Europe, from every country where people were oppressed, came here. And Jefferson was a European liberal. I mean he was an American, but his thinking was European. I mean the country had to be European. It was new.

Q: Why couldn't it just be new?

ALGREN: Well, because the Iroquois were very unprogressive.

Q: Weren't the European intellectuals at the time, like Burke, weren't they astonished by what was going on in America?

ALGREN: Well, they hated it. Burke was—wasn't he—?

Q: No. Burke liked the American Revolution.

ALGREN: Oh, he did. I didn't know. Well, it was attacked. Of course I know Carlyle hated the French Revolution.

Q: Weren't even the French surprised by our Revolution? The French Revolution didn't happen until after the American Revolution. Hasn't the American radical always been most effective when he's gone off on his own hook?

ALGREN: I don't know.

Q: Has he been effective when he's touted somebody else's philosophy?

ALGREN: It's always somebody else's philosophy. No usable philosophy is ever developed by one man. It's always an extension I suppose if you go back far enough, the principles of the French Revolution go back to Greece, to the idea of the Greek democracy.

Q: Well, who do you think the American radicals are?

ALGREN: Are you differentiating between radicals and liberals?

Q: Yes.

ALGREN: I think Jefferson is a liberal.

Q: Who was a radical of Jefferson's day?

ALGREN: I suppose Patrick Henry was a radical. I guess Tom Paine was a radical.

Q: But Patrick Henry didn't think we should go as far as we did go.

ALGREN: Well, I don't know—

Q: Do you feel like naming the people you think were effective politicians and who were also radicals?

ALGREN: Oh, yeah. We've got a tradition.

Q: Who are they?

ALGREN: Thoreau.

Q: Was he an effective politician?

ALGREN: Oh yeah, I think so.

Q: But he was not in politics. All right. Let's not limit it.

ALGREN: He had a political effect.

Q: But only through other men who were in politics.

ALGREN: He was in jail you know.

Q: Let's not limit it. Thoreau. O.K.

ALGREN: Well, does Lincoln pass?

Q: You think he was a radical?

ALGREN: He was extremely radical. He was extremely radical before the Civil War. After all, at the time Polk was President,

Lincoln was the only man in Congress who stood up and denounced the Mexican War, which was considered a great national conquest. Lincoln agreed with Santa Ana when Santa Ana warned the Americans, when he said, "We will welcome you to hospitable graves." Lincoln stood up and he agreed with Santa Ana, which was about as disloyal a thing as a man could have said, and he was a congressman. And I still think that the high point in President Kennedy's career, the most honorable thing he has said, was when he was a senator and he expressed sympathy with the Algerians. He expressed not only sympathy but he said France should get out of Algeria. There is a similarity in those statements. I don't consider Jack Kennedy a great radical, but Lincoln was certainly a radical of his time. Can I get Walt Whitman in there?

Q: Sure.

ALGREN: He never ran for office.

Q: That's O.K.

ALGREN: He wanted to. You know he applied to Salmon P. Chase for a job. Somebody interceded with Salmon P. Chase when Chase was Secretary of the Treasury. The friend wanted to get Whitman a job. Chase said there wasn't any room but could he have an autographed copy of the man's book. It was *Leaves of Grass,* it turns out. He did. He did. It's in Sandburg's book. Sandburg tells about that interview. So Salmon P. Chase was the first Madison Avenue man, you know. He was. And then there was another radical who was a railroad fireman from Terre Haute that isn't so well remembered now.

Q: What's his name?

ALGREN: Eugene Debs. He made a couple of interesting remarks. He was the one who said, "While there is a soul in prison, I am not free," which he got from some Russian. Maybe it was Bakunin or Tolstoi, maybe. But Debs said it here. And when he was still city clerk in Terre Haute, he was asked to issue warrants for the arrest of streetwalkers, and he refused to do it. He challenged the police to arrest somebody. He told the police to go and arrest the people in "high life," as he put it, instead of those girls, which was a pretty radical thing to say. Then he became more radical when he ran for office. He made a speech in Chicago—I think it was in 1914 —when he was opposed to the World War, our entering the World War. His statement there was to the workingman and he said, "You are always making bayonets and always at the wrong end of them," for which he spent the war years in the Atlanta penitentiary. He was a pretty good radical. That's my idea of a radical. I think Darrow was a radical, and I think Dreiser was a radical, and got more radicaler as time went on. Well, that's the end. I don't know of no other effective radical that's come along since.

Q: Since when? Since 1940?

ALGREN: I think Dreiser died in 1945.

Q: We've had no American radical for the last twenty years?

ALGREN: Well, there has been Henry Wallace but—

Q: You think he's a radical?

ALGREN: I think he was in 1948.

Q: Didn't Wallace say that in the 1960 election he voted for Nixon?

ALGREN: I said 1948. Dos Passos was a radical, too, in 1920.

Q: Do you think he was a radical? Wasn't he complaining about modern things, about science, progress, about materialism?

ALGREN: He was a Communist.

Q: But are Communists always radical?

ALGREN: Well, they're considered so. Dos Passos was against the First World War.

Q: Yet there were American Fascists against the First World War.

ALGREN: Dos Passos was certainly a radical. He was involved with many radical organizations in the twenties.

Q: Were the radical organizations in the twenties radical?

ALGREN: Oh, yeah.

Q: Do you mean to say that the American Communist is a radical in America?

ALGREN: Certainly the radicals of the twenties were more radical. We don't have any radicals like that around now. There was a whole slew of radical-thinking people—the poets and the writers: Edna St. Vincent Millay and the *Winterset* guy, Maxwell Anderson, and Vachel Lindsay. Sandburg was a radical. Dreiser was a radical. There was a great radical literary movement in the twenties, which you don't have now. The literary movement is conformist now, unless you want to consider Norman Mailer's challenge to the traffic department of the Provincetown police. Or Allen, what's his name, Howlberg's—you know—all his posturing is just plain crap. I mean it's just typing. Or Gregory Corso or something. To see the difference in the literary scene and how much more unreal it is now than it was in the twenties look at what they are writing. Compare, for instance, Allen Ginsberg, Jack

Kerouac, and Ferlinghetti, and Corso and all the beats with Edna St. Vincent Millay and Theodore Dreiser. It is needless to go on. These were creative people. What we've got now is a bunch of performers. I mean I can't see it any other way. I don't know of a poet who could compare with Edna St. Vincent Millay. I don't know of a playwright who can compare with the plays that were being produced in the twenties. I don't know of a novelist now who can be compared to the best of the twenties. The only aspect of the literary scene in which we are much more skilled than we were in the twenties is in criticism.

Q: How about the theatre?

ALGREN: I don't know what was going on. We had Eugene O'Neill—

Q: Tennessee Williams?

ALGREN: Oh, yeah, yeah, yeah. I really think he's good.

Q: How about Inge?

ALGREN: Oh, that's a very weak pastel sort of a guy. Williams is very strong.

Q: Chayefsky?

ALGREN: Oh, I don't know. That's just a TV writer like Rod Serling or something. Arch Oboler up to date.

Q: What about Arthur Miller?

ALGREN: Oh, Miller is a real serious guy. Miller is somebody you really have to respect and I like to see what he's done, but I'm never much moved by a man who works out of ideas, completely out of ideas. His ideas are sound. Everything he says is genuine and worth seeing, and he doesn't move me at all. To me Miller is never as interesting as a guy like Tennessee Williams, who is a real poet, and Williams is much more full of flaws. You can hardly find a flaw in Miller and you can pick Williams to death. I mean Williams gets silly. He gets ridiculous, but it is because he goes so far. Williams is much more interesting as a playwright for the same reason that a fighter interests me who goes all out and doesn't spare himself, even though that fighter may start bogging down. Williams now and then bogs down, but it's because there are spots that are so strong. Miller works out of caution. He's a perfectionist. He's limited and does a real well-designed job, but Williams works out of a much more human sort of thing and he takes risks that Miller wouldn't dare. Williams always takes the risk of making a fool of himself, and sometimes he does, but what he gets done in between is much more moving, to me, than what Miller does.

Q: Do you think Arthur Miller is an American radical?

ALGREN: He derives from American radicals, yeah.

Q: How about Albee, Richardson, Gelber—the young off-Broadway writers.

ALGREN: I haven't seen the Richardson yet, but I saw Albee, who is very good. I thought that *Zoo Story* was almost unbearably true. I mean there was a point in it at which you wished he hadn't done it, but it's true. I saw the Gelber thing, *The Connection.* I liked it very much. It was original and that's an interesting guy, of course.

Q: We've had it again this time.

ALGREN: We've had it. Well, I can add things to it now, now that we've finished.

Q: Thank you very much, Nelson Algren.

ALGREN: Thank *you* very much, Mr. Donohue.

(At the next meeting)

Q: The last time we spoke you mentioned Albee's *Zoo Story.* What is your feeling about *Who's Afraid of Virginia Woolf?*

ALGREN: I saw it. I think he's stronger than Tennessee Williams. You have to make a comparison with Williams, or at least I do because Uta Hagen was the first actress I saw in a Tennessee Williams thing, *Streetcar Named Desire.* The comparison is of course the compassion. They're both very compassionate people. The play is written out of compassion but I prefer Albee's harshness. It's a harsh compassion with him. He's not as vulnerable. Williams always puts in a kind of a plea and a hope, as he did in *Streetcar Named Desire*— "I've always depended upon the kindness of strangers." Albee doesn't depend on anybody's kindness. He doesn't believe in it. He doesn't believe there is any. It's as harsh as possible and I think it's more tragic. I think it's stronger than Williams and it's also much funnier. There was hardly a moment that didn't strike me as funny, whereas Williams drags at times. Yeah, I think it was a very strong play and the reason his humor is so true is because it is tragic right up to that little dance at the end, that *Who's Afraid of Virginia Woolf* thing. He puts all the pieces together, you know. Williams is more sentimental. The woman asks for your sympathy right away. Blanche Dubois is so pitiful it's almost an open pleading for pity for her, a kindness to her, but

Albee's woman doesn't apparently seem to need anybody.
She's running things pretty well. Seems like a pretty strong,
assertive woman and he takes the reverse route. But at the
end you see she's quite helpless and it's much more moving because you know nobody can do anything. He doesn't
hold out any hope at all. Williams does, and I think it's not
a true hope.

Q: You also saw Zero Mostel in a musical, a completely different
kind of American theatre in *A Funny Thing Happened on
the Way to the Forum.* How did you like that?

ALGREN: Why, it was good burlesque. I couldn't catch it very
well, I sat so far back. It was as good burlesque as Toby, you
know, the *Ten Nights in a Turkish Bath* thing, you know,
where they're running in and out of doors. It was fun.
Mostel is a classic burlesque comedian. Whether you like
burlesque or not, he keeps the thing rolling. He's tremendous.
But I have no idea of what it was about at all. I mean, it's
just entertainment for a couple of hours.

Q: The last time we spoke you said you saw the Gelber thing,
The Connection, and that you liked it very much. I saw
Gelber a couple weeks ago at that same party we went to,
and he said that you've always been very important to him.
Did you know that?

ALGREN: Yeah, he might have implied that, I don't know. He said
he read my stuff. He comes from Chicago's West Side and
he'd read the stuff I'd written, I guess when he was still in
high school, and had been impressed by it.

Q: Have you ever felt that you had an influence on the construc-
tion of *The Connection?*

ALGREN: That *Golden Arm* I think kind of called attention to a
field that, uh, uh, it was the first time that attention had been
called to this field as literature and a lot of people followed
through. I thought he did a much, much better thing than
A Hatful of Rain, which was just plain box-office stuff. Gelber was really trying to show what it's like.

9 *Liberties, Civil and Otherwise*

QUESTION: On the question of the American radicals, what do you think is the influence of the American Negro, not only in the field of literature but his influence on American politics? Do you think that maybe in the field of American radicalism the American Negro is moving to the front?

ALGREN: Well, he's the only man now who is a radical now just by being black; just by his need of asserting himself as a human being he becomes a radical. The whole American radical movement now is the young Negroes in the South. This is the only thing that goes against the trend toward the right. This is the only movement that sustains the old American radical tradition, sustains the original ideal of the country.

Q: You mean the nonviolent Negroes. How about the Black Muslims?

ALGREN: The Black Muslims are radical because they're Negroes, but their thinking is extremely right wing. What you have is extremely orthodox when Malcolm X says you've got to hit back, you've got to defend yourself, but this does not mean that we don't believe in, as he puts it, universal brotherhood. When he says that men should love one another, what he means is love your own kind. In other words, he will love other Black Muslims, and this is really no improvement over the failure of Christianity—for Baptists to love only Baptists and whites to love only Protestant whites and so forth, and so he really isn't offering anything new. He's just repeating the failure of the whites, of white Christianity.

Q: It's Jim Crow in another form.

ALGREN: Yeah, he's only opposing the white ideas, I mean of the white churches of the South. It's Fascist thinking. The Fascists, of course, are radicals in a sense. They always call themselves radicals.

Q: He has given, however, many Negroes a sense of dignity.

ALGREN: Yeah.

Q: That they should be strong.

ALGREN: He has given them, he has, he's given them an image of a perfectly joyless kind of a puritanical Negro.

Q: How do you mean?

ALGREN: No jazz, no joy, and no juice, no smoking, no drinking, no gambling. It's a horror.

Q: How about Baldwin as an American radical? Have you met Baldwin?

ALGREN: Yeah, I met Baldwin.

Q: How did that go?

ALGREN: Why, we didn't hit it off at all. He used the Black Muslim technique of putting responsibility to me as a white man for crimes committed against the Negro.

Q: Didn't you once say he calls you the nicest square he knows?

ALGREN: No, no, he didn't say that. He said very sarcastically, he said, "I'll tell you what you are, you're an honorable well-meaning white square." It was very complex. It was a very interesting little session. It wasn't a little session, it was a long session to which I very innocently brought a French Canadian girl. It must have been sixty-one. Baldwin said some very good things on the radio. He was being interviewed and he said that "if you don't know who I am"—it was the time he published *Nobody Knows My Name* and he's saying, speaking for the American Negro—"if you don't know my name, you don't know your own," which I thought was a very acute and true thing to say, and at the same time this French Canadian girl had read something of his and she was interested in meeting him. So I called her up and he invited us out to a motel on the South Side and I thought it was a good idea to meet him and to bring her because they both speak French. I thought it would be interesting, interesting for both of them to talk about Paris in the native tongue. But I was a little surprised when I got there in that he had about ten, eleven friends there, young studs, all young guys, with a definitely hostile air. Nobody even said hello. He said hello, he spoke, and they were courteous to the girl. And then things got very sullen. Nobody said anything. So, just to get things started, I said, how is it, I said, that, mentioning a mutual friend of ours, a young Negro writer, I said, how is it that this young writer who was so devoted to Reverend King a few years ago seems to have switched over to Malcolm X? Sure enough, that got a rise. Baldwin jumped up and said, "Why do you feel that it's justifiable for the white man to use weapons and to use violence and it's wrong for the Negro?" I said, "The only reason I can think of offhand for being wrong is that he is outnumbered, for one thing." And from there he went on. He said, "Do you realize that it's possible to castrate a man in more ways than one? They can take my nephew down in Montgomery, they can take him out and castrate him." He made several references to his nephew and then later he referred to a couple of the others, one or two of the other young guys there. He said, "You know they can take me out and castrate me?" He was preoccupied with castration and then he went back again and made another reference to what they might do to his nephew. At one point a friend came in and said, "What about your niece, Mr. Baldwin?" Which I thought was a pretty pertinent comment. I don't remember the exact sequence of the events, but then he says, "Of course, you can get out of here, you can go back north, to the North Side, and get out of things without even fighting or feeling any responsibility." I said, "Well, I don't live on the North Side, I live on the West Side, and I'm not, I don't take any particular responsibility for people simply because they're colored." I said, mentioning a colored girl who had written a very bad book, I said, "Are you implying because she's colored, I'm supposed to give it a good review or because a Negro first baseman comes up and he's a bum, I should say he isn't a bum?" I said, "I don't make those allowances at all." Then I said, "I don't take any responsibility for the lynchings in the South either," and I simply declined this assumption of guilt which he seems to have put on the middle class very successfully. So finally we got onto speaking of Richard Wright naturally, because we'd both known him and I knew he hadn't hit it off too well with Wright. They came to a parting of the ways and I said I thought that this idea was a very big idea, too, when Wright brought it out in Bigger Thomas, meaning that Baldwin had picked up from Wright. He picked up a very true thing because Bigger Thomas killed—the only way he could become a man was to commit murder and he was satisfied that he had done it. I went back to the thirties in order to show my respect for Wright and then somebody said, "The thirties are over, you know, that time is dead." I said, "No, the time that we have now comes out of the thirties. We aren't starting all over every ten years." I mean, one decade grows out of another, the way Baldwin has grown out of Wright. Then I thought it was time to go and I said to the girl, "Let's go, that is, if you want to go." She said, "No, I would like to stay, this is interesting." So one of them pops up, one of these guys pops up, and says, "Oh, why don't you just go?" So I said, "Well, to tell you the truth, I never remember leaving when I'm told to go." I sat down. Then we got back into this Wright thing again. One of them, one with the little Dizzy Gillespie beard, said, "You followed Wright around, you attached yourself to Wright after he got to be well known and famous, of course, but you didn't know him before." "Before," I said. "Were you there?" I said, "When I knew Wright nobody knew about him except his mother and his brother." I said, "I never saw him after, I hardly knew him after he was published. I knew him before he was published." So I'm trying to say about five different things at once because they were heckling me with half a dozen different things and then I heard this one guy who had told me to leave before. He said to somebody else in the corner, he said, "Why don't we just have him go?" I was so mad at him I didn't catch onto it. I said, "What are you talking to that man about having me go if it's me you're talking about? What are you telling him for. Why don't you tell me?" He said, "Don't you think I can make you go?" So I looked at him, a pretty big kid about twenty-two. I said, "Well, I know, I know you can make me go, but it's going to take at least forty minutes to get me out the door and you're going to come with me." Then he cooled things off.

Q: Who did?

ALGREN: Baldwin stepped in. He said, "He didn't mean it, he didn't mean it." I got a little hot, I said, "Yeah, he didn't mean it." And there was a little silence and I said to Baldwin, "What do you mean? I should take a lot of shit just because he's colored? That don't mean a fucking thing to me." There was a little silence and I decided, I heard myself saying to the guy, I said, "Listen, *boy*." That broke it up. (*Laughter*) Baldwin jumped up, shaking, waggling his finger, and said, "You *said* it! You *said* it! You *said* it! You *said* it! You *said* 'boy'!" I said, "Yeah. I'm a white supremacist, but it took you six hours to get it out of me. That's what you wanted me to say. That's all you've been driving at." I think this is a little important because his thinking is always aimed to create that gulf. When he was baiting the Attorney General, the challenge he put to the Attorney General to get the President down there to confront Governor Wallace, well, it's an interesting challenge and, uh, all the Attorney General could say was, "What good would that do?" Well, what good it did do, from Baldwin's point of view, was to create a gulf. As he said later with some satisfaction when they asked him afterward if there were still differences, he said, there were no longer differences between them, there was simply, simply a gulf. This is why I have a certain suspicion his basic motives are vindictive, very vindictive indeed. I think he's sore. I think he's vindictive not only about being a Negro, when he would rather be white; I think he's a little put out about being a homosexual, too. I think he would prefer not to be. I mean, I think he feels this. As he says himself, there's more than one way to castrate a man. I think he resents this. I think he resents the kind of a boyhood he had, and rightfully. But it has made him into a very, extremely useful kind of a provocateur. I mean I think he's very needed to say the things he does. He's needed simply to articulate the wrongs done to the colored people and his being on the scene has really, I think, hastened the federal action.

Q: How did the evening end?

ALGREN: Why, the evening ended with a kind of friendliness between himself and the girl, who seemed very pleased with the whole thing. It was just a kind of a standoff. I just had a standoff with him and a thanks and good luck, and that was all. But I sort of watched it going down the stairs. (*Laughter*) I still wasn't sure about that big guy. It was a very interesting evening.

Q: Have you communicated with him since?

ALGREN: No, no, no. He struck me as being a very strange combination of a Negro evangelist merged with a professional Parisienne. It's a very strange combination.

Q: Do you think that the Negro's going to get what he wants, and how will that affect America if he does? If he doesn't get it, how will it affect him?

ALGREN: Well, he'll get and is getting and will get what he needs. I really believe that with the breakdown of segregation that we are going to be so accustomed to seeing Negroes and whites together that the edge will be taken off. The sense of color is going to be blunted. We'll lose our consciousness of skin color. We're going to get so much intermarriage that the Negro won't be such a special creature. All I'm saying is that the importance of color is going to be less sharp. Of course, there are those marriages where the Negro marries the white girl just in order to get into her society and she marries him in order to get out of it.

Q: Are there many marriages in the offing between Negro women and white men? In one of Baldwin's writings he said that the Negro woman was the unsung hero of the Negro's fight for dignity and that she'd never paid attention to white men. I've often wondered why it is that, when people talk about intermarriage, it's primarily in terms of a Negro man marrying a white woman, but I see less and less and I hear less and less of the Negro woman marrying the white man. Why do you think that is? Is there a question of status here? Or does the question interest you?

ALGREN: Yes, it's an interesting question. I can't quite account for it. Almost all the interracial marriages I've known have been a Negro man and a white woman.

Q: Yes. Why is that, do you imagine?

ALGREN: Oh, it might be that the sexual barrier that was set up against the white woman has created—I mean the taboos, the taboo put on the white woman, that nothing, nothing can be worse than to marry a Negro—gives her a means of defying society, and putting the white woman in the league of untouchable of course makes her much more attractive too. It has much more significance. Whereas there has been no taboo put on the Negro woman. I mean, no taboo at all because the white man wanted the Negro woman to be available. The Negro can't look at the white woman, but the white man can come over and have the Negro woman. The Negro woman has been free. She hasn't had that taboo put on her. She's been made available and often served as a mistress in the South, so perhaps that lack of taboo might be a contributing reason for the imbalance of interracial marriages.

Q: Do you think it's important that there's been almost a folk myth built up that Negroes are more sensuous, more passionate, more erotic, and more competent sexually than white men?

ALGREN: I'd like to think this is so, but personally I've never been able to discover it. The colored gals I've known, the colored gals I've slept with, were nothing in particular, nothing to go out of your way for. There's simply as much variation there and emotion—I mean no more passion than the average white woman. They can be quite as frigid as a white woman. But the core of the whole southern thing is in the fear of the Negro's masculinity. I don't think there's that much to fear, but certainly the white man in the South has, out of a sense of inferiority, assaulted the Negro male and resorted to the knife and to castration.

Q: But if there were more intermarriages and people found out that Negroes and whites were pretty much the same, would there be less fear of this?

ALGREN: Yeah, I think the fear has been built up. I mean, it's been built up terrifically beyond its reality.

Q: But if Negroes as people are found out to be as human, with as many strengths and as many frailties as the white man, won't that make for greater understanding between the races?

ALGREN: I don't think it'll be done without bloodshed.

Q: Now that's something that bothers me. Many white intellectuals like Podhoretz of *Commentary* and now more and more Negro leaders almost seem to be asking for bloodshed.

ALGREN: Well, I don't know that it's a question of asking for it.

Q: How much of a need do you think there is to see this actually happen, almost as a kind of expiation of guilt? Is it absolutely necessary that we have this kind of disaster?

ALGREN: Well, I don't think that, I'm not much impressed by, I mean, a warning from Podhoretz is of the same class with me as a warning from your myna bird, you know. . . .

Q: Podhoretz wrote a very good article in *Commentary*.

ALGREN: Did he?

Q: Yeah.

ALGREN: He's still a myna bird.

Q: I think he's a very good man.

ALGREN: I think he's an excellent boy. The fact is that the whites are armed and the Negroes are armed and there's a point at which rationality is lost. . . .

PART V

REPRISE AT FIFTY-FIVE

10 *The Open Society*

QUESTION: As you undoubtedly have gathered, part of the pitch here is that by the actual act of submitting to this interview you are acknowledging—at one level of your consciousness at least—certain changes in you. Other manifestations could be the new agent, the increased travel, the work. You've got books coming out. You are working, you are producing again, right?

ALGREN: Yes.

Q: You've produced more in the last year [1961–62] than in the last three or four years?

ALGREN: Yes, that's right.

Q: You are communicating with people more and more. Are you communicating with friends in Europe?

ALGREN: Oh, yeah. I hear from my friends in Paris, from several friends in Paris.

Q: Do you hear from Sartre at all?

ALGREN: Only indirectly. I hear from some other people there.

Q: This will be our last series of conversations. Do you think
things are getting better? When you got out of college in
1931, things were pretty bad—economically, politically, cre-
atively—for you they were bad. Things have changed since
then. Haven't they?

ALGREN: Yes, they have changed. Comparing this decade with the
thirties, you could say that things are much better or that
things are much worse. Both answers are true. For the creative writer things are much worse in the sense that while
he had economic problems in the thirties—there were almost
no writers I knew of who had economic security—all the
writers who wrote anything in the thirties wrote accidentally
—but the creative writer of the thirties had belief. They saw
the world and they divided the world according to the way
that decade divided it, that is, between human rights and
property rights. That was concentrated in the Spanish Civil
War, and they took sides. It was an easy choice. Anybody
who was anybody believed in the Spanish Civil War—they
were against Franco and in that way it was simpler then. It
was easier to be right then. Injustice was black and justice
was white. It was easier to be creative then.

Q: Why? Because things were clearer?

ALGREN: Things were clearer. There was lynching and there was
anti-Semitism. Things were very serious. The world was dis-
jointed economically. People had a right to howl because they
were going hungry. In that sense it was easier. You had something to write about. Now things, in a certain sense, are
much better. I don't know of any writers now who are going
hungry. The economic situation of writers is much improved,
as it is of painters, actors. There is a much wider chance for
anybody in any of the arts. There's much more money. There

are creative conferences in the creative arts every summer in fifty different places. There are cultural conventions ready to pay a writer five hundred dollars, seven hundred and fifty dollars, to sit on a platform for an hour. My friend John Ciardi tells me of a poem that he had worked on for two years; he was paid thirty-five dollars for it when it was published, but he received seven hundred and fifty dollars to come tell how he did it, by the Arts Club in Chicago. In this sense, things are much better. Take a writer like Jack Kerouac who simply through the courtesy of promotion departments, simply because people have money to buy books, hoping there is something in the books, can become a best-seller with nothing, nothing, nothing to say. And he's not able to write either. He's able to give a performance. In this way the artist is much better off because he doesn't even have to be an artist. There's so much money. Anybody with a real talent, such as Tennessee Williams, becomes greatly renowned. He has a chance to see his work in plays, and on TV, and all over. Nobody would have gambled on a man like Williams, a man whose ideas are so unconventional, in the thirties. So in that sense we are much better off. There are Fulbrights. We didn't know about Fulbrights in the thirties.

Q: Aren't these developments to be wished? Aren't these the things that people in the thirties said *should* happen?

ALGREN: They should happen, but they didn't know what the cost would be.

Q: What is the cost?

ALGREN: The cost is simply that the writer has lost his position. There's almost no way of standing on the same ground that a writer used to stand on, that is, a position in opposition to society—in any society, not necessarily just our own. Every society is always run in a mass way, any society, whether it's Athens, or Rome, or London, or Paris, always has a great "we" feeling, a pro-"us" feeling. The thinking is always led by politicians, the feeling is always that "we" are the image of mankind.

Q: Who? The *hoi polloi?* The square? The bourgeois?

ALGREN: Yeah. If you're a Frenchman at the time of Napoleon, you were the destined people. They thought the same thing in Athens. And the English felt they were born to rule the world, as the Portuguese have felt, as we in our time have felt American "destiny." But there is always in all of these civilizations as they come, there is always somebody as there was Socrates in Athens, as there were men in France, maybe a lot of people whose names are lost, as there were men during the American Civil War and during the First World War, there are always people who stand at the side and say, "You're mad." There's always some singular character who stands aside in opposition to the whole thing, who is either ignored or put away as a bug, or sent to Atlanta, or he's simply the man to whom nobody pays any heed. He's the man who's always ultimately right.

Q: What man was saying that in the thirties? And was right?

ALGREN: Oh, Theodore Dreiser. Dreiser became very strong as he grew older, he became stronger against capitalism. He didn't believe in capitalism and he didn't believe in the justice that he found. This was the theme of *An American Tragedy.* He didn't believe in the morality of the American middle class. Richard Wright was another one of the thirties. Steinbeck, of course, was attacked. So was Farrell.

Q: Did they think there was some other country in the world where they were doing things better than in the United States?

ALGREN: Oh, some of them had that idea I'm sure, at one time.

Q: I mean after the Spanish Civil War, say?

ALGREN: I don't know what they thought. I know before the Spanish Civil War, Wright believed in the Soviet Union. Dreiser believed in it at one time. How long he believed in it, I don't know. A great many American writers, there was a whole—

Q: But were they right about that? Wright was one of the authors, wasn't he, of *The God That Failed?*

ALGREN: You mean were they right about the success of the Soviet Revolution?

Q: No. Were they right about the Soviet being the answer for mankind?

ALGREN: Well, it's kind of plain now. But you can't blame them for lack of foresight that the Soviet Union hasn't gone according to its promise any more than the United States hasn't gone according to *its* promise. You can't blame them though, the people in the early thirties, in the Depression, for having that hope, for really believing that the ideals of the Russian Revolution were to be believed in. I mean, the ideals of the Russian Revolution were as appealing as the ideals of the French Revolution and the American Revolution. They were deceived. Of course it didn't work.

Q: I'm trying to find out what you think should have happened, has happened, and is going to happen in America, particularly since you are a person devoted to the idea of an open society. Am I wrong in this?

ALGREN: I like the idea of an open society very much. I don't know where to find one, though.

Q: And if a college sophomore were to come to you and say, "Where can I find the open society?" wouldn't you talk to him in terms of process and change and development and change and evolution and growth and problems and solution —that it is a never-ending process?

ALGREN: No.

Q: Hasn't the fact that you have seen accomplished many of the things you wanted accomplished then set up new wishes on your part, new campaigns, and new causes? When the unions, for example, got the Wagner Act they also got new problems; they didn't stop there, right? We are not talking about a utopia, which is a place or thing, but we're talking about a process. Is that right? Does that make sense?

ALGREN: Of course. It's always a process.

Q: Now, how much of an anarchist do you think you are, or is that an old-fashioned word to you now?

ALGREN: No. I like the word. I like the word. I would like to think I am basically against government.

Q: Why are you against government?

ALGREN: Well, just off the surface, I like the company of men who are against government. I like the company of Sartre and Brendan Behan and the men who are very firm in the opposition to the establishment, if that's what being an anarchist means, because, to get back to where we were ten minutes ago of whether things now are better or worse, I said they were both, both better *and* worse. They're better because the writer has an easier time; there's more money and he gets more support and all that. At the same time things are worse because the position of the writer has been compromised. In the thirties the writer was told, "We can't use you and we don't want you." Now the writer is besieged on all sides by chances to be used. If there's any sign of talent, TV can use him, advertising can use him. How are you *not* going to take money these days without just standing like a stick saying, "I'm going to live in a garret like they used to"? That's just an affectation. You don't have to be poor.

Q: But you said in an earlier interview that the acceptance of money did not necessarily mean a compromise, that it all depends on what you take the money for, on what you write, on what you actually do.

ALGREN: How are you going to stand in opposition to a host when you're eating at his table? A concrete instance is Linus Pauling. The Nobel scientist picketed the White House against the Administration's program for nuclear testing and then he went in and had dinner with the Kennedys. I think he was wrong to have dinner with the Kennedys. Either he should have gone in and had dinner with them and *not* picketed, or if he's going to picket, he's got to stay outside. But that's the position of the writer. How are you going to have both? How are you going to complain when you're mad as hell and then be like, say, Clifford Odets, who goes to Hollywood for ten years and accepts the soft life and then comes back and says, "They made a whore out of me"? Well, no, they didn't. He made a whore of himself. He took it. But it's becoming increasingly difficult not to become a whore. I mean, where is the place to stand? In this sense Dreiser and Wright's time was easier, because they had no place to stand except what they made for themselves. There's always been a distance between the business society and the writer. Now business assimilates the writer. The business establishment leaves no room for a writer to be an independent voice.

Q: Let's talk about how society should open up. Is the most important thing to you, in general terms, is the most important thing the opening up of human society, a real ventilation of the human spirit?

ALGREN: By "opening up" you mean an opportunity for people to exploit themselves as people, to realize their own possibilities rather than simply to be used? Yeah, I believe in an open society, if by "open society" you mean a society wherein people are given a choice and the opportunity to realize their own possibilities rather than to have no choice except to be used by that society in return for being well clothed and well housed. In other words, an open society would be a society wherein the value of the human being would be given consideration above the value of the machine. This is why I don't see eye to eye with you when you refer to our society as one that is continuing to open up, because to my sight it is continuing to close down.

Q: Have things gotten *worse* in the last thirty years?

ALGREN: Yes, yes, yes. In that sense.

Q: Tell me why.

ALGREN: If I can relate it to disarmament. All this business in Korea and Tibet and why shouldn't we protect Korea and why shouldn't we protect South Vietnam? Well, because it is camouflage. We aren't there because we like the South Vietnamese. We didn't go to Korea because we wanted to bring freedom to the South Koreans. We aren't interested in protecting Tibet from the Chinese because we like the Tibetans.

It isn't that. What we're doing is protecting a society that has to expand, that has to expand technologically. We have a society that—

Q: Where? Where?

ALGREN: Here, in the United States—a society for which such a thing as unilateral disarmament, about which you asked before, would be absolutely disastrous. I suggest that we should disarm, of course, in the abstract, because it would be a great spiritual achievement for a nation to disarm. But it's totally fantastic because such disarmament would cause violent economic chaos, because we are a country which is dependent on our war machine and on our continuing technological expansion. We are now at the mercy of a gigantic technological society, which, in order to keep going, *has* to expand. We *have* to go to Korea. We *have* to keep South Vietnam. We *have* to keep these markets. And Russia, at the same time, has also got a technological monster going which requires her to push, not perhaps quite as hard as we have to to push, because we are already so far ahead of it industrially. We've already developed our West. There is no room there any more. We've gone to our west coast and now we have come back upon ourselves. Russia still has great wastelands to develop, so they don't push as hard outside. We're at a much more desperate, much more crucial economic situation. This is related to the question you asked me about: Are we better off? No, I think we're worse off because as our needs, the technological needs of this society are increased, the human being counts for less and less. So I think the big danger now is of a society continuing to close up on the individual.

Q: When do you think this process started?

ALGREN: It certainly began at the time of the Industrial Revolution, but it proceeded much faster right after the Second
World War, when the necessities of war gave us such technological impetus, and we've taken off since 1946. Just the very
idea that sensible men are investing in space now, in elec-
tronics, can give us an idea of the way the country's machin-
ery is souped up. There isn't any going back to disarm;
nobody would stand for it.

Q: Do you think it's a good thing that more and more people not
only in this country but throughout the world are better fed,
better clothed, better housed, and better educated than they
were thirty years ago?

ALGREN: Yes, I think that's good.

Q: Has that opened up our society at all?

ALGREN: I think it's good just as I think it's better for a man to
have an automobile than not to have one, but if the price of
having the automobile is giving up his freedom, then he's
better off not having the automobile.

Q: How do you feel things should have happened, say, with the
beginning of the Industrial Revolution? Do you feel you
are an anarchist or a Marxist, or would you rather not be
that specific about these things? Would you say you are the
kind of anarchist who feels that even Marxism is a snare and
a delusion, or would you say you are a classical Marxist in
the sense that Kautsky was, you know, that Marx would not
join the First International because it was necessarily an
underground organization and therefore undemocratic. I'm
sure you've read Karl Kautsky on this. His *Social Democracy
vs. Communism?*

ALGREN: No. I'm sure I haven't. And I'm sure I don't have to take membership in Marxism or anarchism or *any* society. I don't feel I want to identify myself as a Marxist when I am not a Marxist.

Q: *Are* you a Marxist?

ALGREN: No, I'm not a Marxist. I feel free to be a Marxist one day if I choose to be. *Or* an anarchist for one day. I don't feel that I have any obligation to be committed to any platform promulgated by Kautsky or Marx.

Q: That's why I even hesitated calling you an anarchist, because obviously you do not wish to be labeled. Being labeled or categorized is certainly an infringement on one's mobility and humanness.

ALGREN: And it changes. If I did commit myself to only one idea, I'd only have to betray the idea.

Q: Why would you have to betray the idea?

ALGREN: Because no program ever works out. You have to keep asking yourself, "Well, is it good for the human being?" As soon as you subscribe to a definite program which is supposed to be good for all human beings, sooner or later you have to betray it.

Q: Why?

ALGREN: We mentioned Dick Wright before. He went for a program which was to benefit all mankind. Then he had to betray it because he saw that the program betrayed mankind.

Q: Did he betray it, or did *it* betray him? If I betray you and you retaliate, can you betray me? You can only betray trust, right?

ALGREN: Well, we certainly have trust.

Q: No-no-no. We do trust each other. But *if* I betray you, then you have no reason to trust me any more, so no matter what you do to me you would not be betraying me because you can only betray trust and trust would no longer exist between us. Does this point interest you?

ALGREN: No. You can't commit yourself to any program or to any person. Sooner or later you have to betray that person or that program. You only go from day to day. I trust you today. I trusted in Stevenson. I don't trust him any more.

Q: But now you cannot *betray* Stevenson, no matter what you do, can you?

ALGREN: I can't betray him now. I could have betrayed him when I believed in him in 1952. But I didn't, I'm proud to say. I went and voted for him.

(The next day)

Q: Now, without talking about political things, will you tell me what you think a *good* culture might be like? Not one we have today or do not have. Do not use examples of bad things we have today.

ALGREN: Well, the people would be relaxed. They would be interested in the things of the moment. They would be people capable of using their lives—it's the failure of our society.

Q: Don't talk about the failure of our society. I mean, don't talk about our society of today, for a minute. We've talked a lot about that.

ALGREN: You asked me what my idea of a good society was, and I can't compare it to any but our own.

Q: *Don't* compare it. Don't compare it. Just state it.

ALGREN: I can tell you what I think it should be by telling you what is missing here.

Q: Well, if that's the way you want to do it, O.K. But it is also possible just to talk about it.

ALGREN: Well, everybody would look better for one thing. Their faces would have more of a look of responsibility. They wouldn't look irresponsible, as many Americans do, irresponsible to themselves, that is. They wouldn't look as incredulous as many Americans do.

Q: You really *can't* talk about good things without knocking America?

ALGREN: There is *no* such thing as talking about good things. You can call it knocking if you want; I'm just calling it observing. You can say I'm knocking the city of Chicago by saying that Chicago is a bleak and joyless city, full of untold thousands of people living bleak and joyless lives. I'm not knocking Chicago. I'm just saying this is the evidence of my eyes.

Q: Go ahead.

ALGREN: I can also say that in this hypothetical society the people will have not only the opportunity but the capacity when they get up in the morning to enjoy the day for its own sake. They will enjoy the weather. They will enjoy everything that is given man to enjoy. The day would not be something simply to be used for the purpose of putting together a week of hard-working days for a year, for twenty-five years to get on a pension. That's a waste. What have you done? You have had nothing.

Q: *Try* not to talk in negative terms about good things.

ALGREN: This is very positive because it means that in our hypothetical society, a *real* society, that in each of those twenty-
five years each person would have enjoyed every day. He
would have enjoyed the weather. He would have enjoyed
food. He would have enjoyed friends. He would have had
love. He would have seen the world. He would have read.
He would have used his mind and his heart and his brain.
He would have *used* himself. Then when he had used himself
up his death wouldn't be anything particularly tragic,
wouldn't be tragic at all. What *is* tragic is the sight of people
dying who have never lived and we've got a *whoooooooole*
civilization full of them. You very seldom see anybody in this
civilization who has a satisfying life in human terms.

Q: Do you know people today who have satisfying lives?

ALGREN: Yes.

Q: Do they come from any one particular stratum of our culture?

ALGREN: No. No.

Q: Any particular race?

ALGREN: No, not at all. They are the people who have had
strength and persistence and a reasonable amount of luck
and have stuck to it. But how many of them are there?

Q: Tell me a little more about that. *How* have they managed to
make it?

ALGREN: Oh, persistence more than anything else—knowing what
they want. Very few people know what they want. I don't suppose one person in a thousand really knows what he wants
and that he wants nothing but *that,* and that he is willing to
work toward that and then is happy when he has that.

Q: Is happiness a result or is it another one of these processes we were talking about?

ALGREN: Happiness is a relative thing. It implies some kind of work that is meaningful, and meaningful work is in short supply. I don't think there is any meaningful work outside of the arts.

Q: What about medicine?

ALGREN: That's an art. Isn't medicine an art? Sure, medicine is meaningful, so is the law—in practical terms of course. But I put the arts in a more meaningful category than either medicine or law, where you are able to save the lives and postpone the deaths in your whole lifetime of a thousand people maybe, or you restore health for a limited number of people, and if you are a very good lawyer you save people from injustice, but that, too, is limited. For the man who paints, however, and the man who writes, or the person who can act, it is unlimited. The work goes from generation to generation. You can reach all of mankind. We still talk about Sarah Bernhardt, and they'll be looking at Picasso, and so forth. I mean there's *no* limit to what you can do if you once interpret the human being to the rest of the race. It lasts. That's the only thing that does last. A successful brain operation only lasts as long as the man's brain is alive. But we'll be reading *David Copperfield* as long as English is read, or as long as any other language is read.

Q: Do you see any of this coming about? Is this kind of culture evolving out of our culture?

ALGREN: Not out of our culture, no.

Q: Do you see it evolving out of any culture in the world today?

ALGREN: No, I don't. But since I'm essentially optimistic, I can't imagine a world in which man is totally decimated or degraded. He's always taken setbacks, he's slipped back, but I can see where our present cultures might be replaced by other, fresher cultures.

Q: Which ones?

ALGREN: Well, certainly new things are happening in Africa. You don't know—it's a beginning of something new. I think a country like Britsh Guiana is beginning something in which they might preserve what we began with and which very obviously we've abandoned.

Q: (*Laughter*)

ALGREN: (*Smiling*) Buried on our expressway somewhere.

Q: If you had charge of our culture—without being an oppressive totalitarian—if you had the influence and the power to make changes in our culture, how would you go about it? How would you open up our society so that we could get this kind of ideal culture?

ALGREN: I'd turn over the narcotics problem to doctors instead of to policemen the way it is now.

Q: What about writers? Would you see to it that they were better paid?

ALGREN: No. I don't think that's a basic thing. I don't think you'd do anything more than if you went around and gave every writer a thousand bucks, anybody who claimed he was a writer. I'd put the ninety-nine billion dollars—whatever it is—that's being appropriated for the Air Force and the Navy, and I'd put it into schools. I'd put it into traveling scholarships. I'd make it possible for thousands of Americans to go to China or Russia, anywhere.

Q: Would you do anything about making an alliance between the United States and Russia against China?

ALGREN: No. I wouldn't be against anybody. I'd have as many Chinese students over here as possible. I'd mix things up as much as possible—I mean racially. I'd have people going to school. I'd try to have enough schools to equip children so that by the time they're fifteen they could do something more than handle a springblade knife—catch their interest in something. Basically what I'd do—in very general terms—would be to try to establish human relationships with other human beings in every aspect of life. I'd make it possible for Russians not just to visit us, but to actually live here for five, ten years, while Americans would go over there not just to go to Russia with preformed ideas of what they are, but to *live* there for five or ten years.

Q: What else?

ALGREN: Well, I've had people tell me—people my own age—casually assure me that I've gotten a great deal out of my life, that I've seen a lot, and that always surprises me because my own consciousness is that I've gotten very, *very* little, a thin trickle of what could be seen, and the reason that the little, little trickle that I've gotten out of fifty-five years seems a lot to them is that they've gotten absolutely nothing. In fact, they don't even know that there is so much to be seen. Fifty-five years isn't enough, and I think most people get absolutely nothing. A few lucky people get a little bit. But I've hardly seen the world. I've seen a few countries. I've had a couple of days here and a couple of days there. I've never seen Africa. I probably never will. I've never seen China. There is no reason why anybody on this earth shouldn't see those countries and shouldn't have time to live there. It seems that we're almost cut off from the natural marvels that people from other times and other places were aware of.

Q: Such as?

ALGREN: If I had all this money that's going into blowing up the Van Allen radiation belt and all that, I'd rather put it into fishponds. Put a big fishpond right in the middle of a city, with a variety of fish in it. I mean, whoever looks at fish? You could spend a whole life looking at fish. I think if you gave kids a chance to look at fish—what a marvelous thing happens there. We never get time to look at a fish or a bird. All I'm saying is I guess what all of us know—that there's no end to the miracles and we're too busy to look at them. I'd bring them around. I'd make for some kind of spaciousness in the city. These springblade kids—my friend Ruth, who runs Jazz Limited in Chicago, said they had a little rumble outside the place the other night. They go outside and three kids try to stick up a cab driver. They stopped the driver, the driver slowed down, a colored guy, and they start whipping him. Two other guys, two older white guys tried to help the cab driver and in no time at all they were both lying on the ground. The three kids whipped both of them. I mean kicked them both senseless, and then they stood around. They stood on the other side of the street and when Ruth came out they were congratulating each other. "You did good, man." They didn't run until about sixteen squad cars came around. Two were caught and one got away. But you don't get any kind of regret out of them. These kids were just born into something that has never offered them anything. They don't even feel anything. There's no pang about hurting anybody. Somebody got in their way. They are just totally unaware that there's anything else to do but to get people out of their way. There *are* other things to do. Only nothing is given to them, and when we don't give them anything they go and get something which can be a little ugly. Chicago is full of such guys. I wasn't even surprised by the story. I've seen guys getting their head kicked off at two o'clock in the morning and I've said something to the other guy, "Let the guy go," or something. And he'd say, "You want some too?" I'd say, "No, I don't want anything," and I'd beat it. But it makes you a little uneasy because you're physically helpless against these guys. That's what I think is wrong. I think there's a much greater danger from these guys, local and otherwise, than there is from the Russians getting a space station on the moon before we do.

Q: Are you aware that if you put all your comments about the United States and Russia together, that you end up with much of the line of the Communist Party in America, although I know you are *not* a Communist?

ALGREN: Well, I don't know what the Party line is. The Party line, so far as I know, isn't a line at all. It's very wavering. If it's a line, it doesn't go straight. The Party line as I remember it is something that changes according to political expediency. But if I said I believe this is so and that, and somebody said, "Well, yes, but you know the Communists say so too," then I say, "Well, good. I'm glad to have them." . . .

Q: You and I disagree about politics. We disagree about sociology. We disagree about history. We disagree about nuclear testing. But I *think* we agree on the worth—no matter how lyrical it sounds—we agree on the worth of the human individual, and his power and glory.

ALGREN: Only on his worth. Spare me the power. *And* the glory.

11 *Writers and Writing*

ALGREN: I thought of something else after we talked about Miss de Beauvoir the other day. I don't know whether or not this is useful, but in reflection I didn't know who the woman was when she first came. I knew she was a Frenchwoman and I liked her. While I was busy showing her Chicago there was a copy of *The New Yorker* there which I didn't open. After she left, I looked at it and there was a profile there, a very interesting woman, Frenchwoman, an Existentialist, and as I read it I began thinking. I began to see a resemblance in this party I'd just spent three days with. I guess I simply had never caught her name. Then I read it a second time and, well, she was just here, you see. I didn't know really that she was a French feminist, femininist, feminist?

Q: Feminist.

ALGREN: Feminist, yeah. But we had already begun a relationship that assumed the secondary status of the female in relation to the male. This was how the relationship got off onto that. It had no philosophical basis. A few years later Miss de Beauvoir found a philosophical justification—but that was a literary discovery and had nothing to do with any living human being. The irony of the title *The Second Sex* is a purely literary irony. In reality there was no irony. Second is where second belongs. It is still interesting to me how a woman may accept the secondary status of the second sex in a personal relationship and the relationship never got off that basis, which contradicts her philosophical premise. I guess this must be very interesting, I don't know. I'm a little bored by it.

Q: I think it's very interesting.

ALGREN: I thought posterity ought to know that.

Q: The look on my face shows I was trying to restrain myself from asking specific questions. . . .

ALGREN: Well, don't restrain yourself. . . . If they're too specific, I'll answer them more specifically than you have.

Q: She was a classical Victorian woman?

ALGREN: I don't know just what you mean by that. She is a rather puritanical woman. She understood that in the relationship between a man and a woman the man is the dominating factor specifically. This was my premise and I hadn't achieved a philosophical basis to reverse it. If this sounds ungallant, I mean it's got to be considered that I never even mentioned my relationship to her until she (*laughter*), until she featured the relationship in a book of her own, and so there is no point in being secretive about it, although I must say that in our relationship from 1946, forty-seven, forty-eight, forty-nine, fifty, up until the publication of *The Mandarins,* not even my friends knew I had this relationship at all. In Paris it became plain enough because we met people there and we were together and very easily accepted there.

Here I never saw any occasion. When we traveled together, I simply said I was going away. I was going down to
the banana country and look around and I never put it in a
"we" sense because I thought this might turn out to be a little
bit awkward, and so it wasn't until after the publication of
The Mandarins, when she volunteered the graphic description of her love life, that I got me some very flattering invi-
tations in the mail. And I quote: "Why don't you spread
your favors around?" "When you get to New York, call me
at the Hotel So-and-So," signed, "P.S. And it will be good."
To these letters I didn't make any answer. Except there was
one I answered. I said, "You'll have to remember that this relationship of which you just read involved a man who was
thirty-nine and I'm now sixty-six, so there's not much point
any more, is there, Dear?"

Q: How did you feel when you saw her writings which included
   you? . . .

ALGREN: Oh I think first I was very much amused. I thought it
   was funny, as though I was reading about somebody else, as
   though I were reading a little gossip column about Hollywood. I enjoy those things You know, Jayne Mansfield
   snitching on somebody or somebody snitching on Jayne Mansfield. But *Time* picked it up and you know *Time*—what
   nails are to the carpenter nastiness is to *Time*. What can you
   do? They send the stuff through the mails, and if you call
   up and complain, they'll compound the injury by reporting
   your complaint too. There's nothing you can do about *Time*.

Q: What I meant was, you had kept quiet about it, about your
   relationship with de Beauvoir. You hadn't flaunted it, or
   flouted it.

ALGREN: Fluted it.

Q: Fluted it. Whatever you're supposed to do, you hadn't done. You didn't do what she did and it was your private affair. Well, I just want to ask you generally—I've asked you this question before and we were talking about it earlier—about literary people and their need to tell everybody what's going on with them sexually.

ALGREN: *Telling all* has its risks. You have to do more than to share the compulsion of Stendhal and Rousseau—if you don't make literature out of confession, all you've done, as with Miss de Beauvoir, is to confess. Not only that, but to confess gratuitously—*telling all* upon the premise that the world has been waiting for the news when the world hasn't been waiting for *anything of the kind*. All the world has been waiting for is for you to shut up for a second. To publicize a relationship existing between two people is to destroy it as a two-person relationship: it shows the relationship could never have meant a great deal in the first place, if its ultimate use has so little to do with love. It becomes something else. See, the big thing about sexual love is it lets you become her and lets her become you, but when you share the relationship with everybody who can afford a book, you reduce it. It no longer has meaning. It's good for the book trade, I guess, but you certainly lose interest in the other party.

Q: I'd like you to explain a couple of things to me. The gang of writers in America these days and for the last ten years, the last twenty years, has been talking about how the individual is being obliterated by the mass and how things are being dehumanized, depersonalized, and yet the same writers who complain about that go out of their way to make a real mockery out of anything personal, private, affectionate, or beautiful. Why do they do that? What are they talking about?

ALGREN: I think you have to be specific here. I've really thought of it as the cult of violence. I don't mean Hemingway. I mean, say, Mailer and Jones and a host of lesser writers, to whom violence is self-sufficient. I don't put either Mailer or Jones far above Mickey Spillane because all three have this antagonism toward personal relationships. The world to Mailer and the world to Jones and the world to Spillane is really the same world of which Budd Schulberg wrote in *What Makes Sammy Run?*, that is, of the man who can operate only on a superiority-inferiority basis. You win or you lose. If you don't, if you don't make the money, if you don't make the girl, you lose the money and you lose the girl. There's no concept, as there was in Hemingway, of having a relationship on a human level in which the primary consideration isn't "Do I win or do I lose?"

Q: I was thinking in terms of the literary gatherings you and I have been to lately where writers, highly talented, established writers, are very critical of our culture, of what they call our culture's "mean aspects," and these same writers are mean themselves.

ALGREN: Well, to go back to what I'm saying, I think we seem to be living in a win-or-lose culture where the ethics of the used-car dealers are not inferior to that of the writer, the critic, or the magazine editor.

Q: But I don't understand the stance or the posture or the position from which intellectuals can complain about the paucity of American life and the coldness of American life and the mechanical love life that we are supposed to have, when they themselves are the greatest priests in the priesthood of this kind of sterile world. I don't understand that. Can you explain it to me?

ALGREN: No, I can't explain it to you. I have observed about the same phenomenon and all I can say is we're living in a time when American literature doesn't know who it is any more.

Q: Well, now, whose fault is that?

ALGREN: Oh, I don't think it's attributable to, to any one group or persons. It's part of the corruption of our own time. I mean, what other time could you turn on a television program and the commercial shows you a woman using two kinds of peanut butter. She discovers with great pleasure that a certain kind of peanut butter doesn't break the bread. A crucial issue is made of what peanut butter, when spread on bread, will break the bread and what peanut butter will not break the bread. This at a time when the threat of racial violence and when the flames are blowing from every direction that can set the world on fire. There is something a little bit gruesome if it weren't so comical. Or a thing can be comical and gruesome too.

Q: You're not answering my question. It's my fault.

ALGREN: Well, I've answered indirectly.

Q: I don't know. It's a great problem for me. And I think it's a great problem for you, too, because very often what you do at these social gatherings is to affect your own stance, you know that? And your stance is that of a clown and you are in absolute control as you do it.

ALGREN: Well, I can't just stand there. I have to react. How deliberate this is, I don't know. I don't have to think beforehand: Now I'm going to clown. You have to have some defense.

Q: I know that. I know that.

ALGREN: And my way of reacting is by mockery. And if I mock myself, I assume that people around don't take themselves any more seriously than I do.

Q: But you know that's not true.

ALGREN: Why? At a cocktail party? I don't take this party seriously that we went to the other night. You took it seriously before we went there and I told you it's not a serious business.

Q: No, I didn't take it seriously in the way you mean. I personally find it disheartening to see our people putting each other on.

ALGREN: I think it was fun.

Q: I find it saddening to find people putting each other on, the same people who complain that it's wrong to put people on.

ALGREN: Well, what are you going to do with people? They put you on, you put them on.

Q: Now I can take care of myself.

ALGREN: If a girl comes up and says with a winning smile, "You're just about the greatest thing that has happened to womankind, not to mention literature," and so forth, I'm going to go along with her and even show her a little bit more than she expected. I mean, she's putting me on and I'm putting her on, and she marvels at her good fortune in meeting me, I'll marvel at my good fortune in meeting her and, ah . . .

Q: Well, then it is all a lot of shit.

ALGREN: What are you there for? I mean, I'm not going to say, "You don't look like a really great actress to me and you've got some mileage on you, too," and she isn't going to say to me, "You're losing your hair for one thing, and is that a plate you've got in your mouth?" No, they are very sharp molars, and I've got a full head of hair. Anything she wants to put out, I'll accept. I mean, if you feel that way, don't go to a party. You know beforehand that it's going to be one spoof after another and some free drinks, and then you forget it. You don't continue those things after the party. You don't write notes saying I'm sorry for what I said if you're not sorry for what you said. You put it out of mind.

Q: How can anyone who agrees with what you've just said complain about nonwriters who do the same thing?

ALGREN: I haven't heard that complaint. I've never complained about nonwriters. That isn't my beef.

Q: Aren't you concerned about the lack of love in our culture? Aren't you concerned about—

ALGREN: At moments when I'm working. But if I have a good horse going at the Big A, or somewhere, I'm going to get out there. I'm not going to wake up concerned with the lack of love in this society. I'm going to go out there and try to get a bet down, and I can't do both things.

Q: O.K. Well, then, you know I have been misinformed about you.

ALGREN: But you know I've never come in here on wings.

Q: No, the purpose of this interviewing is to find out what you think and if I make the error—

ALGREN: When I get ready to take off, I mean, when I do sprout wings, you're going to be the first to know.

Q: If I—

ALGREN: And I'm not going to tell you now, since you've deangel-
ized me, why I've got a very good thing I've been promised
by a jockey, whose brother is also a jockey. When they get
a good thing going, he's going to tell me. His friend, he's going
to tell his friend—

Q: No, the purpose of the interviewing is to find out what you
think and feel, what you've done, who you are, and what you
want to do. And if I start out with any preconceived notions
that are wrong, it's certainly your duty to point out to me
where I'm being naïve or sentimental.

ALGREN: Uh-huh. You're inclined to sentimentality.

Q: I guess I am, yeah, but I don't know what the word means
really, but whatever it is—

ALGREN: Well, I won't tell you.

Q: What is sentimentality? What is sentimental?

ALGREN: Oh, it's an indulgence in emotion. You want men and
women to be good to each other and you're very stubborn
in thinking that they want to be. Sentimentality is a kind of
indulgence in this hope. I'm not against sentimentality. I
think you need it. I mean, I don't think you get a true picture
of people without it in writing.

Q: Go on.

ALGREN: It's a kind of poetry, it's an emotional poetry, and, to
bring it back to the literary scene, I don't think anything is
true that doesn't have it, that doesn't have poetry in it. To
get back to Mailer, I think he carries, you might say, the
seeds of his own disaster in him, inasmuch as there is this
failure of anything poetic. I think even a critic has to have
a touch of the poetic. I don't care how accurate a man's

judgments are, how accurate, that is, according to Freud or according to Marx or according to Bill Buckley or according to anybody. I think the accuracy according to Parrington or according to Veblen—an erudite judgment based on sound academic knowledge, which you have in such a critic as Alfred Kazin, for example, and half a dozen others—is also accompanied by such a total lack of any poetic feeling that it just turns to dust. Nothing, nothing, nothing that a writer like Kazin writes can last for twenty-four hours after Kazin retires because of this lack. I mean, it's journalism. Journalism dies. Some of the older critics, much older, who have this touch—Edmund Wilson, Van Wyck Brooks, and Malcolm Cowley—Malcolm Cowley is the one who caught on to Hemingway, not these much littler people running around. *He* was the one who saw in Hemingway a great nocturnal writer, related to Poe, not at all the war hero. All that these critics who have no sense of the poetic saw in Hemingway was a naturalistic writer who was always out front, an extremely extrovertive kind of man who was always on the firing line somewhere. And they could only see it because they could only see him that way. They could only see him as Hemingway saw himself out front. It takes a touch of the poet to perceive as Cowley did, to perceive that Hemingway was quite the opposite of what he appeared. And I think for this reason Cowley's opinions on Faulkner and on Hemingway are really almost the only ones worth while now, or that will last.

Q: Who is going to last among the young writers, in your opinion? The writers writing today.

ALGREN: I don't know if they're going to last. I have three books that I always bring up. Three great books of our time to my sight line are *Catch-22, Lie Down in Darkness,* and *The Magic Christian.*

Q: Do you think Styron is a writer who'll last?

ALGREN: I think *Lie Down in Darkness* will last. I think *The Magic Christian* will last and *Catch-22* will last. Southern is the comer.

Q: How do you feel about a writer like John O'Hara?

ALGREN: About the same way I feel about John Cheever, except Cheever is possibly better. I think O'Hara and Cheever are the best short-story writers around. I haven't read any novel of O'Hara's since *Butterfield 8* and, ah, what was the other one?

Q: *Appointment in Samarra.*

ALGREN: *Appointment in Samarra,* yeah. Those were great little books. I've never tried his big ones. I understand they're dreadful, but his pieces in *The New Yorker,* the ear is very good and it's always about something. I think he's very good indeed on the short stretch. He writes.

Q: And you feel the same way about Cheever?

ALGREN: Cheever: I've never read a piece that wasn't worth reading of his. Cheever's the only American writer that I can identify without turning the pages of *The New Yorker* back to see who wrote it. I can often tell—I don't know how I can tell—but in the first sentence, even though it's a simple sentence, even though it says nothing more than, "So-and-So got out of the elevator on the fourteenth floor, said 'Good morning' to the elevator starter," I know that, as soon as I see it, I know it's John Cheever.

Q: How about John Updike?

ALGREN: Oh, I've scanned the very glossy surface of his writing. He strikes me as being a very slick, a very intellectual, slick—almost cut to order for *The New Yorker.* I haven't read his books. He doesn't reach me at all. Maybe I haven't tried hard enough. It seems like a literary performance. It's too much performance. There are writers with literary skill who get you, I mean, make you interested, such as this book by Thomas Pynchon. I don't think the best writers writing are literary people at all.

Q: Who are they?

ALGREN: Well, they're almost nameless. I know a couple of people who don't write, really write well at all, but they're, they're tuned in to the American scene much better than much better-known writers. That is, they've had a direct experience with the American scene.

Q: Do you think O'Hara's tuned in to our culture?

ALGREN: Yes, yes, I think he is.

Q: Why doesn't the literary establishment like O'Hara? Why don't the eggheads like O'Hara? I'm talking about the little magazines, college professors, critics, things like that. They don't like O'Hara.

ALGREN: Oh, they don't like O'Hara because he's outside the incubator, pecking around in the yard. The important thing, they feel, is what's going on *inside* the egg. They couldn't catch *Catch-22* either—there was nothing in the yolk to account for it. Well, it's a free country—you can't jail people for thinking W. C. Fields isn't funny. Or that Hemingway was nothing more than an innovator. But it isn't till after you have your bullfight posters hung, your Chianti bottles hung, and your beard is turning white that you're entitled to say this because by then you've done everything Hemingway ever did—but for one detail: he went himself instead of sending somebody. Maybe the invidiousness toward O'Hara is mostly from southern professors—haven't you noticed that he looks more and more like Ulysses S. Grant? These professors don't write—they contrive. Yet, they contrive accurately and make the right connections at *Commentary* or the *Saturday Review,* and they take great care to make friends at writers' conferences everywhere. And then the thing appears at last and all it rates in the *New York Times Book Review* is a half column toward the back. There's hell to pay then. *He* writes the *right* way and O'Hara writes the *wrong* way, but O'Hara gets the whole front page and makes all the money. No wonder the contriver grows bitter young—and gets mad at *me* for praising *Catch-22* because he thinks that *Catch-22* is still *another* book written the wrong way. "What did you *see* in it?" some English department owl is always reproaching me. And of course the classical answer is to fall back on Louis Armstrong's thing, you know: Somebody asked him, "What is jazz?" And Armstrong answered, "If you don't get it, you don't get it, and there's nothing else to say." I mean this English department owl has reached the age of thirty-five or forty—he's totally humorless and he has no ear; he's a man of letters—and then something like *Catch-22* comes along and throws him, and he wants you to justify it. You can't justify it. It's just there. And the curious thing about it—since we mentioned *Catch-22*—is that it strikes so many nonliterary people. I mean, it's liked almost in despite of the literary scene.

Q: You mean "in spite of."

Algren: No, I mean "in despite of."

Q: No, you don't.

ALGREN: Yes, I do, I really do. I really mean that.

Q: You either mean "in spite of" or "despite.". . .

ALGREN: "No, I mean "in despite of."

Q: The hell you do.

ALGREN: The hell I don't. I'm very sure about that. In despite of everything you say, just to be in despite of you.

Q: I asked you to think about American literature. What did you decide?

ALGREN: Well, you asked me what's the matter with American literature and I think the trouble with American literature is it doesn't know who it is. It thinks it's Henry Miller writing to Lawrence Durrell and then again it thinks it's James Baldwin telephoning Norman Mailer, and then it thinks it's Jack Kerouac, subsisting on Coca-Colas on a cross-country ride to nowhere—

Q: What *is* it?

ALGREN: Actually American literature isn't anybody phoning to anybody or anybody writing about anybody. American literature is the woman in the courtroom who, finding herself undefended on a charge, asked, "Isn't anybody on my side?" It's also the phrase I used that was once used in court of a kid who, on being sentenced to death, said, "I knew I'd never get to be twenty-one anyhow." More recently I think American literature is also the fifteen-year-old who, after he had stabbed somebody, said, "Put me in the electric chair—my mother can watch me burn." Even *more* recently, American literature is a seventeen-year-old kid picked up on a double murder charge, two killings in a boat, in a ship off Miami,

who said he was very glad it happened, he had absolutely
no regrets, his only fear was that he might not get the
electric chair. He had no vindictiveness toward those two
people he killed. He said they were pretty good about it.
They didn't know, they had no idea, that he was going to
come up with a knife. He had, in fact, a little bit of admira-
tion for their coolness. One of them, finding himself stabbed,
said, "Why?" He wanted to know. He said, "I can't tell them
why." But I know he's been trying to get out of it since he's
six years old. This is an honors student, you understand, this
is a bright boy from a respectable home. He never remembers a time when he wasn't fully convinced that death was
better than life. And now he was very contented, his only
worry being that he might not get the electric chair. He's
afraid of that. That's the only fear he has, that he might have
to continue to live. I think that's American literature. I think
it's also the thirty-five-year-old Negro who told me recently,
"The only times I ever felt human is when I've been in jail."
The other times he's been on guard, on guard day and night.
He says, "There's no such thing as a friend and you can't
afford love. The only time I've ever let down, let myself have
a relationship with any other person, is when I've been in
jail." I think it's also the girl who says, "It don't matter
what happens to me because it's really happening to somebody else. I'm not really here." I think American literature
consists of these people. It doesn't consist of the, of the con-
trivers of literature who, after a certain number of years on
campus, are entitled to grow a beard to look like Hemingway
although they opposed Hemingway all the time he was alive.
And I don't think it's the public performers. I don't think
it's the stunt men. This is the very reason I like somebody like
O'Hara, because he deals with Americans who seem to me
to be all around. He seems to be one of the few people who

are really in touch with what a bartender does when he goes broke, with what the relationship is with the woman, with the aging woman who comes in and sits on a barstool and expresses her loneliness one way or another. American literature is also the suspect, picked up for carrying an unregistered gun, who answers, when asked, "If you didn't steal this pistol somewhere, why don't you let us have your fingerprints anyhow, just in case you actually steal one someday," with, "Why should I want to steal a pistol when I have eleven thousand dollars in my pocket?" O'Hara is one of the very few people who is writing about something that goes on, and who himself knows *how* it goes on. He didn't send anybody either. At least he's not writing *about* other writers.

Q: At least he's not interviewing other writers.

ALGREN: At least he's not being interviewed either.

Q: Thanks for this. We'll meet again and talk some more.

ALGREN: O.K.

(*At the next meeting*)

Q: What are you working on?

ALGREN: I've finished the *Who Lost An American?* book and I'll be working on the Hemingway book. It's a book of about the length, I guess, of that Lillian Ross book [on Hemingway]—maybe thirty thousand, thirty-five thousand words, something like that. It will just be an elaboration of the piece I had in *The Nation:* That the guy's importance is not that he represented any particular school of writing or that he was an innovator, but that he was one American writer, maybe the *only* American writer, who actually changed the color of his times, who put his personality on the times. He made the times almost represent *him*. There's an awful lot of meat for controversy when I read the pieces in *Encounter* which you gave me, pieces by somebody named Philip Toynbee and Dwight MacDonald. MacDonald's piece is completely true. There's no way of denying any of it. And it's totally false. He's got a way of totally falsifying a thing and making it appear absolutely invulnerable logic. He also has a lot of malice going. But he's much too smart to reveal it. There's a surface thing, "I'm sorry that this happened," you know. And, "You know what happened to Hemingway." He isn't telling what happened to Hemingway. He's telling what happened to himself. I don't think he knows that, but it's true. I mean Hemingway *did* become a public man. He became more and more a part of the public—everybody's friend—and less of a writer. That was a tragedy there. But what MacDonald scissors-cut very carefully is the effect the man had on people. He changed them. He changed people. If what MacDonald says is true, then the guy, Hemingway, had *no* effect. You might as well say the thirties don't exist because Hemingway's color is on them. I mean he changed his times. So in that sense MacDonald's piece is false.

Q: What about the big book?

ALGREN: There is no big book.

Q: Aren't you going to do another big book?

ALGREN: No. I won't do another big book. There's no chance of thinking about a big book. If you do the big book there's no way—at least I have no way—of doing a big book and doing anything else. You don't do anthologies, you don't do essays on other writers. You don't do travel books. In fact you don't do much of anything but get a scene and you live within the scene and keep pushing that particular scene. You've got to push it every day or else you're pushing a snowball. You've got to cut everything else out. You're never free. And you've got to do that for a couple of years before you can make a pattern or cut a scene that nobody else has touched, unless you are able to do stuff that's been done before, like the battle of Chickamauga. If you're able to go to a library and reconstruct fifteenth-century London or something— that's one way to do a book. But I don't have any way of doing a reconstruction thing. The only way I can write is to try to make something that hasn't been done before, and in order to do that you can't just take notes. You have to *be* there. You write about your own reactions to the scene. You identify yourself with the scene. And you have to get all the details that nobody knows about. You have to be specific.

Q: What would the big book be about *if* you were to do it?

ALGREN: It started to be about the people within the narcotics traffic in Chicago. It wasn't a book primarily about drug addiction. It was simply a story about how two people, a man and a woman, were isolated within a city. Because of their addiction they might as well be within a forest fire. You can't get out. Your connection is on the same block. You can't move off the block. You're chained there. I wanted to write about how, under these circumstances, these two people could create a human world of their own, one that has its own humor and its own way of life, the way two people on a desert island might develop their own peculiar morality and language as they develop a human world within an inhuman one. That's what— But it would take a lot of work. It would mean going to a lot of trials. It would mean talking to lawyers. It means talking to cab drivers. It would take two years to write and it would certainly take two more years to write it out, that is, to put it so that one sentence follows another with coherence, so that the sentences stop when they should stop, and so that the whole book is sustained on one level. The main thing is just to be able to keep it going.

Q: Well now, you are fifty-five years old.

ALGREN: That's right.

Q: How many more years of active writing do you think you have?

ALGREN: As many as I want.

Q: Twenty-five? thirty? forty? You have a lifetime of writing ahead of you, don't you?

ALGREN: I also have a lifetime of living, and I hope we are pointing toward the issue that came up in Chicago when you said, "Well, you seem preoccupied with the fear of selling out." But I pulled a reverse on you there.

Q: You mean in the cab here in New York when you said you now think the big danger is in *not* selling out?

ALGREN: I said the big danger has changed. Selling out in the thirties and selling out in the sixties are exactly opposite things. Selling out in the thirties would have meant writing for Hollywood, writing pro-Franco pieces, writing for things you don't believe in, for money. It would have meant that under the guise of being a left-winger you take money to talk right wing. It would have meant selling something you had written out of a human concern, selling it to Hollywood for the swimming pool and everything like that, as a lot of people do. That was a real anxiety writers had in the thirties. Should they go to Hollywood? A lot of them said, "I can get five hundred a week." These were guys who had often gone by without making five hundred a year. These guys would say, *I'm* not going to sell out. *I'm* just going to take five hundred a week until I get two thousand. I can save two thousand and come back to New York and write my novel." I don't know of one who did it. I know several good New York poets—one I recall that I don't hear about any more is Al Hayes—Alfred Hayes was a very good poet. He wrote a poem called "The Port of New York" and it is still the best thing written about New York. I haven't heard from him in years. He was the first one who told me he had taken five hundred a week. I know he went to Hollywood. I've never read another good poem by Alfred Hayes.

Q: How does a writer sell out now?

ALGREN: Now I think a writer sells out by undertaking what you call "the big book," which demands years of his time. I don't know how long Saul Bellow would take to write it—I suppose Bellow maybe could do it in a year or a year and a half. I know it would take me four years. Fifty-five and four is fifty-nine. It would mean that in those four years I would live the life of a single man, a man without a family, a man without any real relationship, living pretty much as a solitary thing, with no assurance that I'd be able to protect it in any way. I've never been able to protect a property. And my last two things were used to enhance the security of a couple of producers, men I don't even know.

Q: You were telling me about selling out *now*.

ALGREN: Well, this Macmillan book and the Hemingway book, which are really just straight journalistic things—I can retain pretty much my own life while I do these things. It isn't an all-out thing. The best thing in Henry Miller, one of the best things Henry Miller ever said, was that art goes all out. It's all out. It goes full length. My criticism of guys like Bellow is that they lack greatness really, no matter how skilled, because they never go all out. It's always with care, with care. The big men—Hemingway and Dreiser and Fitzgerald, maybe Fitzgerald particularly—they went all out. Whether they knew what they were doing or not, they went all out. There's a great penalty to it. Saul Bellow will never do that.

Q: Didn't he do it in *The Adventures of Augie March?*

ALGREN: No, I don't think so. No, I don't think he physically could go all out. He writes out of caution and he writes well. But I have never heard of anybody being great at anything—fighters or writers—who did not go all out. Dylan Thomas was an all-outer. The only way I can really write is to go all out and I no longer see any reason for going all out. I don't believe that this stuff I am doing, I don't deceive myself that it is literature. This is journalism. When you don't go all out, you keep something for yourself. A big book is an all-out book in which you limit your life to things that pertain directly to the book.

Q: Which of your books have been big books where you've gone all out? Was *The Man with the Golden Arm* one?

ALGREN: Yeah, pretty much. And maybe that was the *only* one. I was doing something else with all the other ones. That was the only one in which I was doing *nothing* else.

Q: How long did it take you to write that book?

ALGREN: Oh I think about two and a half years. Before that I did the book of short stories, *The Neon Wilderness,* after the war. I wasn't doing anything but that for a while, for about year, so in that sense *Neon* was an all-out book. I did nothing but put that book together. Then I wrote that *Golden Arm* and I really did almost nothing except think about that book and pushing it. That's the only time I did that. There's a certain cost when you do that. You can't do that and have a personal life. It's just skip and jump, you know, which is all right. Well, forty is a little late for a skip-and-jump life like that. Thirty-nine, or whatever it was.

Q: That's good to hear, because that's my age right now and I am working on the big book.

ALGREN: Um. Well, I'd like to see you going all out with a wife and three kids. I'd like to see it. I'd like to see it done.

Q: You think that's pretty hard?

ALGREN: Well, the visual image I have (*laughter*) is of this burlesque skit, you know, at *This Was Burlesque*. They pulled this old-timer. This guy comes on stage, the clown with the old coat on and with this hat on, really idiotic, and it is a whole series of surrealistic scenes, you know. The guy starts it off by coming into the hospital and says, "Can I see the doctor?" and the nurse says, "Oh, but the doctor isn't in. Just take your shoes off and lay down." Oh, she's a big, good-looking broad, you know. He says, "Oh, yeah," and he's looking around. And she says, "If you need anything— yeah, yeah, yeah—call me," she says. Well, he starts think- ing about that and these absolutely fantastic things happen. He jumps up and screams for the nurse and she runs in and by that time all sorts of intruders come in, dancers, everybody. People come in carrying buckets. And every time the nurse runs in she comes in a little too late. "Well maybe," she keeps telling him, "maybe you imagined it." He's all alone again when this *other* guy comes in. He's got a coat on, you know—a real schlemiel—a red coat and a green tie. And he's got a rope. He's pulling a rope over his shoulder and he walks all the way across the stage from one side to the other pulling this rope, and the rope is still coming even after he walks off the stage at the other side and the rope keeps moving across the stage in one unbroken line and then when the other end of the rope appears it's around the guy's neck and it is the same guy, the same guy who was pulling the rope. (*Laughter*) God, I loved that show! But that was the visual image I had of the way you would go all out on a book with a wife and three kids.

Q: But *you* can go all out again, now, can't you?

ALGREN: Yeah, I could. I'm physically able and I've got carfare to go down to the courts and sit there. But I could be elsewhere. I could be taking a sea tour. I mean, what I mean by selling out is: How long are you going to keep on doing what other people want, instead of what you want? Now what I want is what I want. It's real late, you know. My idea of selling out now would be to do the big book and deny myself a personal life. What right have I to do that? If you were able to write a big book in the thirties and you didn't, you'd be irresponsible because the book was wanted, the book was needed. There were people who wanted answers in the thirties and into the 1950's when McCarthy came along and there were all kinds of conscientious people saying, "Why doesn't somebody write something? Why don't the writers say something about this guy?" Now the scene is changed. There is no feeling of this being wanted. Now the whole atmosphere is, "What's the difference? We won't miss it if it don't appear. We don't need it." There is no feeling, that I can sense, of any kind of spiritual need. There's nobody that's going to say, "Good for you, that's just what we need." I can get that kind of thing out of the criticism I do. I can be as critical as the critics. They say, "Well, good for you." I can get that "good for you" without tying myself up.

Q: Who are writing the big books in American these days?

ALGREN: Oh there are none that I know of. I don't know of any big-book writers. I'm sure there aren't any. There are a lot of good little-book writers.

Q: Who are they?

ALGREN: Oh I always bring up that Terry Southern because of that one book. He's a good little-book guy. Saul Bellow is a good little-book guy. So is John Clellon Holmes. I've had enough of Saul Bellow. He's got something called *Herzog* coming out. I know *Herzog*. I mean I've read Saul. *Herzog* is as much a repetition of Bellow as *Lonigan* is a repetition of Farrell. Saul just keeps doing *Herzog*. I don't mind him doing it, but I won't bother to read it. I'd be more interested in a book by John Clellon Holmes. He changes around. And I'd be very interested in a book by Terry Southern. I'd be most pleasantly surprised as hell by another big book by Joe Heller. *Catch-22* to me is a *big* book. You can always tell a big book because it catches the small people out, in the act of being small. Nobody, it seems, gets so indignant at the appearance of a book that is better than anything for years, than the people who live by books.

Q: Did Heller go all the way in *Catch-22?*

ALGREN: Yeah. I think that's an all-out book.

Q: Well, he did that with a wife and children, by the way. It took him eight years.

ALGREN: Yeah. But he didn't take the wife and kids overseas.

Q: How about William Styron's all-outness? Doesn't he do the big book? He has a wife and children.

ALGREN: Well I don't know. All I know is the way he was reviewed. I know a great deal was expected of him after *Lie Down in Darkness* and his friends were disappointed in *Set This House on Fire*. I know Max Geismar, who really wants a good book from Styron, put in—as critics do—he put in a claim on this guy. He went out for Styron. He says, "Styron is the comer." I mean he wanted to be enough of a critic to see that this guy is a comer, but Geismar was disappointed in *Set This House on Fire*.

Q: How about Katherine Anne Porter's big book?

ALGREN: I don't know anything about her. I never read her. I get her mixed with other women. I know she's very good but I get her mixed up with Katherine Mansfield. Then I get *her* mixed up with Mike Mansfield. You can't win them all.

Q: Does Mailer go all out?

ALGREN: Mailer goes as far as the refrigerator. When he gets there he leans on it. Somebody told him that was how Thomas Wolfe did it. What they didn't tell him was that what Wolfe was doing when he was leaning on the refrigerator was writing.

Q: If you have a lifetime of writing ahead of you and a lifetime of living, what things are you going to write if you are not going to write the big book? I harp on this big book thing because it's hard for me to believe you. I think you have a couple more, two, three, four more big books.

ALGREN: I don't say I absolutely won't.

Q: Can you comment on a reservation some people might have that, if you ever were to do a big book, it would be about dope?

ALGREN: It wouldn't be about dope. The dope would be incidental if I used it at all. It's been used so much I'm hesitant.
It would be a book about racket people. I'd be more interested in showing an operation of how the courts work, of the
whole comedy, the whole comedy. I mean it's not all comedy
either. It's the crazy way that the law works. I'd like to use
the Ciucci case, this guy who was electrocuted, this guy who
died, just as an example. This guy never killed his children.
He never killed his kids. He shot his wife, he shot the mother
of the kids after *she* had killed them. He went to the chair
for killing the kids. It worked out in the sloppiest kind of way,
in the most hit-and-miss sort of way. And yet there have
been murders in Chicago, out-and-out murders where the
guy had no trouble getting off at all. A very hit-and-miss
thing. That whole scene. And, oh, a friend of ours went down
to the psychopathic hospital to visit someone, and I've never
been there, but she described this courtroom there, where
people are assigned, where people are committed. She said
it's just like bargain day at Goldblatt's or the Boston Store
or something. They're just jammed in there with people getting rid of people they don't want around. (*Laughter*) It's
just bing, bing, bing. There's one guy, he's just a little
stewed. And they're really shipping them off real fast. No
trouble in getting *any*body committed at all. It's a riot, you
know, just a riot. I would cover that thing and I'd want to
cover the Narcotics Court. I don't know just what the story
would be. I'd want this one thread. I would like it to be about
a woman caught in the middle of it, a woman with a certain
kind of humor about her—a prostitute with a country-girl
kind of humor about her—and see the thing through her eyes.
I'd like her to keep seeing this scene. I mean I don't want the
writer to come out, you know, and say, "THERE'S-GOT-TO-BE
SOME-CHANGES-MADE-IN-THE-POLICE-DEPARTMENT!" and all

that. Just have the girl laughing her head off at the entire scene, and put in as much as possible. I don't say I wouldn't try it, but I'm certainly not going to try to do it unless I take care of other things first.

Q: Like what?

ALGREN: Oh, like being out of debt . . .

Q: May we speak now about your influence? May I say two things? First, you are more influential than you realize. The other thing is that you are not as influential as you could be. What do you think of your influence as a member of the American writing clan? How influential do you think you are? How would you like to be more influential? What would you like to influence?

ALGREN: Well, there is being influential and then there's being influential. Being influential on the writing people of America isn't my idea of being influential. I imagine I've been influenced, I know I've influenced some people in writing, but this isn't what I mean by influence. I feel that I'm much less influential than you think. I'm sure I could be and ought to be more influential.

Q: How would you like to be more influential? In what way?

ALGREN: I would like to have books that I have written be influential. My idea of an influential writer would be a writer who moves people to action. Hemingway's *For Whom the Bell Tolls*—this moved men's minds. He presented a way of feeling—that men belong to one another. It was very moving and it moved many people. It influenced people. It influenced their hearts. And when Wright came out, Wright was very influential. Even now, on, I believe, July or August 3rd, a Negro is scheduled to die here [in Chicago] in the electric chair and we're uneasy about it. Ever since Wright wrote *Native Son* he's made us uneasy about capital punishment. I call that influence. And Steinbeck's *Grapes of Wrath.*

Q: A friend of mine recently wrote an article for *Commonweal,* the highbrow liberal Catholic review, on dope addiction and how it should be treated as a disease. His name is Will Sparks and he knows a lot about the problem and one of the things that first brought the problem home to him was your book *The Man with the Golden Arm.* That is an example of one direct personal influence. He sent me reprints of the article and I sent one of the reprints to my congressman, John Lindsay, who is a Republican from the so-called silk-stocking congressional district of New York City. This is the same congressman who recently sent out questionnaires to certain constituents and got back twenty-five thousand answers, the majority of which followed the liberal Democratic line. I sent him a reprint of Will's article with a note saying I wanted him to do something about seeing that drug addiction would be treated as a disease. A note came back from his secretary saying he was out of town but my letter would be brought to his attention right away, and meantime would I like to see copies of three bills that Lindsay had already offered to Congress on dope addiction.

ALGREN: Yeah.

Q: The bills were for setting up hospitals and things like that. Sparks's article said that people who wanted drugs should get them by prescription, you know, or even as easily as one can get a quart of whiskey. None of these bills went that far. But they did intend to set up hospitals; the bills were meant to make it easier for drug addicts to be treated more like human beings. All this has happened in the last ten years. And *Hatful of Rain* and *The Connection*—I am not trying to flatter you here, Nelson Algren, but it is the opinion of many other people too that *Hatful of Rain* and *The Connection* would have been a much longer time in coming if it had not been for *The Man with the Golden Arm.*

ALGREN: The book had an effect, but that's not influence. When we were talking about my Hollywood experience what I was trying to convey was that the loss there, the loss in money, was not the irrecoverable thing. That can be recovered. But there *had* been as much of a possibility in this book for influencing the American scene as that *Grapes of Wrath* had. And not only because the book dealt with drug addiction but because it dealt with the disease of isolation. Instead, as a film the book was, well, what was it used for? The book was used in order to, oh, enhance the public image of a couple of ghosts. The book was used to enhance the public image of a good singer, a bad actress, and two hundred pounds of solidified grease.

Q: But millions of people got the message that drug addicts are human beings.

ALGREN: Not from the movie they didn't.

Q: No?

ALGREN: No. They got the idea from the movie that it's something they don't have to bother with if they went to see the movie. It was the use of a public issue for a private purpose. The movie put a tragic situation into a pleasant little representation making it possible to really dismiss the subject. The book should really have been used seriously. But the effect of the movie was, "Well, Sinatra was good in it." That's about it. It was successful. The book was written out of a—well— the writer caught a real cry of anguish. It was the same cry that Ring Lardner heard under the stands, that there is anguish. And the same that Steinbeck heard and reported. Because the Steinbeck movie was a good movie, made with understanding, the voice, the cry as it were, was heard. It was a movie used to communicate the cry. *The Golden Arm* movie was used to make this cry of anguish something that could be sung on a jukebox, that Sinatra could perform to, and that was its whole meaning.

Q: Tell me what would be, to you, for you, what would be signs, indications that you were influential?

ALGREN: If *The Arm* had been used right, then I would have been asked by people who are interested in the drug problem to talk about it. I've seen at least twenty TV panels discussing drug addiction since then.

Q: Have you ever been asked?

ALGREN: No, I've never been asked. I've seen policemen give the policeman's version. I've seen professors talk with sociologists about it. I've seen the backs of heads of addicts and all that. But I've never seen an addict represented articulately. I've never seen the addict's point of view put over on a TV program. I've seen Anslinger, former head of the Narcotics Bureau of the Treasury Department. I've seen him defend the policeman's job. I've *never* seen his opinion forcefully opposed—that you have no more right, I mean in the name of humanity, to punish people for being drug addicts than you have the right to punish them for having tuberculosis. I am a person, at least I have been assured by addicts that I am a person who isn't an addict who understands the addict from the inside. One addict said, "You know as much about it as if you had been on and gotten off." Except I never bothered to get on. And this has value, if people are interested. The book caught interest in that. But as soon as the movie came out it became a pipe dream. It became Otto Preminger bowing as a crusader, and the marvel of Sinatra turning out to be an actor instead of a singer, and a wooden-faced Bohemian girl walking around because she's got a lot of money behind her. This was it. So it was a loss. I think it was a loss to people who are addicts, who are helpless, and to me it was a loss of influence.

Q: Other than your interest in these matters about addiction, what other indications could there be to prove to you that you are influential as a writer?

ALGREN: If somebody asked me to run for office.

Q: For political office?

ALGREN: Uh-huh.

Q: I hope I can take you seriously.

ALGREN: It's no gag. Gore Vidal is taken seriously even though he ran a losing race.

Q: And Michener in Bucks County, P-A.

ALGREN: Gore Vidal would be a very good man to have in office.

Q: How about James Michener?

ALGREN: I don't know much about him but I would certainly vote for him over his competitors.

Q: Being asked to run for office would indicate you were influential?

ALGREN: It would indicate people are really beginning to trust you. Nobody puts you in office unless they have trust and respect, which I don't think they have for writers generally. And I think it's the writer's own fault too, when he gets on this literary thing, as Mailer did—your quote of what Mailer said to Schlesinger—when Mailer replied to Schlesinger's question, "What did you do?" He had some literary achievement as an answer to what he did. He didn't do *any*thing. In that sense there are two kinds of writers: the writers who think they have influence, and the writers who know they don't. Mailer might think he has. I know I don't.

Q: Would you like to run for Congress?

ALGREN: For Congress?

Q: Or have you thought about it this much?

ALGREN: No, I just thought about it this minute. It's just an example. It's just a way of being taken seriously. I don't expect to be asked to run for anything.

Q: Congress would be more influential, say, than—

ALGREN: That would imply an enormous interest and an enormous confidence which I think could hardly happen to any writer in this country. Once somebody tried to get Sandburg to run for something and although Sandburg was tremendously popular, there was immediate opposition among conservative people the second his name came up. They realized he was so well known and so popular in the Middle West that there was actually a possibility he might run for something. The conservative people immediately suggested gently that he just stay on the literary side. They don't want people who believe in changing things, and Sandburg at that time was a man who believed in changing things.

Q: What else would indicate to you that you had influence as a writer?

ALGREN: Oh, I think just by your mail, you know, where your mail comes from.

Q: How is your mail?

ALGREN: I have an overbalance of maladjusted people.

Q: Who write to you?

ALGREN: Uh-huh.

Q: What do they want? Help? Advice? Comfort? Do they want what everybody else wants?

ALGREN: They are dissatisfied people who seem to think that somebody knows all the answers. I run into this at writers' conferences, too. It's a common experience. Women. Especially women, just about the time of their change of life, begin to confuse me with Jesus Christ. One almost killed me. I started telling it to Saul Bellow and this same thing happened to him at Sugarloaf [Breadloaf]. It's almost a psychological pattern. They're very unhappy, you see, usually the victims of a marriage that has gone bad, and they begin to see in you somebody who can save them. They'll tell you, "You can help me." It doesn't do any good to say, "I can't help you, unless you've got a manuscript for me to read, if that's what you mean." She says, "That's not what I mean," very significantly. But this is very dangerous because if you can't help them they might stick something in you. I thought my experience of running into a couple of homicidal women was unique, but it's not unique. Of course I have great influence with them. I have great influence with homicidal women. Women who are halfway between homicide and just general unrest, I influence toward homicide.

Q: Where did this happen?

ALGREN: It happened twice. Once it happened over on Wabansia and Bosworth streets right after the war. The other time was in Missoula, Montana, at a summer writers' conference. On

Wabansia and Bosworth this woman showed up. It was partly my own fault, because I had a letter in the early part of the year, a very sensible letter, from this girl reminding me that she had worked with me in the same office, about nine years before. She said she had been sick the last couple of years. The letter came from West Irving Park, the state hospital for the insane. But the letter was very sensible, very steady handwriting, and she said she had heard I had a book out and she'd like to read it. So I sent her one and put a return address on it, and that was about in February, and it was a June night and my friend de Beauvoir, who also reports the incident, was there. We had been out on the West Side somewhere and we had some wine and came back about twelve o'clock. It was a very narrow little gangway, you know, just two steps, and I was so used to it I just started up, and I could *feel* somebody standing up there so I came down. It was dark and I came down to the alley where I could see. I said, "Who's there?" And this girl calls out her name and I could just see a dim figure. Then I remembered this letter so I told Simone, "It's all right," and we went up. There was this rather heavy-set girl and she said, "Oh, I didn't know you were with somebody." I said, "It's all right, come on and have some coffee." She was very shy, very shy about it, and coming in and all, says, "I don't want to interfere." "No, no, that's all right, come on in." So we came in and this, of course, took Simone entirely by surprise. She didn't know what to make of it. This other woman was very heavy-set, with a little sort of blue and white dress, and I had a bottle of Scotch on the table. I gave the girl a cup of coffee and she says, "Do you mind?" and I says, "No, no, relax, just have a cup of coffee," and she says, "You know, Nelson, everybody thinks so much of you." I said, "Oh, they do?" She says, "Yes, I told the woman downstairs that I was waiting for you and,"

she says, "Do you mind if I have a little Scotch?" I said,
"No, help yourself." So she drank the Scotch—and she said,
"Oh yes, I talked to the woman downstairs and she thinks
the world of you and she asked me to come in and I waited
down there and some other people came in and talked about
you. Could I have a little more Scotch?" "Oh, yeah, help
yourself." And then she said, "We were talking about everybody—could I have a little more Scotch?" So she stood
up. She said, "You son-of-a-bitch! You're responsible for
this!" I looked at her. Her arms were black and blue, you
know, where they had held her in restraint. It was a very quick
change. She was very angry. I said, "Sit down, sit down, sit
down." She was very excited. She was very excited. She got
very excited about it and she said, "Where are your razor
blades?" So I jumped up. There are some on the shelf and I
tried to get them away. I threw them away. I said, "I don't have
any razor blades." So she found one in the little john there and
she jumped into the john. But there was a little window out
on a little porch so I went out onto the porch and I could see
her in the john. She was shaving her arms. Then she came out
with the razor blade. She gave me directions. She pointed at
de Beauvoir saying, "Send this woman home. I've waited a
long time for this night." I said, "No." I said, "You know
this woman's a guest. You've got to be nice to guests you
know." And Simone was dying by this time. She was laughing her head off. She knew I was in some sort of trouble.
And of course I got all the knives and everything out of the
way. The woman's too big to handle and she's quite violent,
you could see. It was the Scotch that did it. If I hadn't fed
her the Scotch, she might have stayed under control. Then
she started shaving her legs. She shaved her legs, then she
went to the mirror in the other room. She shaved herself
under the arms very narcissistically. She said, shaving her

arms, "You know, this will make all the difference in the world." Oh, man, I couldn't get her out of there. And finally I did. I got a cab driver and gave him five bucks to take her to a hotel. Well, the next morning Simone and I are set to go to the track when we look out and there's that girl. She's back, out on the porch. She says, "I've got to see you." She's got to get in there, got to get in. I said, "You can't come in." But I couldn't get her out of there and I didn't want to go out there and fight her. So I said, "Well, I don't like to do it, but—" Well, I called the hospital and I said, "Is anybody missing *there?* We have a woman *here.*" They said, "Oh, yeah, she escaped at six o'clock yesterday." I said, "Would you mind coming and getting her?" And they said, "Oh, no, we don't pick them up. We just send wires to the police station. Tell your local police station." This was all very casual. I guess the escapes are pretty common. So we had to call the station. By that time she had just collapsed. She was just a heap. They came and just put her in the wagon. Routine.

Q: What was the other time?

ALGREN: At Missoula, Montana. I went up there for a summer conference and they gave me an office and the students set time aside for an interview and they'd bring in their man-uscripts and you read them. But this woman walked in for the interview—just walked in on somebody else's time—a big girl with a Scandinavian name. She was about thirty-eight. She started off. She said, "Well, what do you want to talk about?" I said, "Have you got any manuscripts?" "No," she said. I said, "Well, what do *you* want to talk about?" "Sex," she says. "Sex. That's what I want to talk about." So I said, "Oh, well, all right." She says, "Have you ever been knocked down? Really knocked down?" I said, "Oh, I don't remember." She says, "Well I have." She says, "Do you have a car?" So I says, "No, I don't have a car." She says, "Well I have. We'll take a trip Monday or so, you know, go up in the mountains." This was about Friday. Monday came around and I had breakfast with her and I started to get a little uneasy then. I backed out of the trip. I said I couldn't go. And she said, "Well, you know you could help me." I said, "No. I can't help you unless you've got a manuscript." Then she came to the class I was teaching and she sat in the front row and kept interrupting with silly questions. You couldn't say *any*thing but she'd come in with something. So I said, "All right. You either shut up or come up here. You want to take over the class?" She said, "No." So I said, "Then shut up or come up here. One of the two. There are other people here interested in what I'm saying. If you're not interested, that's all right." She got up and she went out. So we got rid of her. It wasn't easy. Next morning she was waiting for me at the dormitory, the men's dormitory where women are not allowed. But early. It must have been seven o'clock in the morning. Somebody told me, "There's a woman waiting for you down there." There she was. She said, "I haven't slept. I haven't done any sleeping. Sit down. Sit down." I said, "No, I'm not going to sit down. I'll see you at the office. What do you want?" She said, "Well, I found out something last night. I was awake all night and I finally found the answer to everything." "How was that?" I said. And she said, "You." "Me?" I said. "Yeah," she said, *you're* the answer." I said, "Well, I'll see you a little later, about nine-thirty." So I got rid of her that time. Then the following Saturday when I was getting ready to go to a movie or something and I had this little room that just had this one exit, one of the guys in the front office says, "There's somebody waiting for you." I said, "Now, who is that?" I had no idea who it was. I said, "Tell her don't bother me. Tell her I'm not here." Then I hear her coming down the hall. I had the door open. I heard those footsteps: *dud-dud-dud-dud*. Very courageously I got up and I locked myself in. Then I sat at the typewriter as if I were typing. I don't hear anything. And she started pushing the door really. She said, "I know you're in there. I know you're in there." She started knocking the shit out of that door. I thought: She's going to break the door down. What'll I do? She's going to come in here and all these other people could hear it. So I got real quiet and I opened the door real fast and went by her. Another act of great courage. I went right up to the desk in front and said, "I'd like to use your phone." She came along and said, "Now let's see what you're going to do. This is going to be comical." She sat on the desk. One guy there saw one of these desk spikes, you know, the spikes that you put things on. One of these guys caught the situation. He just pulled that away. And they were just watching. A real big bitch. I've always had this trouble with big women, you know. If I could find a little one . . . I don't have a chance. She was a big rugged rancher's wife, and evidently her husband, I suppose he was about six six, I suppose he'd been beating her up for about seventeen years. She came down to the conference to beat somebody else up, I don't know. Anyhow she said, "Let's just see what you're going to do now." I called the doctor's office there and I told the doctor, "I teach English here for the summer with the English department and there's a woman here I think needs a little help." He said, "Well, put her on." She got on the phone. And then she changed. She said, "Yes, this is Mrs. So-and-So." She was very rational to him and made an appointment for the next day. The morning after that, the doctor called me up and said, "Well, what goes on here?" I says, "How is she?" He wouldn't tell me at first. I said, "Well, look." Finally he says, "When you get these neurotic women, you've got to report it. You've got to let us know." They'd had a suicide on the campus. It scared them. The year before. He said, "You've got to report it when you've got a neurotic woman in your class." I said, "There's forty-four of them in there. Shall I bring them *all* in? I'll go and get them now." I said, "This woman isn't in any worse shape than the rest." I said, "What would they be doing here? They wouldn't be here if they were in their right minds." I said, "Will you tell me if this woman's a nut? I want to know if she's going to jump out at me from some bush." He said, "No, she's committed." They had called her son. The doctor got her son to write it. They committed her. He said, "She's homicidal." I said, "Well, I never would have guessed." So I told Saul this story and he said he'd been through the whole thing. He escaped with his life, too.

Q: In what *other* ways do you think you are influential?

ALGREN: (*Laughter*) Well—

Q: How about with college students?

ALGREN: Oh, I don't think so now. I don't think so now. I think that about the time *The Man with the Golden Arm* came out, between 1944 and 1950, I think there was a pretty lively interest on campus in this *Neon Wilderness* and *Never Come Morning* and *The Man with the Golden Arm*. But the people on *The Nation,* which makes it its business to find out what kids are interested in now, they say, I believe, that it is Salinger and Golding more than anybody else, and although I would like very much to, I certainly don't have influence. I get invited to talk to college kids about twice a year at different universities.

Q: Do you go?

ALGREN: I always go when I get a chance.

Q: How have you been received?

ALGREN: I've never been asked back, which I suppose means I've had some influence on the students, don't you think? The one in Seattle was pretty good.

Q: How did the students like you?

ALGREN: I got along very well out there. I got to Seattle and also to Ann Arbor. And the University of Missouri. But I don't get a playback on it. I'd like to. I wanted to go back to Seattle.

Q: Didn't *Esquire* have you at a writers' conference?

ALGREN: Yeah. I always run into kids there. It's very flattering. There's nothing more gratifying than a kid asking you questions, and not just about writing. He thinks you know more, somehow, than his parents.

Q: What do you think of the American college kids you've met?

ALGREN: Well, I've run into some awful lively kids.

Q: You've read their stuff?

ALGREN: There isn't much. I've never read anything good off a campus. I went to the University of Kalamazoo, a Protestant denominational school mostly for kids studying for the ministry there and I talked from a pulpit. I talked from a minister's pulpit with a cross overhead. I said, "Now I'm not sure— Do you want me to talk from there?" And I *wasn't* sure. The man said, "No, they have quite a liberal streak. Say anything you want." After hearing what my idea of morality was, these kids crowded around later. They'd been raised on morality, on a very strict morality, and it threw them—a more lenient morality. They are professional moralists. These kids are nineteen or twenty and they're going into the clergy and they're bright kids. One asked me for a specific example of what I consider moral. I said, "Well, consider this moral. If a woman is working as a waitress and she works ten hours a day and makes very little. I mean it is pretty hard work. When she gets through, all she can do is get back to her furnished flat and live to the next week. All she can do is pay her rent. She really has no chance to go anywhere. She can't go dancing because on the weekends she's too tired to do anything. She gets Sunday off, that's all. So she's twitchy. She's tired of it. She's young. She's attractive. She finds out that as a prostitute she can work less hard for three or four evenings a week, just over the weekend, and make enough. She can have the whole week to herself. Now," I said, "the immorality would consist of keeping on being a waitress, whereas she is a more moral person as a prostitute." He said, "How do you figure that?" I said, "Well, because she's getting more out of life. This is the only morality I know of. If you want to pray, then pray. If you want to believe in God, believe in God. That's optional. The important thing is: Keep your life for yourself. That's the only morality. Keep your own life." And the kid wasn't displeased. He was a tall kid, I still remember. It was a sobering thought. It was a complete switch on what he had been taught. So I caused a little furor there and everybody seemed pleased. At all those places when you get a little reaction like that, you want to go back. But I haven't been asked back. Of course, I could just go up there and wait around and get registered. Refuse to leave unless I get to talk again.

12 *The Writer at Fifty-five*

QUESTION: This is going to end up as our last series of interviews, Nelson, and I want us today to talk about what pleases you. How do you enjoy yourself? You enjoy poker, you enjoy horses, you enjoy people, don't you?

ALGREN: I don't think any of those things are really solid enjoyments—playing poker and going to the races—the satisfaction is a little bit tentative. Usually what I have in mind at a game or at the races is not just having fun. I want to walk out of there with some money for other more critical uses. I'm not satisfied just to play poker or go to the races. I enjoy it and I believe I am a good poker player and I believe I'm a good horse player. Neither are necessarily true, but I keep trying to prove it. So those aren't really fun things. Fun things are things you do where you are not really *trying* to gain anything.

Q: What are some for you?

ALGREN: Oh, a physical, a satisfying physical effort in swimming, boating—something where you use yourself physically in a natural scene—where you are up against waves, or sand, or snow—where you come off with a feeling of having used yourself physically. The exhilaration from that is less artificial than the exhilaration you get from winning at poker or the track. I think maybe the ideal life would be one in which you really didn't have to win at anything—you just go and watch the horses run or just play poker, where you wouldn't be aware of debts and all that. Those are the fun things, and all fun things, needless to say, have to be shared. Nothing is really much good by yourself. When a thing is shared, then you really have something that is a little bit more real. It isn't real when it's just yourself, any more than having a really fine dinner with good wine by yourself is real. It's just meaningless. Then you're just eating. The idea of a good meal and good wine has meaning if you are with somebody for whom you have affection—you're sharing it. If you're not sharing it, it's pretty bleak. I'd rather have a bad bottle of wine with somebody for whom I have affection than excellent wine all by myself.

Q: What about friendship? Do you have many friends?

ALGREN: Well, no, not really. I've got many acquaintances.

Q: How about close friends? If you had to get on the phone and call for help—financial, emotional, legal, any kind of help—how many could you call?

ALGREN: For emotional help I wouldn't call anybody because nobody can help you emotionally and all you do if you call for that is to drag somebody else. Financially, if it were a small amount, I'd call Studs Terkel. Studs is very easy to borrow from. There are some people who are good friends that for some reason I never borrow from. Just never. I guess I have three or four good friends in Chicago and New York and a couple abroad, and that's about it.

Q: How about close acquaintances?

ALGREN: I have maybe a dozen or so. Just on my way here I
talked to a guy my age that I've known thirty years, but I
really don't call him a friend. I know a lot of people like that.
But that's sort of limited. You just don't go up and make
friends. Friends just happen to you. All I'm trying to do is
keep the ones I've had a long time.

Q: What kind of people are your friends? Different kinds of
people? The same kind?

ALGREN: They're almost all of them informal people. I don't have
any friends among business people. I really don't. Not that I
couldn't be friendly with business people, but I just don't.
One friend is a mutuel clerk. Another guy has been in the
rackets for many years and now he's out. He's a racket man.
I know a few show people and a few writing people. My
best friends haven't been among writing people. They've
been among racket people.

Q: Or actors?

ALGREN: I don't have any real close friends with actors. I value a
few of them very much but you can't say they are close
relationships. I always see these people and I always like to
see them, but I'm never real close to them. I like to see what
they're doing and they're very good people, but I think the
racket people have a kind of loyalty that you have to reciprocate. It isn't necessary to reciprocate that loyalty among acting people.

Q: Why are you interested in loyalty?

ALGREN: Oh, well, it's a stabilizing thing. It's something that's
always depended on. These two guys whose picture I showed
you or this girl I told you was a hooker when I first met her:

she had that. She had that kind of loyalty, devotion. It's a total thing. There isn't any change in those people. Those people always stay with you. They're with you, that's all. They're not just for now, for this moment. They're not middle-class people. I don't think many people have friends like that. What most people call friends among the middle class, it seems to me, are purely transient things where the main consideration, it strikes me, is whether they are in the same financial league. It's like in the Army where two guys have enlisted together and are buddies and become sergeants together and their wives are living together in town, and one of the guys gets busted to private so the other one tells his wife she'll have to move out because he doesn't want her living with a private's wife. I think that sort of thinking operates pretty much in the middle class: "They can be our friends for as long as they can keep up with us."

Q: How do you know anything about the middle class?

ALGREN: What other class is there? The American working class isn't a subclass. When I say I come from the working class, it is not like saying I come from the people who go down into the mines every day.

Q: How do *you* know anything about the middle class?

ALGREN: Well, our standards are middle class.

Q: Are *your* standards middle class?

ALGREN: I don't think so. But I was raised by them. I don't believe in the middle class.

Q: Are the standards you were raised on the same standards as those held by the so-called middle class these days? Is there any change?

ALGREN: They were the same.

Q: The middle class hasn't changed since you were a member of the middle class?

ALGREN: Oh no, they've become *more* middle class. Because there's more money to be middle class with.

Q: How have you found out about the middle class?

ALGREN: I was raised with them. You don't have to be born into the middle class to live according to middle-class standards. I consider myself to be from the working class because my father made his living with his hands. He wasn't a businessman. He was a man who put tires on cars and fixed machines. But there are no working-class values in that sense. This is a middle-class country. It's a businessman's country and the working class lives according to middle-class standards. My parents' whole life was devoted to achieving all the comforts that made for what the middle class considers success. We never got a car, but what we were trying to do was to get a home and a car because all the relatives were business people and my parents wanted to have as much as they. That is, they wanted to own their own property. Their thinking was in terms of property.

Q: So they *became* middle class?

ALGREN: They never quite succeeded in making it because they never paid off for the house they got. We never got to own a car and we lost the house in the Depression, but we were always striving for it. Certainly my sisters belonged to the middle class. One was an office worker and the other was a schoolteacher. Their standards were of home and family. It's a contradictory thing but most middle-class, most Americans—

Q: What about *you?* You keep talking about *most* Americans. What do *you* personally know as a middle-class American?

ALGREN: I like the things the middle class likes. I want the things that they like.

Q: But are *you* a member of the American middle class?

ALGREN: Not spiritually, no. I'm opposed to the middle class. I don't like the middle class.

Q: Yet you want the things they want?

ALGREN: But I don't want to pay the price.

Q: Your knowledge of the middle class and the price it pays for what it gets is not a matter of personal, active, experiential, existential knowledge, is it?

ALGREN: I've never had any experience with any other class but the middle class.

Q: But your friends are not from the middle class.

ALGREN: Well, *every*body's from the middle class now. Racket people are middle class now.

Q: Are *you* from the middle class now?

ALGREN: I'm *in* it but I'm not *of* it. (*Loud laughter*)

Q: Ah, the serpent coils.

ALGREN: Well, there's no other way to be. How am I going to live? I'm trying to get good-looking drapes for my apartment now.

Q: Why?

ALGREN: Because I want that to look like a nice middle-class home.

Q: Why?

ALGREN: I don't want my middle-class friends to come over there without its being decorated.

Q: Why?

ALGREN: Because it looks better, that's why.

Q: Why does it look better?

ALGREN: Because it looks more cheerful.

Q: Why should you be more cheerful?

ALGREN: Because then I write better and I'll make more money so I can have the flat *re*decorated and get more frustrated and have more and better drapes than my other lower-middle-class friends, and so I'll get into the upper middle class before they will. Hah! See?

Q: When you saw me and my wife at the races—she had a new coat on and I had one of my suits on—we were all having a good time, right?

ALGREN: Um-hmmm.

Q: You came over and said, "You two look like a typical middle-class American couple."

ALGREN: Did I say that? What could I have meant? I must have had a loser. I must have been mad at somebody.

Q: But you didn't tell us whether or not we looked good.

ALGREN: Yeah.

Q: Now tell me: Do you think we looked good?

ALGREN: You looked like enjoyable people enjoying themselves.

Q: I think you thought we looked pretty good and I think you were having fun with us. We had on new drapes, right? We looked as if we had just decorated a flat, right?

ALGREN: Well, I don't want you to give up your myna bird on my account, you know, which is certainly a middle-class frivolity of the—

Q: What else are you doing?

ALGREN: —of the most anti-Marxist sort of—

Q: What are you doing for fun?

ALGREN: What that bird eats, you know, a Chinese kid could live on for a year. Just for conspicuous waste, just for the narcissistic pleasure of waking up in the morning and hearing a bird say, "Hello, Shag!" a little kid has to have rickets in Mexico City. This leaves you cold and hard.

Q: Right. Absolutely. Tell me about your other attempts. What other kind of "new drapes" are you getting? Who's picking out the drapes?

ALGREN: I am.

Q: How about love? Does love interest you?

ALGREN: As I said before, I don't think an unshared experience is an experience. To experience anything you have to experience it through somebody else. Sometimes you have a love feeling and it isn't concentrated anywhere. Sometimes it's very easy. You can look at somebody in the streetcar and you can say, "Well, she'd do." You don't do anything about it. And there have been long stretches of time when I wouldn't say I was not in love, but I was not committed. But I don't think it's a real life without it, without the shared experience which becomes love. Like what's the good of going to the circus and seeing people do tremendous things if you have no reaction to consult with? There's no point. My point in going to the circus is to take somebody who's never seen that. You share her wonder. High-wire artists don't particularly interest me, but if they interest her, then I get something out of it. You get something through the other person. When you go into a restaurant it's just a restaurant, but if it's exciting to the other person, then it's exciting to you. I suppose that's a kind of love.

Q: Do you call your writing a shared experience, then?

ALGREN: No. I don't share that. I don't know how you share writing.

Q: I mean do other people share what you *have* written?

ALGREN: Oh, yeah, yeah. I often get that. I often get that. That's always gratifying, of course, if somebody says, "That story really hit me." Budd Schulberg told me about one of my fight stories. He said, "This is the way a fighter really feels," and since I think Schulberg knows how a fighter feels, that's an achievement—when you get it from people who know what it's like. This drug addict told me, he said, "You know how it really feels." That's about as much, that's about as good as somebody telling an actor that that's how it really is. You've got to be something more than just yourself. It's many things of course. I suppose outwardly the chief thing is it's a way of earning a living. I don't know if I could earn a living another way. The other way I'd earn a living would be as a porter somewhere. I wouldn't be able to work in an office.

Q: If writing is the sharing of your experience, then isn't your writing an act of love?

ALGREN: Oh, yeah, yeah. It gives some dignity to your life. Even if nobody ever read it, you're doing something. You're working on the most important thing. You're not giving yourself to adding a column of figures that you know doesn't matter whether it comes out right or not. You're not writing phony advertisements. You're not doing anything meaningless. You have a chance to reach people who are not even born yet.

Q: Do you think everybody can write?

ALGREN: Oh, no.

Q: What about those people who add up the columns of figures?

ALGREN: They usually like it, I guess.

Q: Should they be mocked for not doing what they cannot do?

ALGREN: I'm not mocking them. I just say I can't do what they do.

Q: How important is sex to you?

ALGREN: Well, I think sex is part of everything. I don't think of sex as just something that happens now and then. I can't imagine writing without the feel of sex. I mean sex is a diffuse feeling. It diffuses everything and only once in a while would it be called sex. Sex is diffused with love and affection and only once in a while it comes to the hard-on point. The feeling is always there, but there isn't necessarily always an erection. I mean I don't think you can make things like that happen. It has to start the other way. Otherwise it's pretty meaningless. Once in Paris I was driving around with a pretty attractive girl who was a little on the loose, a good-looking girl about twenty-eight, took me out to a swimming pool and she drove me home. She talked very frankly about sex. She had the afternoon free and I would have liked to have gone to bed with her but I said, "The trouble with it is I'm leaving Paris—how are you going to start something and then finish it? You can't just say, you know, let me use your cunt and I'll give you my cock and we'll just go at it." She said, "What's the matter with *that?*" I said, "I don't know *what* the hell's the matter with it. I got no heart for it. I don't know, I don't know. I just want to do something more than just *go at it.* I can do without it if that's all there is." I just didn't have the heart, you know. It wasn't hard to do, but the feeling went out. I thought, Oh what the hell, and I said, "Drop me off here." I didn't feel any regret about that. I think I was right. It's got to be the other way around. It's got to be the big thing first and then this other thing is just incidental. When you start planning it and being deliberate about it, it goes wrong. It's usually just when you're both thinking about something else, or rather you're just preoccupied with one another as people, and *boing!* That's when it's all right. But you can't make that happen. You can't say, "Now let's have a big sex deal." That spoils it right away. At first I couldn't figure something out, but it's really very simple, that women who come around looking very persistently for sex, usually married women looking for sex, I thought that this meant that they're sexy. But it means that they are sexless. The worst lay I ever had was a woman who came voluntarily, unsolicited, a married woman showed up and you'd think that was a big thing. But it was just the opposite—quite sexless. It took me a while to put that together. The woman didn't realize that the lack was in herself. So she's shopping all around for this thing that isn't going to happen. And it's sexlessness, not sex, which I think is the big thing at *Playboy* —something of the same sort of search. I think it's basically a sexless thing. I think the people who like sex stay home. I mean I don't think they make a big thing out of it.

Q: How about you and marriage?

ALGREN: I wouldn't say I plan to be married again, but I would like to be. It's not such an easy thing to do. I haven't quite reached the Schliemann stage. Do you know Schliemann? The old German archaeologist? Remember him? Well, there's a good story on him.

Q: Oh yes. He uncovered Troy.

ALGREN: He started uncovering Troy when he was about six years old. Somebody gave him a book on Troy and he decided it was a real city. He had one unsuccessful marriage when he was about twenty and then he lived as a single man, became a very successful grocer, made a million dollars by the time he was thirty, and devoted it all to the excavation of Troy. He didn't know anything about archaeology; he would just go there and dig. Then, when he was fifty-six years old and he hit on the ultimate spot where he figured Troy was, he stopped and he wrote to the village priest of this little Greek town and said, "I want a Greek wife." So the priest went out—he was very glad to find a wife for a well-to-do fifty-six-year-old German—the kids are running all over the place. So the priest picked the best-looking girl in the village, sixteen years old. The old man says, "You've got to marry him." This was a very Teutonic way of doing things. "Find me a Frau!" you know, good-looking and all that. But as it turned out, from the book I read on him, it was a hell of a marriage. The girl was very bright and she dug like mad. She fell in love with the old man and between the two of them they had a few very good years. That's a very Germanic thing. I'd rather do my own finding.

Q: As a heterosexual man, do you feel that the homosexual world is growing or that simply more of it is being discussed more honestly?

ALGREN: I think if it isn't growing at least they've got uniforms now. I think that's an improvement. That is interesting in New York. I never saw that before—about the narrow pants and this very obvious thing, which shows it now has prestige. It always had a terrible stigma. In fact, it was unheard of, you know. There were secret rumors when I was a kid that something's wrong there with someone, but nobody spoke of it.

Q: But now it is a new status symbol?

ALGREN: Yeah, it seems so. In my own neighborhood it's not a new strange thing now, as it was.

Q: But you don't feel threatened by any kind of homosexual on-slaught? You don't think our culture is going to be taken over by homosexuals?

ALGREN: Well, it's becoming an effeminate culture. Look in the ads. Look at the dress of men. Listen to their voices. It's a very common complaint.

Q: How do you feel about this? Do you mind?

ALGREN: Yes, I mind. I would prefer to live in a masculine cul-ture. I don't mean that everybody has to knock somebody's head off to prove he's a man. But I prefer masculinity in writ-ing, simply because it's stronger. And I like a country to be mas-culine. It's a weakening thing. I'm not talking about moral-ity. I'm talking about the kind of *thinking* that goes with homosexuality—it is a very inferior kind of thinking because it's a very cold way of thinking. I'm fully capable of admir-ing the homosexual writers. But all the same there is a coldness that comes along with it that we didn't have when the great writing was being done by men like Mark Twain. Homosexuals can't write like this. They don't have the warmth. They have a humor but it's a cold humor. It's a dehumanized thing. What a homosexual is, he's an inferior woman. I think that sort of culture is an inferior culture. So far as good masculine writing goes and good feminine writing goes, the masculine writing I believe is better. Just like a good male horse will always beat a female horse. It's stronger. It makes a better animal and it makes a better thinker. The people who have hit the high points in this country were very well balanced sexually I think. Anyway I think of— Oh, boy, I really got into it that time. (*Laughter*) I just ran into Walt Whitman. Well, I wouldn't do without Whitman, but the big voices of America, I think, from Jefferson to Lincoln and Jackson have been masculine voices.

Q: Tell me about the kind of woman you might like to marry. How old should she be?

ALGREN: Well, she can't be too young.

Q: How young? What if I were to introduce you to a sixteen-year-old?

ALGREN: I'd tell her to come back in three years.

Q: Say she's a beauty, very bright, very mature, very nice, and looked good. You'd tell her to come back in three years?

ALGREN: Well, I certainly wouldn't stick my neck out on that.

Q: Oh, because of the law.

ALGREN: Oh, no, not because of the law.

Q: And if she expressed an interest in you?

ALGREN: Oh if she expressed interest, I'd encourage her, I'd encourage her. I certainly wouldn't turn her down, but I'd go
very, very easy because with any girl like that I wouldn't feel
able to deal with her.

Q: Why not?

ALGREN: Because she's too smart, too intuitive. She could make
an ass out of me almost momentarily. (*Laughter*) I wish she
would.

Q: So a wife should be a little older than that?

ALGREN: I think if I met a very attractive woman, say, about
thirty-six, still at the childbearing age, who didn't have a
great repugnance for raising kids—I wouldn't even care if she
had a kid or two by somebody else, although I wouldn't want
to just raise somebody else's kids—a woman of thirty-two or
so, thirty-three, thirty-four maybe. She's got to be sort of
joyous and she's got to be good-looking and she's got to
know how to wear clothes. She's got to be presentable. She's
got to know how to cook.

Q: Any preference about blondes or brunettes?

ALGREN: Oh no, no. It just depends on the woman.

Q: Long? Tall? Skinny? Pleasingly plump?

ALGREN: Well, I've never gone for fat six-foot heavy-set blondes,
but I wouldn't rule them out. It just so happens I've always
gone for smaller women. Maybe they make me feel taller, I
don't know. I just like darkness in a woman, I don't know why.

Q: Do you think you *are* going to get married again?

ALGREN: There's probably a fifty-fifty chance, probably a pretty
fair chance within a couple of years. Not before that, I
don't think.

Q: By the time you are fifty-seven?

ALGREN: That's a fair, reasonable, fifty-fifty bet.

Q: Where will you live?

ALGREN: I'll leave that up to her. See, I don't know her yet.

Q: Tell me about your writing plans. What other novels do you want to write?

ALGREN: I'd still like to write about a prostitute in an American city—just the comings and goings of a woman practicing her trade, without giving it any morality, just explain the trade as a trade.

Q: Do you think you'll ever write about the affluent society.

ALGREN: No, no. I never will. I don't see any chance of doing that. I don't feel any impulse to do it.

Q: Will you ever write a political novel?

ALGREN: No. Never. Never.

Q: How about a boxing novel?

ALGREN: That would be too hard to do. I don't know enough about it. The only way I'd do that would be if I could buy a fighter and live with him. If I could buy a welterweight's contract for fifteen hundred dollars and have a place where he could train and bring him along—go down to New York and talk to fight managers and do as though I were in the fight game, really get *in* the fight game.

Q: Do you think you *will* do that?

ALGREN: If I had the money, I'd like to do it. I wouldn't rule it out. I'd like to do that kind of book because it would be about more than just boxing. This guy would come into it only incidentally—it would just be a way of writing about New York actually, and it would just be a reporting job. I wouldn't try to do more than discover details and get the speech down, at the same time try to create enough interest in the main character. . . . I just noticed my socks are mismatched. I thought they were the same, thought they were matched.

Q: I want to ask you specific questions about writing because I'm an American writer and so are you an American writer.

ALGREN: With mitch-matched socks.

Q: With mitch-matched, mix-matched . . .

ALGREN: With mismatched socks, yeah.

Q: With mismatched socks.

ALGREN: Yeah.

Q: When you've finished, as you come toward the end of a book, do you have a feeling that you'd been with it too long and, at the same time, you hate to finish it, to give it up?

ALGREN: Oh, yeah, yeah, yeah. I do have that deep reluctance to let it go, yeah, just hanging on and hanging on and hanging on until it almost has to be pried away from you. I've had that.

Q: As you've been writing a book, have you found that it revealed to you the profound feelings about a number of disturbing things?

ALGREN: No, I wouldn't say so. I do know that when you have a book under way and are working well that you feel much better about your own relationship to the world, and the way to feel good all the time is to always have a good book going. But I'm not conscious of any particular strain about it.

Q: Well, do you end up exhausted toward the end of each book you do?

ALGREN: No, no, I don't recall ending up exhausted. Just impatient, that's all, just feel impatient with the feeling of a lot of tag ends. While I'm finishing a book it's a little bit like tying a lot of knots that keep slipping and you're just impatient to get it done. And then you have to go all the way back in, in order to tie it up, and you find you just can't tie it up at the end. You have to go all the way back and tie it up. And once I've done that I don't feel any sense of exhaustion about it. I just feel a sense of completion.

Q: Are you pleased with what you've completed?

ALGREN: Well, not entirely. I always have the feeling that, why didn't I put this in there or that in there. There's always the misgivings and—that you have to brush aside and the stuff that you didn't get in. . . .

Q: How do you brush it aside?

ALGREN: Oh, you don't, you pay the misgivings no heed. First they bark just like little dogs inside you, they keep barking and you just keep walking away. You can't do anything about it any more. The book is out of your hands. After a while they quit barking and a new set come in and take over and start barking.

Q: Have you ever felt on any of your books that you were really doing something good and that it made things easier for you?

ALGREN: Oh, yeah, yeah. When you have a good story you know it's good and then you feel better for it. It's about the only thing that makes you feel really good.

Q: What kind of writing do you think is coming up? I mean, your books have beginnings, middles, and ends. You don't write the anti-novel. You deal with people's emotions. You care about what happens to them. You care about telling a story. Do you think this kind of writing is becoming less and less the fashion?

ALGREN: Yes, it seems so.

Q: What's taking its place?

ALGREN: Well, I think maybe we're coming into a time where the writing is much more detached and much less compassionate, much less concerned with the individual. I mean, we're living so much in a world where personalities count for so little. Society's become so depersonalized that it'd be pretty difficult now to write a book that would depend simply on strength of character, in which the people are attractive simply by force of their personality. We don't seem to be writing about individuals now. We're writing about society. Writing is likely to become more documentary, in the way that Sinclair Lewis wrote. His people were just one-dimensional people. I mean you could tell what kind of people they were just by the names he stuck on them. I have an idea that we're going to get more of this thing and less of the kind of personalized American: the man or woman with many dimensions and human complexity. I'm just guessing. I don't know, but I don't see anybody writing any . . .

Q: How about the style of writing? Uh, do you think there'll be less naturalism, less—that there is less and less naturalism?

ALGREN: Most people are writing from other writers. They're not writing first person directly from life as Hemingway did. This is the sort of novelist we're going to have: the no-novelist.

Q: When you're working on a book, do you schedule the day or does it fall into any kind of pattern?

ALGREN: Oh, a general over-all pattern, I guess. I don't make a schedule. I just have a general feeling that I ought to be typing.

Q: Do you enjoy writing?

ALGREN: It's pleasant in a tedious sort of way.

Q: Are you much of a rewriter?

ALGREN: I rewrite all the time. I never stop rewriting.

Q: Tell me something. Do you think there's any purpose to life?

ALGREN: Well, no ultimate purpose. The purpose is to live it. It has its own purpose. Its only purpose is part of itself. You're alive. That's its only purpose. The only meaning that life has is to have it while you've got it, to use it while you've got it. Life's meaning simply comes in within your senses. That's your only justification—just sight and smell and sound. And you keep those as sharp as you can for as long as you can and then you go out as fast as you can. You've lived successfully or not depending on how much you got out of life in terms of living, not in what you acquired. Although, of course, if you acquire something, you probably get more out of life.

Q: What do you mean, "go out of it as fast as you can"?

ALGREN: Well, it's a terrible drag to go out one toe at a time and I think Hemingway must have felt this. When he started dropping off, I think he lost sixty pounds, something like that. When he started being reduced to a vegetable, he went, which makes sense because he was just going to be reduced to a heap of garbage in another six months and he'd always respected himself as a man. As a physical being I guess he just couldn't take that, ah, humiliation.

Q: Your health is good now?

ALGREN: Yes, it is.

Q: Although you don't sleep properly, you don't eat properly?

ALGREN: That's true. I don't, I don't.

Q: How come your health is good?

ALGREN: Well, I don't know. I'm fortunate that way, and I, ah (*knocking on wood*), I have just not been afflicted with the common afflictions, the countless multitude of afflictions you can have, beginning with A, arthritis, and ending with Z, zilicosis of the veins or varicose veins. I haven't been struck. I had a backache a few years ago which simply terrified me.

Q: What was it?

ALGREN: It was just a little backache. It was one of these things that double you over a little bit—not at all an uncommon thing. I was immediately terrified—what if I can't straighten up again? And I guess some people can't. So I never let myself get complacent about it because I feel I may wake up someday with a splitting headache, a sore jaw, sinus, a hacking cough, rheumatism—all at once. All of these things are going to hit me at once. But I've really had good health and I would like to have more of it if I may. And I did it without prayer. I don't pray. I smoke too much. I drink too much. I eat too much. I don't exercise.

Q: You swim, don't you?

ALGREN: I swim a little bit and I don't say my prayers.

Q: Tell me once again about the last time you saw your mother.

ALGREN: Well, the last time I saw her she'd been dying for six months. She was supposed to be dead in January, and in July she was still sitting there just too strong to go. She wanted to go and it was time to go, so I came in and I lit a cigarette. She was reduced at this time to just simply a little mess of shaking bones.

Q: How old was she?

ALGREN: Eighty-six. And she would just sit there and shake, just that prolonged, perpetual discomfort, and I lit a cigarette and she said, "Give me one." I thought at first she was kidding. I said, "No, you don't want to smoke, Ma, do you?" She said, "Well, I have to do *something.*" So I gave her the cigarette and she smoked it. The nurses came around and watched.

Q: Had she ever had a cigarette before?

ALGERN: Once or twice. But she simply wanted to do something so she smoked the cigarette. The attendants watched, really quite amazed. She died the next day.

Q: That's about all the questions I have.

ALGREN: She added one thing. That morning she said—there was sort of a murmur of steam or something from the radiator, some sound in the radiator—and she said, "Voices are coming up from below." But she said it in this rhythm, with a certain rhythm to it that surprised me very much. I was surprised that she should put her last strength into trying to make a poem.

Q: One more question: Are you glad that you are alive?

ALGREN: Yeah.

Q: When are you *not* glad you're alive?

ALGREN: Oh, I've never been not glad. I've always been glad to be alive.

Q: Even when things go badly?

ALGREN: Oh yeah, yeah. They couldn't go *that* badly. I just can't imagine anything going *that* badly.

Q: Have you ever contemplated suicide?

ALGREN: No. I've thought about it in a very abstract way, but I couldn't do that. I couldn't even chop off the end of my little finger, and I'm sure I would never have the nerve to put a gun in my mouth as the Great White Hunter did in Idaho. In fact, I'm afraid if I found out what he found out—that he had cancer, that it made no sense to go on—I'd pin myself on some abstract hope that somebody was going to come up with some magic penicillin. I don't think I'd give up. I don't think so.

Q: At fifty-five, does the world look like an interesting place to you?

ALGREN: It's getting more and more diverse, more and more wild. More and more people are around who don't know what they're doing, and there are more and more things to see.

Q: Is it more fun?

ALGREN: Oh there's more fun to be had. It's getting harder and harder to get at it. (*Laughter*) I keep having to go home and work. But there are certainly more things to do.

Q: Would you rather be the age you are now, or is there some other time of your life you'd like to get back to again?

ALGREN: Oh, thirty-nine is the time.

Q: Thirty-nine? My age now?

ALGREN: Yeah. Yeah. Yeah. Yeah. The time between the time I got out of the Army in 1946 and 1950. That was a very good time.

Q: The time you got out of the Army and wrote *The Man with the Golden Arm?*

ALGREN: Uh-huh. A very fresh time.

Q: You are the first man I've ever met who thinks the 1940's were the good old days. Is there anything you want to add about yourself, or about the interview?

ALGREN: Well, just put in that I'm well-dressed, attractive, and single.

Q: What's your address?

ALGREN: 1958 West Evergreen. Third floor. Just walk in.

Q: And the zone?

ALGREN: Zone twenty-two.

Q: What's your name?

ALGREN: Nelson Algren. A-l-g-r-e-n. Army serial number 36679611.

Q: Right.

ALGREN: 125th Evacuation Hospital. That's all I have to say. That's all I have to tell. *And I may be a spy!* Nobody'll ever know, for *sure!*

Notes

About the Book

The book should have a subtitle. It should be called *Notes Toward a Biography,* even though the whole thing started out as a magazine article.

In my opinion, Nelson Algren is one of the most important American writers—certainly he has been important to me in my twenty-year attempt to write. I had heard that he had made no money from Hollywood for two of his books: *The Man with the Golden Arm* and *A Walk on the Wild Side.* How could this be? Why had such a "tough guy" permitted this to happen? Why had *anyone* permitted this to happen to the man who had been awarded the first National Book Award for *The Man with the Golden Arm?*

A national magazine seemed interested in the answers, and at the time, late February, 1962, I was writing articles while working on my own novel, my first. So I went to Chicago and visited him for two days where introductions were made (and facilitated by Studs Terkel, Mr. and Mrs. Herman Kogan, and William Alton).

I went back to Chicago with a tape recorder on March 26 and stayed for three days. March 28, 1962, was Nelson Algren's fifty-third birthday, and because of his birthday perhaps, or other imponderables, comments by him and questions by me ranged far beyond Algren's "war with the United States as represented by Kim Novak." It became apparent that, while we liked and trusted each other, we were two entirely different kinds of people, and we disagreed about many things.

The magazine which had shown interest in the article about Algren and Hollywood no longer found it to their liking, but he and I began a personal—sometimes friendly, sometimes carping—correspondence. A mutual friend who had introduced us, Candida Donadio, suggested other interviews. Then she suggested a book.

In late April and early May, Algren visited New York and agreed to more interviews. We talked about his ancestors, childhood, youth, the Depression, his Army days, and writing. Before he left for his long sea voyage to the Far East, I visited him again in Chicago for three more days that May.

A draft of the interview was done, with the Hollywood section moved to the middle to strengthen the material's chronological tone. The publishers of this book suggested we return to certain sections in order to explore more thoroughly different parts of his life and his opinions. The suggestions seemed sensible to me. Algren agreed. By this time it was 1963. In late May and early June of that year, Nelson and I met in New York for three more sessions.

This book, then, is a result of two years of talk, letters, and thirteen specific meetings, eleven of which were recorded—about thirty hours' worth, or almost two hundred thousand words.

Since a man's life and work were being discussed, the decision was made early and often to leave the sequence of questions and the development of themes to the mercies of the open, or "unstructured," interview. Until he heard the questions, Nelson Algren rarely knew what he was going to be asked. Quite often, as the dialogue shows, I did not know either.

As each part of the original transcript was prepared, through the

supreme efforts of Miss Martha Blankenship, I had ample opportunity to tidy up the sequence, to smooth roughness completely
away, to make all one hundred thousand words of interrogation
seem ordered, cohesive, rehearsed. This I could not do. The subject
of this book is Nelson Algren, talking—openly, as candidly as he
can, spontaneously, extempore. To meddle with the result would be
more than mere tampering, it would be anti-Algren, that is, hypo-
critical.

To be sure, editing was done; one half of the transcript was
not used. And this is not the actual way Algren talks. He hangs
onto key words and phrases, for instance, in almost every sentence he speaks. He enjoys too many double negatives. For em-
phasis he often leans on the fancy word "ain't." He likes to
swear and curse. Obscenities are to him not a curse. And in the
two years we discussed things, many events changed, both for him
and for me. So, while many of these earmarks have been minimized,
enough have been retained so that he knows that what appears in
this book is what he thought he was trying to say.

He checked the finished manuscript. But it is my choice when
an earthy adjective appears, or when ramblings seem at first to
lead nowhere, or when awkward questions are permitted to stand
next to foolish answers. These blemishes, along with contradictions
and inconsistencies on both our parts, have been retained because
the attempt has been made here to present the thoughts and feelings of one of America's best writers in the form and style of his
own speech.

For those affronted by my projection of myself into many areas
of the conversations, I can only offer the experiential defense: If
by such projections I was able to elicit certain responses, then to
report only the responses would have been to present a distortion
of what actually happened. There is also the feeble personal
reply: Let anyone talk to Nelson Algren for very long and remain
uninvolved, disengaged, aloof.